Psychology and Management
A text for managers and trade unionists

Psychology for Professional Groups

Series Editors: Antony J. Chapman and Anthony Gale

Psychology for Professional Groups is a new series of major
textbooks published with the British Psychological Society.
Each is edited by a teacher with expertise in the
application of psychology to professional practice and
covers the key topics in the training syllabus. The editors
have drawn upon a series of specially commissioned topic
chapters prepared by leading psychologists and have set them
within the context of their various professions. A tutor
manual is available for each text and includes examination
questions, practical exercises and projects, further reading
and general guidance for the tutor. Each textbook shows in a
fresh, original and authoritative way how psychology may be
applied in a variety of professional settings, and how
practitioners may improve their skills and gain a deeper
understanding of themselves. There is also a general
tutorial text incorporating the complete set of specialist
chapters and their associated teaching materials.

Published with this book
Psychology for Teachers. David Fontana
Psychology for Social Workers. Martin Herbert

Subsequent titles
Psychology for Physiotherapists. E. N. Dunkin
Psychology for Occupational Therapists. Fay Fransella
Psychology and Medicine. David Griffiths
Psychology for Nurses and Health Visitors. John Hall
Psychology for Careers Counselling. Ruth Holdsworth
Psychology for Speech Therapists. Harry Purser
Psychology and People: A tutorial text. Antony J. Chapman
        and Anthony Gale

Psychology and Management

A text for managers and trade unionists

Cary L Cooper

First published 1981 by THE BRITISH PSYCHOLOGICAL SOCIETY
and THE MACMILLAN PRESS LTD.

Distributed by The Macmillan Press Ltd, London and
Basingstoke. Associated companies and representatives
throughout the world.

ISBN 0 333 318 560 (hard cover)
ISBN 0 333 318 757 (paper cover)

Printed in Great Britain by Wheatons of Exeter

Note: throughout these texts, the masculine pronouns have
been used for succinctness and are intended to refer to both
females and males.

The conclusions drawn and opinions expressed are those of
the authors. They should not be taken to represent the
views of the publishers.

Contents

Foreword

This book is one of a series, the principal aims of which
are to illustrate how psychology can be applied in particular professional contexts, how it can improve the skills
of practitioners, and how it can increase the practitioners'
and students' understanding of themselves.

Psychology is taught to many groups of students and is
now integrated within prescribed syllabuses for an increasing number of professions. The existing texts which teachers
have been obliged to recommend are typically designed for
broad and disparate purposes, and consequently they fail to
reflect the special needs of students in professional
training. The starting point for the series was the
systematic distillation of views expressed in professional
journals by those psychologists whose teaching specialisms
relate to the applications of psychology. It soon became
apparent that many fundamental topics were common to a
number of syllabuses and courses; yet in general introductory textbooks these topics tend to be embedded amongst
much superfluous material. Therefore, from within the
British Psychological Society, we invited experienced
teachers and authorities in their field to write review
chapters on key topics. Forty-seven chapters covering 23
topics were then available for selection by the series'
Volume Editors. The Volume Editors are also psychologists
and they have had many years of involvement with their
respective professions. In preparing their books, they have
consulted formally with colleagues in those professions.
Each of their books has its own combination of the
specially-prepared chapters, set in the context of the
specific professional practice.

Because psychology is only one component of the various
training curricula, and because students generally have
limited access to learned journals and specialist texts, our
contributors to the series have restricted their use of
references, while at the same time providing short lists of
annotated readings. In addition, they have provided review
questions to help students organize their learning and
prepare for examinations. Further teaching materials, in the
form of additional references, projects, exercises and class
notes, are available in Tutor Manuals prepared for each
book. A comprehensive tutorial text ('Psychology and
People'), prepared by the Series Editors, combines in a

single volume all the key topics, together with their associated teaching materials.

It is intended that new titles will be added to the series and that existing titles will be revised in the light of changing requirements. Evaluative and constructive comments, bearing on any aspect of the series, are most welcome and should be addressed to us at the BPS in Leicester.

In devising and developing the series we have had the good fortune to benefit from the advice and support of Dr Halla Beloff, Professor Philip Levy, Mr Allan Sakne and Mr John Winckler. A great burden has been borne by Mrs Gail Sheffield, who with skill, tact and courtesy, has managed the production of the series: to her and her colleagues at the BPS headquarters and at the Macmillan Press, we express our thanks.

Antony J. Chapman
UWIST, Cardiff

Anthony Gale
University of Southampton

May 1981

Introduction
Cary L. Cooper

Before we can begin to understand how psychological research
and theory can contribute to the skills and performance of
managers and those working on behalf of the trade union
movement, we must first explore the nature of their roles,
functions and activities at work. What overall functions do
different managers and trade unionists perform in the course
of their normal working week? What are the activities that
are common to both groups, and those that are distinct?

We would have no trouble finding definitions of the role of
managers or management from among the best-sellers of Drucker
or other management gurus, but the approach that appeals to
me is to try and categorize the different types of managers
by acknowledging the reality that individual managers behave
in quite different ways. This allows us to get a feel for
the generic role of management; all the activities that
should be performed if 'superman-ager' existed.
   Handy (1976) recently remarked that 'the last quarter
century has seen the emergence of "the manager" as a
recognized occupational role in society'. He then goes on to
suggest that managers seem to be increasingly playing two
primary sets of roles: the manager as a person or the
manager as a GP. The manager as a person alludes to the
increasing professionalization of managers, so that managers
are acquiring a set of skills which are, and arguably should
be, independent of any organization for whom he does, or
could, work. Since organizations seem to care less for the
home/work interface concerns of their managers than previously (Cooper, 1979b), it is in their interest to make
sure they continue to make themselves marketable by further
education and career-management. The manager as a GP concept, on the other hand, is based on the premise that the
manager is the 'first recipient of problems' which require
solutions or decisions. It is the role of a manager in this
context to carry out four basic activities at work: (i)
identify the symptoms in the situation; (ii) diagnose the
cause of trouble; (iii) decide how to deal with it; and (iv)
start the treatment or make the decision or create the
action plans. Handy argues that all too often the symptoms
are treated like diseases in the 'industrial wards' of the

country, and that managers who do not follow the medical model above in dealing with issues and problems, but stop at stage one, find that the illness or sources of grievance return in the same form or in disguise. Frequently we find managers who can diagnose the symptoms, such as poor morale or bad communications, but then provide solutions without knowing the cause: for example, poor communications - start in-house journal; late arrivals to work - introduce time-clocks, etc. In order to identify adequately and accurately problems or situations, it is absolutely essential to understand the needs of individual workers, be they other managers or unskilled labourers. Diagnosis not only involves understanding individual behaviour but also the dynamics of groups within the organizations and the consequences of action plans that may affect groups outside.

Handy also suggests that the manager as a GP, when considering strategies for improving the health of the organization, should consider and be aware of three sets of variables; the people, the work and the structure, systems and procedure of the organization. In terms of 'people concerns', he should be aware of individual needs, training and education potential, career development, motivation, need for counselling or support, etc., whereas in terms of the organizational structure and systems he should be aware of the nature of roles, inter-group conflict, small group behaviour, decision making, negotiating processes, reward systems, etc. The general practitioner manager is not only expected to be aware of these factors and processes but also to understand their interaction: that is, how change in one may produce change in another.

And finally, a crucial characteristic of any skilled manager is to be aware of change and how to implement it. This requires an understanding of learning theory, the various strategies for change (counselling, behaviour modi-fication, etc.), the dilemmas people experience at differ-ent times in their lives, identifying an initiating person or group, creating an awareness of change, and so on. This is part and parcel of any GP role whether in the medical field or in organizations:

To obtain a further and more amusing yet informative view of the role of the manager we turn to Mant's (1977) historical styles of management, which has its contemporary meaning in today's managers (by sleight of author's li-cence). First, there is the RESPECTABLE BUCCANEER or the British proto-manager. This is the swashbuckling Sir Francis Drake type who uses 'who he knows' and 'who he is' to achieve results. The success of this style depends to a large extent on a highly developed sense of social skills and timing, but little else. He is the entrepreneur in its most extreme form.

The next managerial prototype is the AGENT. He acts on behalf of others, takes no decisions himself and has histor-ical roots in the commercial world of nineteenth-century England. His contemporary counterpart is the 'middle manager' of today, who feels, not by choice, that his power and ability to influence decisions is declining (due to the power of the trade union movement, greater participative decision making, etc.).

The SCIENTIFIC MANAGER is another breed of executive who is seen in organizational jungles from time to time. He tends to make decisions based on what appear to be rational and appropriate data, but frequently ignores the 'people problems' that result from his decisions or are created by them. Sheldon writing in 1923 (quoted in Mant, 1977) summed it up from a historical perspective: 'management is no longer the wielding of the whip; it is rather the delving into experience and building upon facts'. In contrast to the factual manager is the MANAGERIAL QUISLING, or as Mant puts it, 'the manager in the role of the pal'. This stems from the human relations school of management of the 1940s and 1950s. This prototypic manager is one who is supposed to be concerned with the quality of worklife and the well-being of workers. It is my view that this species of manager comes in different varieties. First, there is the GENUINE QUISLING, who really is concerned about the worker's health and well-being. Incidentally, this type of manager is usually so naïve about the politics of his organization that he fails to achieve his objectives, or achieves them at the expense of other people. Second, there is the ENTRE-PRENEURIAL QUISLING, who 'appears to care' but is really using the 'flavour of the month' managerial style to achieve recognition, or enhance his own image, or accomplish some political manoeuvre. He is the classic Milo Minderbinder in Heller's Catch-22; 'it's all in the syndicate and everybody has a share'.

Another managerial prototype is the MANAGER AS A TECHNOCRAT. He is a breed that grew up as the technology around them developed, particularly during the 1940s when we were increasingly looking to engineers for our salvation. This type of manager handles all issues as if they were technical problems capable of stress analysis, critical pathanalysis, etc. His concern for the 'people component' is once again a mere 'given' in the decision-making process.

And finally, there is the MANAGER AS A CONSTITUTIONALIST. This form of managerial style seemed to emerge from the Glacier Metal Company study undertaken by Brown (1965). This style of management is not unlike the Tavistock approach to applied problems in industry, in that it relies heavily on contractual arrangements. That is to say, it believes fundamentally that psychological contracts between individuals or representatives of groups are essential for harmonious relationships at work. Managers are effective, according to this strategy, if they work with their subordinates and colleagues in designing contractual arrangements on most issues of importance. This reduces ambiguity and heightens the boundaries on tasks, roles and organizational units.

What Mant (1977) has done in trying to identify managerial types is to suggest implicitly that each of the caricatures of prototypic executives is ineffective, but in different ways. And although some managers utilize (consistently) one or more of these styles than others, the well-rounded and Twenty-First-Century manager will require a behavioural repertoire that encompasses nearly the whole range, but used flexibly and appropriately. We need to educate and train managers to understand the needs of people so that they take a scientific or diagnostic approach to problems and decision, but with a socio-technical, humanistic, and risk-taking orientation as well. To do this, one might follow the advice of many managers that 'behavioural scientists are incapable of telling us anything we don't already know'. This was epitomized in a piece that appeared in 'The Financial Times' a few years ago:

> Good evening gentlemen, welcome to the X management education establishment. You will have noted, perhaps with relief, the absence of faculty or curriculum. This is a regular feature of this programme and a closely-guarded secret of its alumni, present and past. If you should require any inducement to keep this secret you may be influenced by the £500 in crisp ten-pound notes which is to be found in a brown envelope in your bedroom. This represents half the fee paid by your employers and approximated expenditure that would otherwise have been incurred with respect to teaching staff salaries and related costs. In the meantime, meals and other services will be provided and the bar will remain open at normal opening times. You will have discovered that your colleagues are drawn from similar organizations to your own and contain amongst them a wealth of practical experience in all manner of managerial roles. There is also a first-rate library at your disposal. How you decide to pass these six weeks is your own managerial decision; we trust you will enjoy it and find it beneficial. Thank you.

On the other hand, we could begin to provide managers with information that behavioural scientists have accumulated over the last 30 years of empirical and theoretical development. It is this latter approach that we have decided to take in this volume, to make available psychological knowledge that may be of some use in dealing with individual, interpersonal, group and organization behaviour, and in creating change among individuals and organizations.

Trade unionists

Many trade union officials carry out a variety of tasks similar to many managers (discussed above) working within industrial and public sector organizations. They have the job of having to deal with a variety of different people they help to organize, to understand the dynamics of group situations (committees, negotiating groups, etc.) and to understand the structure and functioning of organizations and groups within them. In addition, they require other skills, which most, although not all, managers do not use on

a regular basis (e.g. negotiating and bargaining, interviewing, etc.).

One of the classic studies which has helped us to
understand the major duties of various trade union officers
was carried out by Clegg, Killick and Adams (1966). In their
work they identified the main constituents of the job of
full-time officers, branch secretaries, and shop stewards,
among others.

It can be seen from table 1 that each category of trade
unionist engages in quite different activities. In other
words, they each need slightly different bits of psychological knowledge and training. Whereas full-time officers
have to get involved quite regularly in high level negotiation exercises of one kind or another, this is not quite
the case for branch secretaries or shop stewards (where
their roles in negotiations are much more circumscribed).
Shop stewards, on the other hand, require greater emphasis
on interpersonal skills in their dealings with local
management, grievances with foremen and other first line
managers. Although the emphasis is different, the need for
understanding and skill development in various psychological areas is of great importance to all trade union
representatives. Indeed, it might be argued that many
industrial relations disputes, which start as local matters,
develop further because of the lack of psychological insight
by both local management and the shop stewards into the
'real' underlying problems and their causes, and their
consequent inability to deal with them at that level.

The role of the shop steward is critical, therefore,
because of his unique set of boundary roles between the work
group, the management and union officials. Torrington and
Chapman (1979) suggest that the shop steward requires skills
in at least six different and demanding tasks. First, he
must have skills as a spokesman and negotiator, both for his
fellow workers but also for management and 'the union' as
well. Second, he is responsible for recruitment of union
members among the employees. This means approaching new
employees and maintaining contacts with older ones, which
requires a high level of social and interpersonal skills.
Third, the shop steward is responsible for the dissemination
of information; on current working practices, on union
policy, on management attitudes, etc. Fourth, he must
possess the skills to counsel members with difficulties, or
deal with advice to members about services available. Fifth,
they must ensure, from time to time, the compliance with
union rules in an effort to adhere to agreements or sustain union policy. And finally, but perhaps most importantly, shop stewards have to act as an important communications
link between the workers, management, and the union officials. Goodman and Whittingham (1969) reflect this in the
following:

He will be expected to state grievances from the shop
floor and, having reached an agreement with the
management, will be expected to carry his members with

Table 1
___

Importance of main duties of full-time officers, branch secretaries and shop stewards (across a number of unions)
Source: Clegg, H. A., Killick, A. J. and Adams, R. (1966)
Trade Union Officers, Oxford: Blackwell.

Main duties	Full-time officers (%)	Branch secretaries (%)	Shop stewards (%)
Negotiation	24	8	
Correspondence	18	16	6
Helping others	17	13	
Branch and other meetings	21	16	8
Recruiting new members	12		
Other office work	5		
Financial work	3	20	
Benefit claims and payments		12	
Arrears and meeting notices		6	
Branch minutes		5	
Membership transfers and resignations		4	
Discussions with members and shop stewards			32
Negotiations with management above foreman level			21
Taking up grievances with foremen			16
Works' committee, Joint Consultative committees, etc.			11
Rate fixing			6

Table 2

Shop stewards' view of their role
Source: Batstone, E., Boraston, I. and Frenkel, S. (1977).

	Staff (%)	Shop floor (%)
Promote socialism, trade union principles	12	16
Protect members, improve wages and conditions	31	100
Maintain unity and union organization	12	13
Ensure harmony with management	38	19
Solve problems in accordance with agreements	6	23
Act as communications channel with the membership	50	16
Total respondents	100%	100%
Number of respondents	16	31
Number of answers	24	58
No answer	3	–

him. As such, management may have a vested interest in his strength, regarding him as both representative and advocate. Additionally he will be expected to lead, as well as reflect, shop floor opinion. The steward's representative role may be further emphasized by participation in joint consultative committees, about which he should also disseminate information.

Although these six roles are the main functions performed by shop stewards, there are differences in emphasis between stewards depending on what group of workers they are representing. Batstone, Boraston and Frenkel (1977) found this in their study on 'Shop Stewards in Action'.

It can be seen from table 2 that staff stewards saw their role as 'ensuring harmony with management' and 'maintaining a communications channel with their membership', while shop floor stewards overwhelmingly saw their role as 'protecting members, improving wages and conditions'. While the balance between these various role functions can differ, the need for training in human relations skills and other aspects of human behaviour is crucial to effective trade unionism. Indeed, the Commission on Industrial Relations has suggested, in terms of the training need of shop stewards, that

> it is necessary for him (the shop steward) to combine the skills of negotiation with those involved in communicating not only with management but with his members, fellow stewards and full-time officers. He needs analytic abilities in preparing cases and dealing with problems, and understanding of techniques such as work study and job evaluation.

It is hoped that various chapters in this book will aid the shop steward and other union officials in understanding and being able to carry out some of the 'people aspects' of their job. We are attempting to deal with only the cognitive or informational part of these skills; further work will have to be done by the unions themselves in action skills through various forms of experiential learning (Cooper, 1979a).

How to use this book

Most of the contributions written for this book are of value to both managers and trade union officials. Obviously some chapters are of more practical use to trade unionists (e.g. bargaining and negotiating) than managers, and vice versa, while some are not of any direct pragmatic value but are of greater foundational use in helping one to become more aware generally of human behaviour at work. The book is divided into five sections. The first section explores a number of topics that help to enhance our understanding of individual behaviour. The second section examines dyadic, inter-personal, group, and social behaviour. Section three highlights intergroup and other facets of organizational behaviour. In the fourth section, we attempt to bring together the individual, interpersonal and organizational factors of the previous three sections to focus on one of the most pressing and increasingly disruptive problems in contemporary organizations today, stress at work. This chapter not only highlights the major sources of stress acting on people at work in organizations, but also attempts to give the reader some insight on how important it is to take a multi-faceted view of organizational problems if we are to deal with the root causes and not the symptoms of conflict. And the final section explores change, the process and methods of personal, group and organizational change.

Individual behaviour
We start off this section by examining the concept of the self. Bannister asks a series of questions which it is essential for us to answer if we are to begin to understand anything about basic human needs and behaviour: what is the self, how do we know ourselves, do we change ourselves, how is our self-image related to others' view of our self, and what are the obstacles to self-knowledge and self-change? It

is necessary to begin any understanding of human behaviour by starting with the basic unit, the person. From there we should proceed to grapple with how the person came to be. What are the developmental sequences or episodes or events that are responsible for the creation of the self? Kline's chapter attempts briefly to provide us with a series of snapshots of various personality theories that help us to understand the processes that have been posited to explicate the development of the person.

An integral part of any theory of personality is motivation. Evans provides a brief review of a number of the motivational theories of interest to industrial psychology, by focussing on basic stimulus response theory, Maslow's hierarchy of needs (which is used extensively by managers and trade unionists alike in trying to explain work behaviour and the needs of workers), achievement motivation, trait motivation and motivation by anxiety. In addition, and very importantly for contemporary industrial life, he encourages us to think about achievement motivation in societal terms. Most of the theories discussed in this chapter are critical for a deeper level understanding of our current industrial relations dilemmas, as well as a portent of the future if organizational life is not changed to meet the developing needs of people at work; managers, clerical employees, skilled and unskilled workers alike.

And finally in this section Fontana provides us with an interesting and stimulating chapter on learning. In it he briefly examines a number of theories of learning and then turns his attention to the nature of the learner. In the latter part of his chapter, he highlights a group of factors within the learner which influence his ability to learn. An awareness of these individual-specific factors is essential for anybody attempting to influence others, whether in a managerial role or as a trade union official. Cognitive factors such as intelligence and creativity are explored as well as affective, motivational, maturational, demographic, and personal factors (e.g. the learner's age, sex, social background, etc.). In addition to material about the learner, the author also provides the management or trade union educator with information about other aspects of learning that are crucial in the educational process: the importance of the nature of the knowledge to be learned and the nature of the learning process (e.g. motivation, apprehending, acquisition, retention, recall, generalization, performance and feedback).

Interpersonal and social behaviour
In the second section of the book we focus on interpersonal, group, inter-group and social interaction. This is one of the more critical parts of the volume, because these are the areas of everyday importance to both managers and shop stewards, as was highlighted earlier in this chapter in the discussion of their job functions and roles. Of particular significance are the chapters by Wicks and Morley. Knowledge

of interviewing and the skills necessary to carry out such activities are vital for any shop steward in the course of his day-to-day activities. This is also an important aspect of first-line management and certain specialist managerial functions (e.g. personnel). And even more obviously the skill and process of bargaining is invaluable to trade unionists. Here, Morley explores the models of negotiation, the 'system' view of industrial negotiations, theories of labour negotiations and bargaining, the decision-making process, power and influence and the conflicts that many trade unionists and industrial relations specialists face in the process of negotiation. This chapter is not only a 'must' for trade union officials in exploring the psychology of bargaining and negotiations, but also of vital importance to the managers of industrial relations. In this context, there is an interesting quotation from Len Deighton in defining chess, which is appropriate for our industrial relations climate currently: 'a pejorative term used of inexperienced players who assume that both sides make rational decisions when in full possession of the facts. Any history book provides evidence that this is a fallacy and war-gaming exists only because of the fallacy'.

The final chapter in this section is also of enormous conceptual and practical importance. It looks at the nature of social behaviour which is fundamental to all aspects of human interaction. Argyle starts by providing a model of social skill behaviour, accounting for a sequence of social interaction. His model provides us with a framework for the development of social skills training for managers and trade unionists later in the chapter. He then goes on to explore the various forms of verbal and non-verbal behaviour, a knowledge of which is crucial for successful interaction. In addition, he highlights the importance of person perception and the necessity of perceiving oneself and others accurately in the course of social interaction. From there we move on to interpersonal influence: reinforcement, power, reciprocation of favours and other persuasive strategies. One of the most informative aspects of the latter strategies is 'how to handle groups', which is an essential function of managers and trade unionists. Here, Argyle explores group formation, conformity, leadership, committee chairmanships, etc. And finally, the improvement of social skills or competence is addressed. A variety of social skills techniques is examined in detail, from role-playing, modelling and video-playback to experiential small group methods.

This section of the book is full of psychological material which is invaluable to anyone working with people in industry or the public sector, be they managers or foremen or shop stewards or the Managing Director.

Organizational behaviour
In understanding the dynamics of individuals and groups within organizations, and their role in the growth or decline of organizations, Payne asks the fundamental

question: why are organizations the way they are? He then
attempts to answer this question systematically, by exploring the internal and external influences on organizational
structure, the nature of roles and the informal organization, and their impact on institutional life. In the second
part of his chapter, Payne begins to examine the psychological concepts relevant to understanding the behaviour of
people in organizations. In this section he relates many of
the concepts of the first section of this volume to the
behaviour of individuals within organizations, such as
motivational and need theories, learning theories and work
behaviour, leadership in organizations, and bases of social
influence. And finally, he focusses on one of the most
prominent approaches to change: organizational development
(OD). A model of a six-phase OD programme is presented
which highlights a total systems approach to organizational
change. He concludes by expressing concern at the increasing
pressure and level of stress found in the contemporary work
organization and how this affects the professional manager
and trade union official.

Stress in the workplace
Leading on from Payne's final remarks, it was thought to be
important to highlight the sources of organizational stress
currently affecting people at work. There were two reasons
for bringing it in at this stage of the volume. First, it is
a topic of growing importance in industry and in the public
sector. Stress-related illnesses such as coronary heart
disease have been on a steady upward trend over the past
couple of decades in the UK. In England and Wales, for
example, the death rate of men between 35 and 44 nearly
doubled between 1950 and 1973, and has increased much more
rapidly than that of older age ranges (e.g. 45-54). By 1973,
41 per cent of all deaths in the age group 25-44 were due
to cardio-vascular disease. In fact, in 1976 the American
Heart Association estimated the cost of cardio-vascular
diseases in the US at $26.7 billions a year. Industrial
accidents and short-term illnesses (through certified and
uncertified sick leaves) have been estimated in one year
alone in the UK to represent 300 million working days lost
at a cost of £55 million in national insurance and supple-
mentary benefits payments alone, aside from the costs to
industry in lost labour, retraining, etc. Second, the
sources, or causes, of stress at work are multi-factorial:
that is, they are usually the result of several inter-
related stressors. In this chapter we explore the individual, interpersonal/social and organizational sources of
stress and how they interact to create unnecessary and
damaging pressure on people at work. As the author of this
chapter I attempt to bring together much of the material
previously discussed to bear on this topic; examining how
certain personality types are more prone to stress than
others, the problems of role conflict, the pressure of poor
interpersonal relationships at work and the importance of

organizational structure and climate in creating trust or tension. Only by being made aware of the stressors operating in work organizations can managers and trade unionists begin to improve the quality of worklife by managing stress rather than 'being managed' by it.

Change

The final section of the book deals exclusively with change. One of the purposes of this volume is to make managers and trade union officials aware of individual, group and organizational behaviour, so that ultimately they are able to understand the needs of people at work, to identify problem areas in organizations, and to take action to change or minimize adverse work environments. It is vitally important, therefore, that we explore various theories and strategies of change. We start with a chapter by Hopson on understanding and managing personal change. One of the most important facts of life that many people in responsible positions fail to recognize (or do not want to acknowledge) about the people they manage or represent is that their personal life is not static! Life events are frequently occurring in an individual's personal and social circumstances that can adversely affect them at work. It is important to appreciate these, in order to understand fully the 'complete working person'. For employers entirely to disregard the private lives and circumstances of their employees is not only morally reprehensible but also managerially inept. Hopson provides us with a view of what can befall individuals in the course of various life events and, crucially, what people can do to help themselves to adapt. His strategies for self-help are both interesting and practically useful for those of us involved in managing or representing or interacting with people at work.

The final two chapters are less experiential than the previous one in this section, but they provide the reader with two different theoretical and practical approaches for the changing of behaviour.

Beech focusses on behavioural approaches to change, highlighting their theoretical foundations, advantages, potential usages, and disadvantages. Although many management educators as well as industrial relation specialists would cringe at the thought of using behavioural modification or other behavioural approaches in trying to change people in the workplace, Beech at least makes us aware of what these techniques can do and of their potential utility in a variety of situations. His summary of rational-emotive therapy is one example of a cognitive behavioural approach which, adapted for industrial use, could be of some value to individuals in a work context. The important point about this chapter is that it provides a 'window' into an approach for change which is growing in use in a variety of situations.

The final chapter explores a host of techniques one might find useful in industry to help people or groups of people. Although Hopson entitles his chapter 'Counselling and helping', he provides the interested manager or trade unionist with a compendium of training techniques that have been used to improve human relations or social skills at work. He explores the experiential or humanistic approaches, client-centred techniques, Gestalt therapy, etc. While this chapter is of particular use to management or industrial relations educators, it should provide the ordinary manager or trade unionist with a comparative framework of the various counselling or human relations training approaches currently available and being used to improve interpersonal relationships, to reduce tensions in work groups, to help develop organizational trust and communications and so on.

References

Batstone, E., Boraston, I. and Frenkel, S. (1977)
Shop Stewards in Action. Oxford: Blackwell.
Brown, W. and Jacques, E. (1965)
Glacier Project Papers. London: Heinemann.
Clegg, H.A., Killick, A.J. and Adams, R. (1966)
Trade Union Officers. Oxford: Blackwell.
Cooper, C.L. (1979a)
Learning from Others in Groups. London: Associated Business Press.
Cooper, C.L. (1979b)
The Executive Gypsy. London: Macmillan.
Goodman, J. and Whittingham, T.G. (1969)
Shop Stewards in British Industry. London: McGraw-Hill.
Handy, C. (1976)
Understanding Organizations. Harmondsworth: Penguin.
Mant, A. (1977)
The Rise and Fall of the British Manager. London: Pan.
Torrington, D. and Chapman, J. (1979)
Personnel Management. London: Prentice-Hall.

Part one

Individual Behaviour

I

Knowledge of Self
D. Bannister

Definition is a social undertaking. As a community we
negotiate the meaning of words. This makes 'self' a
peculiarly difficult term to define, since much of the
meaning we attach to it derives from essentially private
experiences of a kind which are difficult to communicate
about and agree upon. Nevertheless, we can try to abstract
from our private experience of self qualities which can
constitute a working definition. Such an attempt was made
by Bannister and Fransella (1980) in the following terms.

**Each of us entertains a notion of our own separateness from
others and relies on the essential privacy of our own
consciousness**
Consider differences between the way in which you communicate with yourself and the way in which you communicate with
others. To communicate with others involves externalizing
(and thereby blurring) your experience into forms of speech,
arm waving, gift giving, sulking, writing and so on. Yet
communicating with yourself is so easy that it seems not to
merit the word communication: it is more like instant recognition. Additionally, communicating with specific others
involves the risk of being overheard, spied upon or having
your messages intercepted and this contrasts with our
internal communications which are secret and safeguarded.
Most importantly, we experience our internal communications
as the origin and starting point of things. We believe that
it is out of them that we construct communications with
others. We know this when we tell a lie because we are aware
of the difference between our experienced internal communications and the special distortions given it before trans-
mission.

**We entertain a notion of the integrity and completeness of
our own experience in that we believe all parts of it to be
relatable because we are, in some vital sense, the
experience itself**
We extend the notion of me into notion of my world. We think
of events as more or less relevant to us. We distinguish
between what concerns and what does not concern us. In this
way we can use the phrase 'my situation' to indicate the
boundaries of our important experience and the ways in which
the various parts of it relate to make up a personal world.

We entertain the notion of our own continuity over time; we possess our biography and we live in relation to it

We live along a time line. We believe that we are essentially the 'same' person now that we were five minutes ago or five years ago. We accept that our circumstances may have changed in this or that respect, but we have a feeling of continuity, we possess a 'life'. We extend this to imagine a continuing future life. We can see our history in a variety of ways, but how we see it, the way in which we interpret it, is a central part of our character.

We entertain a notion of ourselves as causes, we have purposes, we intend, we accept a partial responsibility for the consequences of our actions

Just as we believe that we possess our life, so we think of ourselves as making 'choices' and as being identified by our choices. Even those psychologists who (in their professional writing) describe humankind as wholly determined, and persons as entirely the products of their environments, talk personally in terms of their own intentions and purposive acts and are prepared to accept responsibility, when challenged, for the choices they have made.

We work towards a notion of other persons by analogy with ourselves; we assume a comparability of subjective experience

If we accept for the moment the personal construct theory argument (Kelly, 1955, 1969) and think not simply of 'self' but of the bipolar construct of self versus others, then this draws our attention to the way in which we can only define self by distinguishing it from and comparing it to others. Yet this distinction between self and others also implies that others can be seen in the same terms, as 'persons' or as 'selves'. Our working assumption is that the rest of humankind have experiences which are somehow comparable with, although not the same as, our own and thereby we reasonably assume that they experience themselves as 'selves'.

We reflect, we are conscious, we are aware of self

Everything that has been said so far is by way of reflecting, standing back and viewing self. We both experience and reflect upon our experience, summarize it, comment on it and analyse it. This capacity to reflect is both the source of our commentary on self and a central part of the experience of being a 'self'. Psychologists sometimes, rather quaintly, talk of 'consciousness' as a problem. They see consciousness as a mystery which might best be dealt with by ignoring it and regarding people as mechanisms without awareness. This seems curious when we reflect that, were it not for this problematical consciousness, there would be no psychology to have problems to argue about. Psychology itself is a direct expression of consciousness. Mead (1925) elaborated this point in terms of the difference between 'I' and 'me', referring to the 'I' who acts and the 'me' who reflects upon the action and can go on to reflect upon the 'me' reflecting on the action.

The question 'do you know yourself?' seems to call forth a categorical 'yes' by way of answer. We know, in complete and sometimes painful detail, what has happened to us, what we have to contend with and what our thoughts and feelings are. We can reasonably claim to sit inside ourselves and know what is going on.

Yet we all have kinds of experience which cast doubt on the idea that we completely know ourselves. A basic test (in science and personal life) of whether you understand someone is your ability to predict accurately what they will do in a given situation. Yet most of us come across situations where we fail to predict our own behaviour; we find ourselves surprised by it and see ourselves behaving in a way we would not have expected to behave if we were the sort of person we thought we were.

We also sense that not all aspects of ourselves are equally accessible to us. There is nothing very mysterious in the notion of a hidden storehouse. We can confirm it very simply by reference to what we can readily draw from it. If I ask you to think about what kind of clothes you wore when you were around 14 years old you can probably bring some kind of image to mind. That raises the obvious question: where was that knowledge of yourself a minute ago, before I asked you the question? We are accustomed to having a vast knowledge of ourselves which is not consciously in front of us all the time. It is stored. It is not a great step to add to that picture the possibility that some parts of the 'store' of your past may not be so easily brought to the surface. We can then go one stage further and argue that although parts of your past are not easily brought to the surface they may nevertheless influence the present ways in which you feel and behave.

The best known picture of this kind of process is the Freudian portrait of the unconscious. Freud portrayed the self as divided. He saw it as made up of an id, the source of our primitive sexual and aggressive drives; a super-ego, our learned morality, our inhibitions; and an ego, our conscious self, struggling to maintain some kind of balance between the driving force of the id and the controlling force of the super-ego. Freud argued that the id is entirely unconscious and a great deal of the super-ego is also unconscious, and that only very special strategies such as those used in psychoanalytic therapy can give access to the contents of these unconscious areas of self. We do not have to accept Freud's particular thesis in order to accept the idea of different levels of awareness, but it may well be that the enormous popularity of Freudian theory is due to the fact that it depicts what most of us feel is a 'probable' state of affairs; namely, that we have much more going on in us that we can readily be aware of or name.

Indeed, if we examine our everyday experience then we may well conclude that we are continually becoming aware of aspects of ourselves previously hidden from us.

A great deal of psychotherapy, education and personal and interpersonal soul-searching is dedicated to bringing to the surface hitherto unrecognized consistencies in our lives.

How do we know ourselves?

There is evidence that getting to know ourselves is a developmental process: it is something we learn in the same way that we learn to walk, talk and relate to others. In one study (Bannister and Agnew, 1977), groups of children were tape-recorded answering a variety of questions about their school, home, favourite games and so forth. These tape-recordings were transcribed and re-recorded in different voices so as to exclude circumstantial clues (names, occupations of parents and so forth) as to the identity of the children. Four months after the original recording the same children were asked to identify their own statements, to point out which statements were definitely not theirs and to give reasons for their choice. The children's ability to recognize their own statements increased steadily with age, and the strategies they used to pick out their own answers changed and became more complex. Thus, at the age of five, children relied heavily on their (often inaccurate) memory or used simple clues such as whether they themselves undertook the kinds of activity mentioned in the statement; 'That boy says he plays football and I play football so I must have said that'. By the age of nine, they were using more psychologically complex methods to identify which statements they had made and which statements they had not made. For example, one boy picked out the statement 'I want to be a soldier when I grow up' as definitely not his because 'I don't think I could ever kill a human being so I wouldn't say I wanted to be a soldier'. This is clearly a psychological inference of a fairly elaborate kind.

Underlying our notions about ourselves and other people are personal psychological theories which roughly parallel those put forward in formal psychology.

A common kind of theory is what would be called in formal psychology a 'trait theory'. Trait theories hinge on the argument that there are, in each of us, enduring characteristics which differentiate us from others, who have more or less of these characteristics. The notion that we or someone else is 'bad-tempered' is closely akin to the notion in formal psychology that some people are constitutionally 'introverted' or 'authoritarian' and so forth. The problem with trait descriptions is that they are not explanatory. They are a kind of tautology which says that a person behaves in a bad-tempered way because he is a bad-tempered kind of person. Such approaches tend to distract our attention from what is going on between us and other people by firmly lodging 'causes' in either us or the other person. If

I say that I am angry with you because I am 'a bad-tempered person' that relieves me of the need to understand what is going on specifically between you and me that is making me angry.

Environmental and learning theories in psychology have their equivalents in our everyday arguments about our own nature. The fundamental assertion of stimulus-response psychology, that a person can be seen as reacting to his environment in terms of previously learned patterns of response, is mirrored in our own talk when we offer as grounds for our actions that it is all 'due to the way I was brought up' or 'there was nothing else I could do in the circumstances'. Those theories and approaches in formal psychology which treat the person as a mechanism echo the kinds of explanation which we offer for our own behaviour when we are most eager to excuse it, to deny our responsibility for it and to argue that we cannot be expected to change.

Any theory or attempt to explain how we come to be what we are and how we change involves us in the question of what kind of evidence we use. Kelly (1955) argued that we derive our picture of ourselves through the picture which we have of other people's picture of us. He was arguing here that the central evidence we use in understanding ourselves is other people's reactions to us, both what they say of us and the implications of their behaviour towards us. He was not saying that we simply take other people's views of us as gospel. Obviously this would be impossible because people have very varying and often very disparate reactions to us. He argued that we filter others' views of us through our view of them. If someone you consider excessively rash and impulsive says that you are a conventional mouse, you might be inclined to dismiss their estimate on the grounds that they see everyone who is not perpetually swinging from the chandelier as being a conventional mouse. However, if someone you consider very docile and timid says that you are a conventional mouse, then this has quite different implications. You do not come to understand yourself simply by contemplating your own navel or even by analysing your own history. You build up a continuous and changing picture of yourself out of your interaction with other people.

we change ourselves? That we change in small ways seems obvious enough. Looking at ourselves or others we readily notice changes in preferred style of dress, taste in films or food, changes in interests and hobbies, the gaining of new skills and the rusting of old and so forth.

Whether we change in large ways as well as small involves us in the question of how we define 'large' and 'small' change. Kelly (1955) hypothesized that each of us has a 'theory' about ourselves, about other people, and about the nature of the world, a theory which he referred to as our personal construct system. Constructs are our ways of discriminating our world. For many of them we have overt labels such as nice-nasty, ugly-beautiful, cheap-expensive, north-south, trustworthy-untrustworthy and so forth. He also distinguished between superordinate and subordinate constructs. Superordinate constructs are those which govern large areas of our life and which refer to matters of central concern to us, while subordinate constructs govern the minor detail of our lives.

If we take constructs about 'change in dress' at a subordinate level then we refer simply to our tendency to switch from sober to bright colours, from wide lapels to narrow lapels and so forth. If we look at such changes superordinately then we can make more far-reaching distinctions. For example, we might see ourselves as having made many subordinate changes in dress while not changing superordinately because we have always 'followed fashion'. Thus at this level of abstraction there is no change because the multitude of our minor changes are always governed and controlled by our refusal to make a major change, that is, to dress independently of fashion.

Psychologists differ greatly in their view of how much change takes place in people and how it takes place. Trait psychologists tend to set up the notion of fixed personality characteristics which remain with people all their lives, which are measurable and which will predict their behaviour to a fair degree in any given situation. The evidence for this view has been much attacked (e.g. Mischel, 1968). Direct examination of personal experience suggests that Kelly (1955) may have been right in referring to 'man as a form of motion and not a static object that is occasionally kicked into movement'.

Psychological measurement, to date, suggests that people change their character, if only slowly, and have complex natures so that behaviour is not easily predictable from one situation to another. Psychologists have also tended to argue that where change takes place it is often unconscious and unchosen by the person. The issue of whether we choose change or whether change is something that happens to us is clearly complex. One way of viewing it might be to argue that we can and do choose to change ourselves, but that often we are less aware of the direction which chosen change may eventually take.

A person in a semi-skilled job may decide to go to night-school classes or undertake other forms of training in order to qualify themselves for what they regard as more challenging kinds of work. They might be successful in gaining qualifications and entering a new field. Up to this point they can reasonably claim to have chosen their direction of personal change and to have carried through that change in terms of their original proposal. However, the long-term effect may be that they acquire new kinds of responsibility, contacts with different kinds of people, new values and a life style which, in total, will involve personal changes not clearly envisaged at the time they went to their first evening class.

On the issue of how we go about changing ourselves, Radley (1974) speculated that change, particularly self-chosen change, may have three stages to it. Initially, if we are going to change, we must be able to envisage some goal; we must have a kind of picture of what we will be like when we have changed. He argued that if we have only a vague picture or no picture at all then we cannot change; we need to be able to 'see' the changed us in the distance. He went on to argue that when we have the picture then we can enact the role of a person like that. That is to say, we do not at heart believe that we are such a person but we can behave as if we were such a person, rather like an actor playing a role on stage or someone trying out a new style. (This may relate to the old adage that adolescence is the time when we 'try out' personalities to see which is a good fit.) He argued that if we enact in a committed and vigorous way for long enough then, at some mysterious point, we become what we are enacting and it is much more true to say that we are that person than that we are our former selves. This is very much a psychological explanation, in that it is about what is psychologically true, rather than what is formally and officially true. Thus the student who qualifies and becomes a teacher may officially, in terms of pay packet and title, be 'a teacher'. Yet, in Radley's terms, the person may still psychologically be 'a student' who is enacting the role of teacher, who is putting on a teaching style and carrying out the duties of a teacher but who still, in his heart of hearts, sees himself as a student. Later, there may come a point at which he becomes, in the psychological sense, a teacher.

However, we are also aware that there is much that is problematic and threatening about change. The set expectations of others about us may have an imprisoning effect and restrict our capacity to change. People have a picture of us and may attempt to enforce that picture. They may resist change in us because it seems to them unnatural, and it would make us less predictable. Phrases such as 'you are acting out of character', or 'that is not the true you', or 'those are not really your ideas' all reflect the difficulty people find and the resistance they manifest to change in us. Often the pressure of others' expectations is so great that we can only achieve change by keeping it secret until the change has gone so far that we can confront the dismay of others.

This is not to argue that we are simply moulded and brainwashed by our society and our family so that we are merely puppets dancing to tunes played by others. We are clearly influenced by others and everything, the language we speak, the clothes we wear, our values, ideas and feelings, is derived from and elaborated in terms of our relationships with other people and our society. But the more conscious we become of how this happens, the more likely we are to become critical of and the less likely automatically to accept what we are taught (formally and informally), and the more we may independently explore what we wish to make of ourselves as persons.

Equally, when we attempt to change we may find the process personally threatening. We may lose sight of the fact that change is inevitably a form of evolution: that is to say, we change from something to something and thereby there is continuity as well as change. If we lose faith in our own continuity we may be overwhelmed by a fear of some kind of catastrophic break, a fear of becoming something unpredictable to ourselves, of falling into chaos. Whether or not we are entirely happy with ourselves, at least we are something we are familiar with, and quite often we stay as we are because we would sooner suffer the devil we know than the unknown devil of a changed us. Fransella (1972) explored the way in which stutterers who seem to be on the verge of being cured of their stutter often suddenly relapse. She argued that stutterers know full well how to live as 'stutterers'; they understand how people react and relate to them as 'stutterers'. Nearing cure they are overwhelmed with the fear of the unknown, the strangeness of being 'a fluent speaker'.

Monitoring of self

One of the marked features of our culture is that it does not demand (or even suggest) that we formally monitor our lives or that we record our personal history in the way in which a society records its history. True, a few keep diaries and practices such as re-reading old letters from other people give us glimpses into our past attitudes and feelings. For the most part, our understanding of our past is based on our often erratic memory of it. Moreover, our memory is likely to be erratic, not just because we forget past incidents and ideas but because we may actively 're-write' our history so as to emphasize our consistency and make our past compatible with our present.

Psychologists have tended to ignore the importance of personal history. The vast majority of psychological tests designed to assess the person cut in at a given point in time; they are essentially cross-sectional and pay little heed to the evolution of the person. It would be a very unusual psychology course that used biography or autobiography as material for its students to ponder. There are exceptions to this here-and-now preoccupation. In child psychology great emphasis is laid on the notion of 'development' and a great deal of the research and argument in child psychology is about how children acquire skills over a period, how they are gradually influenced by social customs and how life within the family, over a period of years, affects a child's valuing of himself. Additionally, clinical psychologists involved in psychotherapy and counselling very often find themselves engaged in a joint search with their clients through the immediate and distant past in order to understand present problems and concerns. This does not necessarily argue that a person is simply the end product of their past. We need to understand and acknowledge our past, not in order to repeat it but in order either to use it or to be free of it. As Kelly (1969) put it, 'you are not the victim of your autobiography but you may become the victim of the way you interpret your autobiography'.

Obstacles to self-knowledge and self-change

To try and understand oneself is not simply an interesting pastime, it is a necessity of life. In order to plan our future and to make choices we have to be able to anticipate our behaviour in future situations. This makes self-knowledge a practical guide, not a self-indulgence. Sometimes the situations with which we are confronted are of a defined and clear kind so that we can anticipate and predict our behaviour with reasonable certainty. If someone asks you if you can undertake task X (keep a set of accounts, drive a car, translate a letter from German and so forth) then it is not difficult to assess your skills and experience and work out whether you can undertake the task or not. Often the choice or the undertaking is of a more complex and less defined nature. Can you stand up in conflict with a powerful authority figure? Can you make a success of your marriage to this or that person? Can you live by yourself when you have been used to living with a family? The stranger the country we are entering the more threatening the prospect becomes; the more we realize that some degree of self-change may be involved, the more we must rely upon our understanding of our own character and potential.

In such circumstances we are acutely aware of the dangers of change and may take refuge in a rigid and inflexible notion of what we are. Kelly (1955, 1969) referred to this tendency as 'hostility'. He defined hostility as 'the continued effort to extort validational evidence in favour of a type of social prediction which has already been recognized as a failure'. We cannot lightly abandon our theory of what we are, since the abandonment of such a theory may plunge us into chaos. Thus we see someone destroy a close relationship in order to 'prove' that they are independent or we see teachers 'proving' that their pupils are stupid in order to verify that they themselves are clever.

Closely connected to this definition of hostility is Kelly's definition of guilt as 'the awareness of dislodgement of self from one's core role structure'. Core constructs are those which govern a person's maintenance processes; they are those constructs in terms of which identity is established and the self is pictured and understood. Your core role structure is what you understand yourself to be.

It is in a situation in which you fail to anticipate your own behaviour that you experience guilt. Defined in this way guilt comes not from a violation of some social code but from a violation of your own personal picture of what you are.

There are traditional ways of exploring the issue of 'what am I like?' We can meditate upon ourselves, ask others how they see us, or review our history. Psychologists have devised numerous tests for assessing 'personality', though insofar as these are of any use they seem to be designed to give the psychologist ideas about the other person rather than to give the people ideas about themselves. Two relatively recent attempts to provide people with ways of exploring their own 'personality' are offered by McFall (in Bannister and Fransella, 1980) and Mair (1970).

McFall offers a simple elaboration on the idea of talking to oneself. His work indicated that if people associate freely into a tape-recorder and listen to their own free flow then, given that they erase it afterwards so that there is no possible audience other than themselves at that time, they may learn something of the themes, conflicts and issues that concern them; themes that are 'edited out' of most conversation and which are only fleetingly glimpsed in our thinking. Mair experimented with formalized, written conversation. Chosen partners wrote psychological descriptions of each other (and predictions of the other's description) and then compared and discussed the meaning and the evidence underlying their written impressions.

Although we have formal ways of exploring how we see and how we are seen by others (the encounter group), and informal ways (the party), it can be argued that there is something of a taboo in our society on direct expression of our views of each other. It may be that we fear to criticize lest we be criticized, or it may be that we are embarrassed by the whole idea of the kind of confrontation involved in telling each other about impressions which are being created. Certainly if you contemplate how much you know about the way you are seen by others, you may be struck by the limitations of your knowledge, even on quite simple issues. How clear are you as to how your voice tone is experienced by other people? How often do you try and convey to someone your feelings and thoughts about them in such an oblique and roundabout way that there is a fair chance that they will not grasp the import of what you are saying?

Psychologists are only very slowly seeing it as any part of their task to offer WAYS to people in which they may explore themselves and explore the effect they have on others.

Role and person

Social psychologists have made much use of the concept of 'role'. Just as an actor plays a particular role in a drama it can be argued that each of us has a number of roles in our family, in work groups, in our society. We have consistent ways of speaking, dressing and behaving which reflect our response to the expectations of the group around us. Thus within a family or small social group we may have inherited and developed the role of 'clown' or 'hardheaded practical person' or 'sympathizer'. Jobs often carry

implicit role specifications with them so that we perceive
different psychological requirements in the role of teacher
from the role of student or the role of manager from the
role of worker. We are surprised by the randy parson, the
sensitive soldier, the shy showbusiness person. Society also
prescribes very broad and pervasive roles for us as men or
women, young or old, working-class or middle-class and so
forth. It is not that every word of our scripts is pre-
written for us, but the broad boundaries and characteristics
of behaviour appropriate to each role are fairly well
understood. These social roles can and do conflict with
personal inclinations and one way of defining maturity would
be to look on it as the process whereby we give increasing
expression to what we personally are, even where this
conflicts with standard social expectations.

Kelly chose to define role in a more strictly personal
sense in his sociality corollary which reads: 'to the extent
that one person construes the construction processes of
another he may play a role in a social process involving the
other person'. He is here emphasizing the degree to which,
when we relate to another person, we relate in terms of our
picture of the other person's picture of us. Role then
becomes not a life style worked out by our culture and
waiting for us to step into, but the on-going process
whereby we try to imagine and understand how other people
see the world and continuously to relate our own conception
to theirs.

the paradox of self-knowing

We reasonably assume that our knowledge of something does
not alter the 'thing' itself. If I come to know that Guatemala produces zinc or that the angle of incidence of a light
ray equals its angle of reflection, then this new knowledge
of mine does not, of itself, affect Guatemala or light.
However, it alters me in that I have become 'knowing' and
not 'ignorant' of these things. More pointedly, if I come to
know something of myself then I am changed, to a greater
or lesser degree, by that knowledge. Any realization by a
person of the motives and attitudes underlying their
behaviour has the potential to alter that behaviour.

Put another way, a person is the sum of their understanding of their world and themselves. Changes in what we
know of ourselves and the way in which we come to know it
are changes in the kind of person we are.

This paradox of self-knowledge presents a perpetual
problem to psychologists. An experimental psychologist may
condition a person to blink their eye when a buzzer is
pressed, simply by pairing the buzzer sound with a puff of
air to the person's eyelid until the blink becomes a response to the sound of the buzzer on its own. But if the
person becomes aware of the nature of the conditioning
process and resents being its 'victim' then he may not
condition at all, or at least take much longer to condition.
The person's knowledge of what is going on within him and

between him and the psychologist has altered the person and invalidated the psychologist's predictions. Experimental psychologists seek to evade the consequences of this state of affairs by striving to keep the subject in ignorance of the nature of the experimental process or by using what they assume to be naturally ignorant subjects: for example, rats. But relying on a precariously maintained ignorance in the experimental subject creates only a mythical certainty in science. Psychotherapists, on the other hand, generally work on the basis that the more the person (subject, patient, client) comes to know of themselves, the nearer they will come to solving, at least in part, their personal problems.

This self-changing property of self knowledge may be a pitfall for a simple-minded science of psychology. It may also be the very basis of living, for us as persons.

References

Bannister, D. and Agnew, J. (1977)
The Child's Construing of Self. In A.W. Landfield (ed.), Nebraska Symposium on Motivation 1976. Nebraska: University of Nebraska Press.

Bannister, D. and Fransella, F. (1980)
Inquiring Man (2nd edn). Harmondsworth: Penguin.

Fransella, F. (1972)
Personal Change and Reconstruction. London: Academic Press.

Kelly, G.A. (1955)
The Psychology of Personal Constructs, Volumes I and II. New York: Norton.

Kelly, G.A. (1969)
Clinical Psychology and Personality: The selected papers of George Kelly (ed. B.A. Maher). New York: Wiley.

Mair, J.M.M. (1970)
Experimenting with individuals. British Journal of Medical Psychology, 43, 245-256.

Mead, G.H. (1925)
The genesis of the self and social control. International Journal of Ethics, 35, 251-273.

Mischel, W. (1968)
Personality and Assessment. New York: Wiley.

Radley, A.R. (1974)
The effect of role enactment on construct alternatives. British Journal of Medical Psychology, 47, 313-320.

Questions

1. Discuss the problem of defining 'self'.
2. Examine the way in which a person's idea of 'self' is affected by the nature of their work.
3. Discuss the nature of sex differences in ideas about 'self'.
4. How can we 'keep track' of ourselves?
5. What does Kelly mean by 'hostility'? Give examples.
6. Outline one theory of 'self' you have read about.

7. Describe some way in which you have increased knowledge of self.
8. Comment on Radley's idea of change through role enactment.
9. Outline Freud's picture of self as made up of id, ego and super-ego.
10. How would you go about teaching a course in 'self-knowledge'?
11. How do parents influence their children's ideas about 'self'?
12. To what extent is our picture of our self influenced by our physical state and appearance?
13. Some institutions require their staff to meet regularly and formally to discuss how their personal differences affect their work. Is this a good idea?
14. We come to understand ourselves through our relationship with others. Discuss.
15. Examine the way in which social customs inhibit our revealing of 'self'.
16. Self is just a product of our environment. Discuss.
17. People are born with a fixed character which they cannot alter. Discuss.
18. Adolescence is the time when we experiment with self. Discuss.
19. Write an essay on 'roles'.
20. Can psychologists measure personality?
21. What, in your view, are the main hindrances of self-knowledge?
22. Write an essay on 'guilt'.
23. 'He is not himself today.' What triggers off this kind of comment, and does it say more about the speaker than the person of whom it is said?
24. How can we go about changing ourselves?
25. What idea about 'self', proposed by anyone (psychologist, poet, friend or whatever) has impressed you most? Why?
26. Your family teaches you what to think of yourself. Discuss.
27. Your job enables you to express yourself. Your job prevents you being yourself. Discuss.

annotated reading

Axline, Virginia M. (1971) Dibs: In search of self. Harmondsworth: Penguin.
> A finely written description of a withdrawn and disturbed child who in the process of psychotherapy comes vividly to life. It casts light on our early struggles to achieve the idea of being a 'self'.

Bannister, D. and Fransella, F. (1980) Inquiring Man: The psychology of personal constructs. Harmondsworth: Penguin.
> The second edition of a book which sets out the way George Kelly sees each of us as developing a complex personal view of our world. The book describes two

decades of psychological research based on the theory and relates it to problems such as psychological breakdown, prejudice, child development and personal relationships.

Bott, M. and Bowskill, D. (1980) The Do-It-Yourself Mind Book. London: Wildwood House.
A lightly written but shrewd book by a psychiatrist on the ways in which we can tackle serious personal and emotional problems without recourse to formal psychiatry.

Fransella, F. (1975) Need to Change? London: Methuen.
A brief description of the formal and informal ways in which 'self' is explored and change attempted.

Rogers, C.R. (1961) On Becoming a Person. Boston: Houghton Mifflin.
Sets out the idea of 'self-actualization' and describes the ways in which we might avoid either limiting ourselves or being socially limited and come to be what Rogers calls a fully functioning person.

2

Personality
P. Kline

Personality tests

Personality tests can be divided into tests of temperament and mood. Temperament tests measure how we do what we do, and temperamental traits are usually thought of as enduring and stable, such as dominance or anxiety. Dynamic traits are concerned with motives: for instance, why we do what we do, and include drives such as sexuality or pugnacity. Moods refer to those fluctuating states that we all experience in our lives: anger, fatigue or fear. Let us now look at each of these three categories in turn, and discuss how the psychologist attempts to measure them.

Temperament tests

The most used type of temperament test is the personality questionnaire. This consists of lists of items concerned with the subject's behaviour. Typical items are: 'Do you enjoy watching boxing?', 'Do you hesitate before spending a large sum of money?' Items come in various formats. Those above would usually require subjects to respond 'Yes' or 'No'; or 'Yes', 'Uncertain' or 'No'. Sometimes items are of the forced choice variety. For example, 'Do you prefer: (i) watching boxing; (ii) going to a musical; or (iii) sitting quietly at home reading?'

CONSTRUCTION OF PERSONALITY QUESTIONNAIRES: given that these items are used, readers may wonder how personality questionnaires are constructed and how are the items chosen? In fact, the selection of items by item analysis is briefly described because this gives an insight into the effectiveness of personality questionnaires.

* Item writing: in the first place, items will be written which are face valid, that is, they appear to be relevant to the variable which we are trying to measure. For example, if we were attempting to measure anxiety we should include items that seemed to touch on the symptoms and feelings of anxiety both as we experience it and as we have found it delineated in the literature, such as finding it difficult to get to sleep, worrying over things one has done, feeling miserable for no good reason, having palpitations, poor appetite, and so on.

* Item analysis: in the construction of tests, the item analysis by which items are selected for a test is the critical issue. The rationale of item analysis is simple: if we are trying to measure a variable (say anxiety) then each selected item should be shown to measure anxiety. Furthermore, if the test is to be discriminating, then each item should be answered in one way (yes or no) by not more than about 80 per cent of the sample. Obviously, our sample for item trials should be drawn from the population for whom the test is intended. Item analysis therefore requires a statistical procedure which will reveal this information: that each item measures a common variable, and that each item is discriminating. Three methods are used: (i) factor analysis: the items can be correlated and the correlations are then subjected to factor analysis. Items loading on a general factor (unless constructing several scales at once) are selected. This method automatically eliminates items of low discrimination, since they will not load up properly. The items should be tried out again on a new sample to eliminate those loading by chance in the first item trial. (ii) Correlations of item and total score: a more simple method and one with less technical problems than factor analysis is to correlate each item with the total score for each scale separately. Items are chosen which correlate beyond 0.3. The endorsement rate for each item is also checked and any items of poor discriminatory power are removed. Finally, all results should be checked on a new sample. Results from this method are similar to method one. (iii) Criterion-keying: here the items are administered to criterion groups and those that can discriminate between the groups are selected. The problem here is to establish sufficiently clear criterion groups to make the technique robust. Thus an anxiety scale might be given to a group of anxious patients and a control non-anxious group. In addition, if the groups differ on more than one variable - if, for example, anxiety is confounded with intelligence - the resulting scale could be heterogeneous. Thus this method is not, in our view, as powerful as methods one and two.
* Validation of the scale: finally, the scale produced by the item analysis must be validated.

These methods are used in the construction of all psychometric tests which contain items (therefore excluding projective tests: see below), not only personality questionnaires. Method one was used to construct Cattell's 16PF personality questionnaire, method two for our own Ai3Q, a far less well-known test than the former, and method three was used to construct the MMPI (the Minnesota Multiphasic Personality Inventory).

The disadvantages of questionnaires are considerable, yet in spite of them many valid and highly useful

personality questionnaires have been constructed. The disadvantages are: (i) they are easy to fake, that is, subjects
may not tell the truth, for one reason or another, and this
makes them difficult to use in selection, although for
vocational guidance or psychiatric help, where subjects
have no reason to fake; this is not too serious; (ii) they
require some self-knowledge, and some subjects (while
attempting to be honest) may respond quite unrealistically;
(iii) they are subject to response sets. An important set is
social desirability, the tendency to endorse the socially
desirable response: that is, to present yourself in what you
consider to be the most favourable light. For example, to
the item, 'Do you have a good sense of humour?', the response 'Yes' would be given by about 95 per cent of subjects.
The other serious response set is that of acquiescence, the
tendency to put 'Yes' as an answer or agree with it regardless of content. Balanced scales, with some responses keyed
'No', obviate this to some extent.

Objective tests
Objective tests, defined by Cattell (cf. Cattell and Kline,
1977) as tests of which the purpose is hidden from the
subject and which can be objectively scored, have been
developed to overcome the disadvantages of questionnaires.
The aim is to reduce the possibility of faking response sets
or acquiescence though the reader might wish to challenge
their face validity. Ironically, because their purpose is
hidden from subjects, considerable research is necessary to
establish their validity, and as yet most are still in an
experimental form. These tests will probably take over from
questionnaires when the necessary research has been done.
The following examples indicate their nature.

* Balloon-blowing: subjects are required to inflate a
  balloon as much as they can. Measures taken are the size
  of the balloon, time taken blowing it up, whether they
  burst it, and if they delay in beginning the task. This
  test may be related to timidity and inhibition.
* The slow line-drawing test: subjects are required to
  draw a line as slowly as possible. The measure is the
  length of line over a fixed time.

In fact more than 800 such tests have been listed and more
can easily be developed depending upon the ingenuity of the
researcher. The technique is to administer a large battery
of such tests and to determine experimentally by validity
studies what each measures.

Projective tests
Projective tests essentially consist of ambiguous stimuli to
which the subjects have to respond. These are some of the
oldest personality tests and one, the Rorschach Test (the
inkblot test), has achieved a fame beyond psychology. Most
people have heard of inkblots. The rationale of projective

tests is intuitively brilliant: if a stimulus is so vague that it warrants no particular description, then any description of it must depend on what is projected on to it by the subject. Projective testers believe that projective tests measure the inner needs and fantasies of their subjects. Their ambiguity disarms the subject, thus enabling the tester to sidestep his defences, or his desire to please or to fake.

A serious problem with projective tests lies in their unreliability. Very complex responses have to be interpreted by scorers, and often considerable training, experience and expertise is necessary. Inter-marker reliability is low. Generally, too, it is difficult to demonstrate test validity. However, the present writer has experimented with entirely objective forms of scoring these tests and some evidence has now accrued that this is a useful procedure.

PROJECTIVE TEST STIMULI: although any ambiguous stimulus could be used as a test, generally the choice of stimulus is determined by the particular theory of personality the test constructor follows. For example, a psychoanalytically orientated psychologist would select stimuli relevant to that theory, such as vague figures who could be mother and son (the Oedipus complex) or figures with knives or scissors (the castration complex). The TAT (Thematic Apperception Test) developed by Murray uses pictures which, it is hoped, tap the inner needs held by Murray to be paramount in human behaviour.

Mood and motivation tests
Mood and motivation tests are essentially similar to temperament tests. Indeed, relatively little work has been done with these and their validity is not so widely attested as that of temperament tests.

Mood tests generally use items that concentrate as might be expected on present feelings rather than usual ones. With such tests, high test-retest reliability is not to be expected. However, the fluctuations in scores should not be random but should be related to external conditions. Thus experiments can be conducted in which scores, if the tests are valid, can be manipulated. Samples can take the mood test and then some can be angered, others sexually aroused, and the tests can be retaken. If the experimental manipulations are good and the tests valid, the relevant scores should change.

Motivation tests should be similarly fluctuating, according to whether drives are sated or frustrated. In a well-known study by the present author the scores of a single subject over a 28-day period were related to a diary recording all that happened to her and everything she felt or thought. In fact, the relations of scores to diary events were close. For example, the fear drive rose each weekend, and at weekends the subject went touring in a dangerous car. The career drive was flat except on one day where it became high. On this day the subject was interviewed for a course in teacher training.

Motivation tests can be of the questionnaire variety although objective and projective tests are more frequently used. For moods, questionnaire items are easy to write. They suffer, of course, from the same response sets as bedevil questionnaire measures of temperamental traits.

Interest tests

The tests of motivation described above are very general: that is, they measure variables thought to account for a wide variety of human behaviour. Vocational and industrial psychologists, however, have long felt the need for more specific measures of motivation, assessing the variables which seemed of immediate relevance to them, such as interests. For example, we all know of motoring enthusiasts who seem to have an all-embracing interest in cars. It would seem to make sense to think of an interest in cars as accounting for much of their behaviour and conversation.

Thus a number of interest tests have been developed which attempt to assess the major interests: outdoor, mechanical or an interest in people, for example. Some of these are tied closely to occupations. In some tests, the scoring of items which are face valid, for example, 'Do you enjoy working with children?', is in terms of groups. The performance of specific occupational groups on the tests is known and if, for example, foresters score high on an item then this item contributes to the interest in forestry score. In other tests, the scoring involves little more than subjects having to rank jobs. In other words, interest tests of this type are like formalized interviews.

Generally, as has been pointed out in Buros (1972), the correlations of interest test scores with success in a job relevant to the interests are modest and little better than the correlation obtained with response to the question of whether a subject thinks he would enjoy a job.

Attitude tests

Social psychologists have attempted to measure attitudes for many years now. Generally, the attitudes tested are important aspects of a person's life, such as attitudes to war, or to coloured people (in white populations) or to religion. Obviously, if efficient measures of such attitudes are possible then progress can be made in understanding how such attitudes arise and are maintained; important knowledge, it is thought, in a complex multi-racial society. There are three kinds of attitude test, differing in their mode of construction.

* THE THURSTONE SCALES: in these tests items are given to judges to rank 1-11 (favourable-unfavourable) in respect of an attitude. Items are selected about which there is good agreement among the judges. The subject then taking the test is given the highest judged rank

score of the items with which he agrees. The reason for this is clear if we consider a few examples. (1) 'War is totally evil' would probably be ranked high as unfavourable to war. (2) 'Wars sometimes have to be fought if there is no alternative': this is clearly against war but not strongly. (3) 'Wars are not always wrong': this is yet further down the scale, while the item (4) 'Wars are good: they select the finest nations' is favourable. Thus a subject who agreed with (1) would not agree with (2), (3) or (4). Similarly, a subject agreeing with (3) would not agree with (4).

These tests are difficult to construct because much depends on obtaining a good cross-section of judges. A more simple alternative is the Likert Scale.

* LIKERT SCALES: in the Likert scales statements relevant to the attitude being measured are presented to the subject who has to state on a five-point scale the extent of his agreement. Thus 'a Hitler' would score 100 on a 20-item attitude to war scale; 'a Ghandi' would score zero, one presumes. To make the scale less obvious, items are so written that to agree with items represents both poles of the attitude.

* THE GUTTMAN SCALE: this is a scale so constructed that if the items are ranked for positive attitudes, then any subject who endorses item 10 will also endorse items 1-9 below it. While this tends to happen by virtue of its construction with the Thurstone scale, such perfect ordering rarely occurs in practice. Guttman scales are not much used because they are extremely difficult to construct, and as Nunnally (1978) has pointed out, this perfect ordering of items can usually only be achieved by leaving huge gaps between the items (in terms of attitude) which means few items and rather coarse measurement.

The factorial description of personality

Personality questionnaires have been subjected, over the years, to factor analyses in the hope of discovering what are the basic temperamental dimensions. The main researchers in this area have been Cattell (working in Illinois), Eysenck (in London) and Guilford (in California). Although superficially each has produced what looks like a separate set of factors, recent research in this field has enabled some sort of consensus to be arrived at (see Cattell and Kline, 1977; Kline, 1979, for a full discussion of this work). In effect, the study of individual differences has led to the establishment of the main dimensions of personality. These dimensions are therefore those that demand study, and are as outlined below.

Extraversion
The high-scoring extravert is sociable, cheerful, talkative, and does not like to be alone. He enjoys excitement, takes risks and is generally impulsive: an outgoing optimist,

active and lively. The introvert is the opposite of this: cold, retiring and aloof. This dimension has been related by Eysenck to the arousability of the central nervous system. Scores on tests of this factor have a large genetic component.

Neuroticism (or anxiety)

The highly anxious subject is one who worries a lot, is moody and often depressed. He is highly emotional and takes a long time to calm down. He tends to sleep poorly and to suffer from psychosomatic disorders. This variable is claimed to be related to the lability of the autonomic nervous system.

These variables are both measured by the Cattell 16PF test and Eysenck's EPQ (the most recent version of the Eysenck personality tests). If we know an individual's status on these two factors, then already we know a good deal about his temperament.

Psychoticism (P)

This variable has not been as extensively studied as extraversion and anxiety and only recently (1975) has it appeared in a published questionnaire, the EPQ. Nevertheless, the nature of psychoticism is clear. The high scorer on this dimension is solitary, uncaring of people, troublesome, lacking in human feeling and empathy, thick skinned and insensitive. He is cruel, inhumane, hostile and aggressive, reckless to danger, aggressive even to his own family. Naturally enough, most normal individuals score low on P, but many criminals score high. This factor has been related by Eysenck to 'maleness'.

It is to be noted that these three factors have not only been clearly identified from the factor analysis of questionnaires: there is also a considerable mass of experimental data supporting their identification and nature.

These are the three second-order factors claimed by Eysenck to be the most important in accounting for temperamental differences. Second-order factors are factors arising from the correlations among first-order factors: that is, the factors accounting for the original correlations (see our discussion of factor analysis above). These first-order, or primary, factors are more problematic than the second orders but, as the work of Cattell has shown, can be of considerable power in applied psychometrics.

In brief, the factorial analysis of personality has revealed three basic dimensions, each tied to the basic physiology of man and hence largely heritable.

Of course, this factorial analysis of personality is essentially a theory of personality postulating that these three factors, physiologically and largely genetically determined, account for most of the differences in behaviour between individuals. It is interesting, therefore, to contrast this theory which is closely based upon measurement with some earlier theories of personality based on clinical observation and inference.

Psychoanalytic theories and theories of personality

Perhaps the most famous theory of personality is the classical psychoanalytic theory of Freud. Freud was a psychiatrist working in Vienna from the turn of the century to just before the outbreak of the Second World War. Eysenck has attacked psychoanalysis because it lacks quantification, is hard to verify and is not, in his view, highly successful as a therapy. Against this one must bear in mind the fact that it has attracted intelligent men all over the world because of its ability to throw light on a diverse array of human behaviours, such as totemism, painting, scientific endeavour, literary production, dreams and neuroses. Our brief description can do little justice to Freud's 24 volumes of collected papers.

Data base
The data on which psychoanalytic theory is based are the free associations of patients and their free associations to dreams: what Freud called 'the royal road to the unconscious'. Free association is the process by which a patient is required simply to say whatever comes into his head regardless of its nature.

The unconscious
A critical feature of Freudian theory is the emphasis placed upon unconscious mental activity: this is highly important in determining behaviour. Unconscious mental activity (primary processes) is chaotic, illogical and bizarre, demanding immediate satisfaction of the drives and needs within the unconscious. Only by understanding the unconscious can we understand personality. Preconscious ideas are unconscious but capable of recall: for example, telephone numbers.

The mind
In psychoanalytic theory the mind is divided into three parts. The id, unconscious, is the repository of basic drives, sex and aggression, and what has been repressed into it. The id is the source of mental energy, demanding immediate expression. This, however, in modern society cannot be permitted. To kill and copulate at whim leads only to prison. The id is controlled, therefore, by two other mental provinces. First, the ego, developed by identification with the same sex parent and the repository of our moral values (these being those of our parents as seen at about the age of five when the super-ego develops: see below). Thus mental health depends upon the correct balance of these three systems: too much control and the individual leads a narrow inexpressive life. If the super-ego is too strong we feel guilt-ridden and anxious, yet if there is too little control we become psychopathic criminals. The aim of psychoanalytic

therapy is to make man as rational as possible: where id was, there shall ego be.

The ego maintains control by the use of mechanisms of defence, which satisfy the conflicting demands of id and super-ego and which are unconscious. The system of defences we use profoundly affects our behaviour.

Successful defences (sublimation) allow expression of the instinctual, forbidden id drive: unsuccessful defences simply prevent its expression. This is important because in Freudian theory an instinctually barred expression still demands outlet. Hence unsuccessful defences have to be used over and over again, as the id drive persists in seeking expression: the basis of the tension and weariness of neurotic illness.

Defence mechanisms

1. SUCCESSFUL DEFENCES (sublimation): sublimation involves the deflection of instinctual drives so that they are expressed in a manner acceptable to the ego. For example, in Freudian theory anal drives, the desire to smear and handle faeces, are sublimated in the exercises of painting and pottery-making. Children's love of playing in mud and puddles is another example of such sublimation.

If drives are blocked, the energy remains in the system and demands different outlets. Sublimation is important because it allows the expression of otherwise forbidden drives. Indeed, Freud (1933) regarded sublimation as the cornerstone of civilized life: the arts, the sciences, all are sublimations of sexuality. Free expression of the id, sexuality and aggression is the road to barbarism.

2. UNSUCCESSFUL DEFENCES

* Repression: one of the most important mechanisms of defence. There are two phases in repression: primal repression, where the ego denies the instinct entry into consciousness, and repression proper, where the instinct and all connected with it are kept out of consciousness. The energy still remains in the system and is expressed as anxiety. Thus repression is critical in the development of neurosis. It is, of course, unconscious.
* Denial: this is similar to repression, except that here the ego wards off the external world by altering perception. Denial of age is a common example: the middle-aged paunch crammed into tight jeans, combined with an Afro hair-cut and cowboy boots.
* Projection: here unacceptable impulses are attributed to others. A woman's neurotic fear of sexual attack may result from her projection of her own sexual drive and even lead to agoraphobia.
* Reaction-formation: the feelings in the conscious are the opposite of those in the unconscious. Thus love becomes hate, while shame, disgust and moralizing are

reaction-formations against sexuality. The delusions of
persecution found in paranoia are in Freudian theory
attributed to reaction-formation against homosexuality.
Thus, 'I love him' becomes 'I hate him', which becomes,
by projection, 'he hates me'.

* Regression: to avoid conflict, people resort to earlier
modes of behaviour. Thus the person regresses to earlier
modes of responding which were appropriate then, but not
in the present. The ego cannot solve the conflicts created by the need to develop new responses appropriate
to present circumstances.

* Isolation: here feelings and emotions are separated from
the experiences which normally produce them: for
example, the man who can have sexual relations only with
women he despises; the isolation of love and sex.

* Undoing: here an action 'undoes' an imaginary or real
action. For example, the obsessional who washes everything he touches because he feels, being himself dirty,
that he has made them dirty.

From this, the importance of defence mechanisms in understanding personality must be obvious. The quality of the
dynamic balance depends upon the strategy of our defences.
However, another aspect of psychoanalytic theory relevant
to personality is Freudian psychosexual developmental theory
and this is described below. As we shall see, it is in this
that the importance of the first five years is emphasized.

Psychosexual development
'Sexual life does not begin at puberty, but starts with
plain manifestations soon after birth' (Freud, 1940). Indeed
Freud described the infant, to the outrage of his
contemporaries, as a 'polymorphous pervert'. This is
because, as Freud (1940) continued, 'sexual life includes
the function of obtaining pleasure from zones of the body -
a function which is subsequently brought into the service of
reproduction'. The infant derives pleasure initially from
the stimulation of any part of the body, and this pleasure
is sexual: hence the term 'polymorphous pervert', for Freud
defined any sexual activity which does not have reproduction
as its aim as a perversion.

* The oral stage: very soon in the infant's life the
sexual drive begins to manifest itself through the
mouth, which becomes the principal erotogenic zone.
There is an oral-erotic phase, sucking, and an oral-
sadistic phase, biting. The erotogenic pleasure is known
as oral eroticism.

* The anal stage: at about two years of age, the anus
becomes the most important erotogenic zone. Anal erotism
also has two phases: there is pleasure in expelling
faeces (anal-expulsive) and later in retention (anal-
retentive).

* The phallic stage: around the age of four the penis and
clitoris become the chief erotogenic zones; this is

phallic erotism. Then, after the Oedipus and castration complexes, the child enters the latency period, during which he usually experiences less sexual conflict, until the final stage of sexual organization is established at puberty.
*   The mature genital stage: here previous stages are reorganized and subordinated to the adult sexual aim of reproduction.

The Oedipus complex

Freud regarded the Oedipus complex not only as his greatest discovery but as one of man's greatest discoveries. It explains how, in spite of our instincts, we become law-abiding citizens, strive for perfection, and develop a conscience. Every male child is fated to pass through the Oedipus complex. At the phallic stage the boy becomes his mother's lover; he desires to possess her physically, to assume his father's place: his father becomes a rival.

However, the Oedipus complex is 'doomed to a terrible end'. It is repressed through fear of castration - a punishment for infantile masturbation - which the boy imagines will be inflicted on him by his powerful rival, his father. The result of this is that the boy identifies with his father (through fear of castration), and thus the super-ego is born. Since the child cannot have his mother sexually (as the id wishes), he adopts the compromise of vicarious pleasure through identifying with his father. This identification involves not only sexual pleasure but subsequently the father's ideas and beliefs. Thus the cultural values of our generation are passed on to the next. Clearly, these complexes are critical for the development of the male personality.

Penis envy

For the girl, however, there is a different process. At the phallic phase she suffers from penis envy: inferiority feelings about the clitoris vis-à-vis the penis. She then turns against her mother who, she feels, has castrated her; in her mother's place she puts her father as an object of love. Thus the Electra complex begins. Oedipal attitudes are more likely to remain in women, as there is no castration complex to end them. It is through fear of losing love that the girl identifies with the same sex parent and develops the super-ego which, according to Freud, is likely to be less strongly developed in women. It follows that women are less idealistic and less troubled by conscience.

Psychosexual theory and personality

Two facts contribute to the importance of psychosexual theory in understanding personality.

*   Pregenital erotism cannot all be directly expressed. Thus defence mechanisms have to be used, producing other apparently unrelated behaviours. For example, direct expression of anal erotism (sodomy) is actually illegal

in Britain. Direct expression of oral erotism is allowed: connoisseurs of food, specialists in oral sex. Indeed, permanent character traits, according to Freud, are either unchanged expressions of these original instincts or defences against them. Defences against oral erotism are the oral traits of dependency, talkativeness and optimism. Defences against anality embrace the famous anal character of parsimony, perseverance, obstinacy and orderliness. Parsimony is a sublimation of the desire to retain the faeces; orderliness a reaction formation against the desire to smear them.

* Fixation at the pregenital level: we may become fixated at a particular level, as a result of being over-indulged or not sufficiently indulged during the relevant stage of infancy. Thus fixation at the oral level can be caused by sudden weaning or indulgent demand feeding. Similarly, different kinds of toilet training can cause fixation at the anal level. Fixation implies that undue importance is attached to a particular developmental phase. Fixation is also partly determined by constitutional factors, such as the sensitivity to stimulation of the particular erotogenic zone. This, of course, interacts with the environmental variables discussed above.
* The Oedipus complex: this is regarded as the kernel of neurosis. For Freud, truly maturing involves breaking away from the parents. In the neurotic this is never done. This unconscious conflict affects our lives in ways of which we are unaware. Attitudes to women (do we like women like our mother?), attitudes to employers and superiors and attitudes to authority itself (rivalry of father) are all examples of this. The castration complex, too, is also powerful. This may be reflected in attitudes to vivisection, to surgery, to blood itself. Homosexuals in psychoanalytic theory are held to have the castration complex. Their homosexuality stems from their inability to face penisless beings or beings that bleed from their private parts.

This brief account of psychoanalytic personality theory makes clear its complexity in that it can account for a huge variety of behaviours. However, it does so with a surprisingly small number of concepts.

Objections to Freudian theory

We have already mentioned the objections on scientific grounds, to psychoanalysis, objections most widely broadcast by Eysenck. These concern:

* the lack of clear raw data;
* the poor sampling: the patients under Freud's care are clearly not samples of all mankind;
* the lack of statistical analysis;
* the ambiguity and vagueness of the concepts;

* the difficulty of falsifying the theory;
* the failure of the therapy to show itself efficacious.

Even if all these objections are admitted, does this inevitably mean that Freudian theory should be abandoned as worthless?

The scientific study of psychoanalytic theory

A previous work (Kline, 1972) has dealt extensively with this problem. The essence of the case that psychoanalytic theory has some scientific validity and is deserving of further investigation is set out below.

* Psychoanalytic theory can be broken down into sets of testable hypotheses. In this sense, Freudian theory is a collection of theories as Farrell has claimed.
* When this is done and the theories are put to a scientific test, using proper samples, validated tests and adequate statistics, certain of the psychoanalytic propositions can be shown to hold. For example (see Kline, 1972), there is reasonable evidence for repression and the Oedipus complex. To summarize the findings in this huge area: much of Freudian theory has received some objective support and it would be flying in the face of the evidence to reject it out of hand.

Other psychoanalytic theories

Of course, over the years there has developed a large number of variants of Freudian theory: the work of Jung, Adler, Fromm, Horney, Sullivan and Melanie Klein being amongst the most well known. In general, these theories have differed from those of Freud in their lesser emphasis on sexuality. For Adler the great drive was the aim of achieving superiority (hence his use of the inferiority complex). For Jung the profoundest aspects of the mind were the contents of the collective unconscious, the accumulated wisdom of the ages. While Freud believed that mental health lay in controlling the instincts of the id, Jung believed that only by allowing oneself proper contact with the collective unconscious could one develop one's full potential.

Other theories of personality

Psychoanalytic theories, especially those of Jung and Freud, have had enormous effects on the Zeitgeist; their ripples have spread far beyond the confines of psychology. For this reason alone psychoanalytic theory deserves critical scrutiny.

However, there are many other personality theorists whose work, even if influenced by dynamic theories, can in no way be called psychoanalytic. To summarize these briefly and with justice is hardly possible. However, many of these theories are old, so that a brief acquaintance is perhaps all that is necessary. More recently theories of personality have been eschewed because the field is so large. The age of grand theorizing is gone. Indeed, the nearest thing to a coherent modern personality theory is in fact the factor-analytic work of Eysenck and Cattell, which we have already discussed. To conclude this brief account of theories of personality, let us simply select a few items from various different theories to illustrate the range and scope.

The work of McDougall

McDougall, a psychologist not now held in high repute, claimed that the mainsprings of human activity lay in a number of native propensities, and sentiments within which these propensities are organized. McDougall (1932) listed 18 propensities among which were: food seeking, rejecting noxious substances, sexual propensities, fear, exploratory drive, protective and gregarious propensities, to name but seven. However, McDougall regarded one sentiment as all important; the self-image, the master sentiment around which much of what we do revolves. Other sentiments are (for example, money-seeking, job-seeking and so on) cultural avenues for expressing the basic propensities.

This kind of psychologizing is mainly of historical interest (i) because it is speculative rather than empirical and (ii) because the very concept of propensity is circular: that is, we observe a behaviour, such as food seeking, explain it by hypothesizing a food-seeking propensity and then use the behaviour which it seeks to explain as confirmation of the hypothesis. However, we mention it because recent factor-analytic work by Cattell in Illinois (see Cattell and Kline, 1977) gives some support for there being a number of basic propensities and sentiments, although by no means as many as McDougall claimed. It could be the case that McDougall will become more highly esteemed as more empirical work is carried out. McDougall's theory suffered neglect because of a distaste among psychologists, which lasted from the Second World War until quite recently, for any theory which was based on the notion of inborn propensities or instincts.

Murray

Murray was another important personality theorist who, in 'Explorations in Personality' (1938), attempted to develop a new subject, 'Personology'. His work was based on the analysis of interviews, biographies, projective and experimental tests and involved brilliant clinical intuition from a huge amount of data from each subject. He postulated a large number of needs to account for human behaviour together with corresponding environmental presses. Although the factor analysis of motivation has not supported his list of needs, for example, to abase, to affiliate, to achieve, to be aggressive, to be different, it seems likely that Murray was looking at surface clusters of behaviours rather than the larger more basic factors of factor analysis. One of his drives, nAch, the need to achieve, has been extensively studied by McClelland and colleagues and does seem an important determinant of entrepreneurial performance at least. Murray's work is valuable because it lays stress on the importance of studying the whole person in all his aspects, yet not to the extent that generalizable laws of behaviour cannot be formulated. This is a good counter-balance against large-scale statistical studies where the unique individual can be lost.

Physique and personality

Two researchers, Kretschmer (1925) and Sheldon (Sheldon and Stevens, 1942) have claimed that physique is related to temperament. Kretschmer observed from his clinical work that schizophrenics tend to be thin, and manic depressives fat, extreme examples, in his view, of tendencies in the normal population that moody individuals are likely to be rotund, and aloof, withdrawn people of slender build.

Sheldon in his work on physique and character attempted to classify body build into three dimensions, each on a seven-point scale. Most individuals are high on one of these dimensions which are measured precisely from different parts of the body. A cluster analysis (a simple form of factor analysis) of ratings of temperament showed a close relationship between body build and character, findings which have been challenged on grounds of computing error (not that uncommon in large-scale correlational studies calculated by hand). The results were in accord with common sense and literary stereotypes. The fat individual was of Falstaffian temperament, the muscular rugby-playing type was pushy and insensitive, and the thin ectomorph cold and withdrawn.

Modern studies conducted by Eysenck and colleagues at the Maudsley and Cattell and co-workers at Illinois give only modest confirmation of this link. Nevertheless, it is research that has been neglected, perhaps surprisingly, and large-scale investigations of Sheldon's typology relating it to the main personality dimensions might prove useful.

In all these theories which we have so far mentioned it must be noted that there are common problems. These relate to the proper quantification of temperament and dynamics. None of these researchers had personality tests of proven validity and reliability.

Finally, the approach of two other psychologists must be mentioned so that psychological testing in relation to personality can be put into a different perspective. Our view, as is obvious, is that precise measurement is the 'sine qua non' of any adequate personality theory. Concomitant with this is our claim that factor analysis is the instrument by which good tests can be constructed and validated. This indeed is the psychometric view, the implicit underpinning of the work of Eysenck and Cattell.

Allport

Allport (1938), however, has explicitly argued against this. He admits that statistical analyses of tests can reveal common dimensions. However, he stresses the importance of the unique components of personality that each individual alone possesses, dependent upon the experience that he alone has undergone. For Allport it is these personal data that are critical to understanding personality.

Two important points are raised here. First, if Allport were correct, a science of personality would be impossible, for each individual is essentially unique. We can, given sufficient time, understand him but this would not help us to understand anyone else. Thus no statements about regularities of behaviour can be made. The second point follows from this. If Allport were correct, it would not be possible to predict real-life behaviours from tests of personality. In fact, however, this can be done, as the extensive handbooks to the better personality inventories, the 16PF test, the EPQ and the MMPI, illustrate. Allport, therefore, must have exaggerated his case. Even so, the existence of personality scales is not incompatible with the notion of uniqueness. In any one sample, individuals will have very different profiles across a range of scales. This does not mean they will not share certain characteristics or groups of characteristics in common with other members of the sample.

Situationalism

Mischel (e.g. 1977) has been highly influential in recent personality theory to such an extent that many writers have abandoned the notion of traits entirely, and hence the measurement of personality is regarded as impossible and worthless.

He attacks traits on the old behaviourist ground of redundancy. We see a man violently attacking another and say he is high on aggression, and that this aggression is causing the behaviour. While this logical argument is sound, it can be refuted empirically if in fact wide clusters of behaviour do cohere together such that a concept of aggression can parsimoniously account for them.

His second argument is empirical. He argues that in fact there are few cross-situational similarities in behaviour. Behaviour to Mischel is situation-specific. To understand a behaviour we must examine the stimuli which elicits it.

Intuitively this is not sensible since in everyday life we do find people to be consistent. We think of A as cheerful, B as testy and so on. This is regarded by Mischel as but a halo effect, reflecting the stereotype of the observer. Thus we form a view of an individual and remember the behaviour that confirms it, forgetting what fails to fit our picture: fighting Irishmen, sad Russians, loudly-checked English gentlemen, just for example. Thus our everyday observations are set at nought.

Further, Mischel argues that the traits which raters use reflect only the categories of behaviour which raters hold, rather than any real categorization of observed behaviour, citing as evidence studies where ratings of virtually unknown subjects revealed the same factor structure as ratings of known subjects.

Finally, situationalists cite investigations where traits and ratings fail to correlate with observed criterion behaviours, thus casting doubts on the cross-situational generality of such measures.

The answer to situationalism is again an empirical one. If there is no cross-situational generality, if the responses to personality questionnaires are specific to the tests, how can it be that there are meaningful educational, clinical and occupational discriminations and correlations? These, if Mischel were correct, should not occur, yet they do and this fact alone seems to us to refute the situationalist case.

Enough has been said about theories of personality. Generally, most flounder through a lack of sound quantification and a consequent reliance on clinical impressions. Those theories that argue that common traits can never reveal the uniqueness of the individual are destroyed by the evidence, as is situationalism. The fact is that personality traits can be reliably and validly measured and these do have substantial correlations with a wide variety of external criteria. As such they should become the data base of any theory of personality.

References

Allport, G.W. (1938)
Personality: Psychological interpretation. New York: Chilton.

Buros, O.K. (1972)
VII Mental Measurements Year Book. New Jersey: Gryphon Press.

Cattell, R.B. and Kline, P. (1977)
The Scientific Analysis of Personality and Motivation. London: Academic Press.

Freud, S. (1933)
New Introductory Lectures. London: Hogarth Press & Institute of Psychoanalysis.

Freud, S. (1940)
An Outline of Psychoanalysis. London: Hogarth Press.

Kline, P. (1972)
Fact and Fantasy in Freudian Theory. London: Methuen.

Kline, P. (1979)
Psychometrics and Psychology. London: Academic Press.

Kretschmer, E. (1925)
Physique and Character. London: Methuen.

McDougall, W. (1932)
The Energies of Man. London: Methuen.

Mischel, M. (1977)
On the future of personality measurement. American Psychology, 32, 246-254.

Murray, H.A. (1938)
Explorations in Personality. New York: Oxford University Press.

Nunnally, J. (1978)
Psychometric Theory. New York: McGraw-Hill.

Sheldon, W.H. and Stevens, S.S. (1942)
    The Varieties of Temperament. New York: Harper & Row.

Questions

1. What factors contribute to the efficiency of psychological tests?
2. What are the main types of psychological test? Give a brief description of them.
3. Compare projective and questionnaire personality tests.
4. Discuss the main types of attitude tests.
5. Discuss the concept of intelligence as factorially defined.
6. What are the main factors of personality?
7. Outline the Freudian developmental theory as applied to the first five years of life.
8. Discuss the Oedipus complex.
9. Discuss the castration complex.
10. Write an account of the Freudian theory of dreams.
11. Write an account of the Freudian theory of slips of the tongue.
12. Discuss defence mechanisms.
13. Discuss the objections to trait psychology by situationalists.
14. Compare the work of McDougall and Murray.
15. Give a simple description of factor analysis.
16. If individuals are unique, how can they be measured by tests of universal dimensions?
17. If individuals are unique, how can there be a science of personality?

Annotated reading

Cronbach, L. (1976) Essentials of Psychological Testing. Chicago: Harper & Row.
    A clear comprehensive discussion of psychological testing and tests.

Cattell, R.B. and Kline, P. (1977) The Scientific Analysis of Personality and Motivation. London: Academic Press.
    A full account of the factor analysis of personality, in which the results are related to clinical theories.

Freud, S. (1978) New Introductory Lectures. Harmondsworth: Penguin.
    A brilliantly told account of Freudian theory by the Master himself.

Hall, G.S. and Lindzey, G. (1973) Theories of Personality. New York: Wiley.
    A good summary of a variety of theories of personality.

Vernon, P.E. (1979) Intelligence, Heredity and Environment.
San Francisco: Freeman.
    Another useful book on this topic.

3

Motivation
Philip D. Evans

Introduction

Poetically speaking, motivation may be considered to be
about the 'springs of action'. More prosaically, the
motivation theorist asks himself why any bit of behaviour
occurs: what are the necessary and sufficient conditions
which make any organism, human or animal, give up one
activity and take up another, in the ever-flowing stream
that constitutes behaviour?

In everyday life, people answer essentially motivational
questions by giving 'reasons' or 'intentions' for their
actions, but these are often given after the event and
cannot be said to explain behaviour in any scientific
fashion. The psychologist is more interested in specifying
conditions beforehand which, if they pertain, inevitably
lead to a prediction that some behaviour probably will (or
will not) occur. Where do we find these all-important
conditions? Traditional wisdom, in the case of human behaviour, has until this century always taught us that the
answer to questions about why we behave lies inaccessibly in
the mind, whatever that may be. The mind wills the body,
and since the will is supposedly free, we might as well give
up any attempt to predict human behaviour! Fortunately the
work of Charles Darwin changed all that and all animal
behaviour, including human behaviour, became fair game for
systematic and scientific enquiry. Like other areas of
psychology, then, empirical research in the field of motivation has been largely a twentieth-century endeavour.
First of all, let us very briefly sketch in the historical
aspects of our subject matter.

**Historical
perspective**

When Ivan Pavlov (1849-1936) discovered the phenomenon of
the 'conditioned reflex', the scene appeared to be set for
explaining all behaviour as the sum of responses and conditioned responses, which in turn could be traced inexorably
back to their controlling stimuli. The answer to the question 'What motivated that particular response?' would simply
be: that particular stimulus. This was the revolutionary
behaviourism preached in the 1920s by the American
psychologist, John B. Watson.

In the 1930s, this strident behaviourism was somewhat
moderated by the ideas of Clark Hull, perhaps the most

influential theorist of motivation and behaviour right up to
the 1950s. Like Watson, Hull believed that all behaviour
could be seen as stimulus-response chains. However, he was
also influenced by the work of an earlier psychologist
called Thorndike, who had shown how animals can learn to
solve certain problems by 'trial and error' if successful
responses were reliably followed by important consequences
such as food for a hungry animal or escape for a confined
one. Hull believed that such consequences 'reinforced' a
connection between a stimulus and a response and built it
into a habit. In trying to define the nature of reinforcement of this kind, Hull committed himself to a belief in
internal mediators of behaviour, hidden sources of motivation. Briefly, he believed that physiological needs
resulting from deprivation of food, water, etc., brought
about a general motivational state within the organism
called 'drive' which goaded it into activity. When such
activity finally resulted in the animal finding a source of
satisfying the need, drive reduction would take place. It
was this drive reduction which Hull identified as the basis
of reinforcement. Thus, for Hull, the performance of any act
was the result of two basic types of variables: the strength
of the habit being considered and the motivation, resulting
from drive, to perform the habit. The two variables were
assumed to act multiplicatively; thus if drive is zero the
animal will not perform the response however well it 'knows'
how to perform it: that is, however great the habit
strength. Conversely, the animal will not perform the response however great its motivational drive if it does not
know how to perform, that is, if habit strength equals
zero.

This theoretical approach may seem over-simplified and
applicable more to laboratory rats in simple mazes than
human beings in more complex situations, but Hull assumed
that more complex motives could be acquired by association
with more primary ones, through conditioning procedures of
a Pavlovian kind.

One of the major embarrassments to Hull's early theory
came from findings which suggested that, even in the case of
simple animals in mazes, sources of motivation could not be
confined to the internal drive variable. It appeared that
the reinforcer itself seemed to have incentive properties,
which acted to 'pull' the animal towards a goal, as much as
the assumed drive force was taken to 'push' it there. An
animal's running speed to a goal would reflect, for example,
the quantity and quality of the reinforcement given. Hull
did not like the mentalistic notion that animals could be
motivated by expectations of some future event in the goal
box, but he was forced to admit a new motivational term into
his theoretical model to account for such incentive motivational effects. The fact that he phrased such incentive
effects in mechanistic stimulus-response language reflects
only a bias of vocabulary.

The modern era

Hull's intention had been to build up a complex and general model of all motivated behaviour, human and animal. Despite increasing complexity the endeavour failed. Predication on such a grand scale was impossible. The modern trend within psychology as a whole has been to develop mini-theories which can tell us something useful about more limited areas of behaviour, and particularly human behaviour. Whereas Hull had been content to speculate that human motives could be ultimately traced back to biological imperatives shared by all organisms, that formidable task of tracing the development of motives has lost ground to theories which simply assume motives, arising perhaps out of particular human needs, demonstrate that the strength of the motive can be effectively measured, and then propose predictions about how such specified motives interact with an environmental context to produce behaviour related to that motive. The approach is still vaguely Hullian, but by being more narrow in its scope offers greater opportunity for useful application. There are two areas of research which we outline in the next section which illustrate this. First, work on achievement motivation, that is, striving behaviour in human beings: this is described immediately after a general theory of human needs is outlined. Second, research in the field of anxiety as a motive is examined. The research in both areas has been done with human beings and has scope for application. Lastly, we return to the animal laboratory to show that results from that quarter can themselves be very illuminating when discussed in the context of human problems.

Maslow's theory of human needs

Maslow, like Hull, believed that actions spring from needs but, unlike Hull, was not interested in the derivation of all needs and motives from a few primary biological survival needs. Rather he put forward the interesting idea that the major human needs could be put into a hierarchical order. Having done this, he postulated a theoretical prediction that needs higher up the 'ladder' would only produce striving for fulfilment when those lower down the ladder were satisfied. His categories orders from lowest to highest were:

* biological survival needs: for example, need for food, water, oxygen, etc.;
* safety needs: for example, need to avoid danger, need for security;
* affiliated needs: for example, love, friendship, acceptance by others;
* self-esteem needs: for example, self-acceptance, success in life;
* self-actualization needs: for example, achievement of one's full potential.

Although Maslow's ideas were not earth shattering, they were put forward at a time (just after the Second World War) when people were becoming receptive. Particularly ready to receive them were the growing number of management training establishments. Managers of industry were of necessity becoming interested in the question of what motivated men to work in modern society where it had to be taken for granted that survival needs would be taken care of by at least a token Welfare State. Nineteenth-century notions of keeping a man at work by keeping the wolf of hunger at his door were no longer practically or ethically possible. Maslow's theory was soon taken up by business schools particularly in the USA, and was used to generate ideas about how work conditions could be arranged to satisfy higher-level needs, rather than just provide a pay-packet at the end of the week. Applied researchers were stimulated to ask whether a particular job allowed affiliative needs to be satisfied; alternatively, did another job foster a sense of personal responsibility which could satisfy self-esteem needs?

Although Maslow's theory could not be said to be predictive of behaviour (it is too general for that), it was generative of much piecemeal research which paid dividends in terms of productivity and job satisfaction. It was also a reference point for later, more specific, theories of work motivation which related performance to an interaction between non-monetary need variables and monetary incentive variables (see Murrell, 1976).

Maslow's views of human motivation have also been taken up in the field of psychotherapy. Traditionally, psychotherapy has been concerned with resolving, in Maslow's terms, problems with affiliative and self-esteem needs. Maslow's theory, however, hints that a person who is reasonably well satisfied with respect to these needs will inevitably turn his attention to satisfying self-actualization needs: that is, fulfilment of full potential. The idea that so-called 'normal' people may seek 'therapy' to help themselves along the road to full growth is no more than a necessary corollary of Maslow's theory. It is less than surprising, therefore, that the human 'growth' movement, with its encounter groups and sensitivity training groups and so on, should have grown up particularly in the rich state of California, where lower-level needs may have been satisfied to a point of boredom!

hievement motivation

If Maslow's theory of needs lacks predictive power and is instead a useful and productive way of looking at human behaviour, the same is not true of the next motivational theory, which does generate quite specific predictions about how different people react in different situations. In many areas of life one could point to standards which define excellence, achievement, success. A person's motivation to achieve these standards has been called 'need achievement motivation' or nAch for short. One of the pioneers of research in this area, a psychologist called McClelland, was the first to demonstrate that a person's hidden reserves of

nAch could reliably be measured by looking at their fantasy
life in certain controlled conditions. By using a 'personality test', in which the person invented stories around
certain pictures on cards, McClelland found that he could
score these stories for the number of achievement-related
themes in them. The scores which resulted were reliable
enough to differentiate low nAch people and high nAch
people. More importantly the scores also had validity: that
is, they would to an important degree predict real differences in 'striving' behaviour in real contexts of an
achievement kind. In the laboratory, for example, high nAch
subjects could be shown to persist longer at some task or
other than low nAch subjects. Outside the laboratory,
studies have shown that high nAch subjects are more likely
to be 'upwardly socially mobile' in terms of changing socio-
economic status, whilst low nAch subjects are more likely to
stay still, or even move down the scale.

However, it became clear to the early researchers that
achievement-related behaviour was powerfully affected by
more than just the nAch motive. In particular, certain
subjects seemed to behave in such striving situations as if
their primary motivation was to avoid failure rather than
simply succeed. By using a questionnaire to measure this
'fear of failure' trait, it was possible to make predictions
about real achievement behaviour in a more exact fashion.
A psychologist called Atkinson, one of the foremost of
modern motivation theorists, proposed a modified theory of
achievement behaviour, incorporating two major motives, nAch
and fear of failure, together with certain contextual variables, notably the perceived probability of success (or
failure), and the incentive (or 'negative incentive':
'shame' if you like) associated with success (or failure).
The probability variables are related in a complementary way
to their respective incentive variables. This is common
sense in a way, since if a task is very easy (i.e. the
probability of success is very large), then the incentive
attached to succeeding is not very high. Conversely, if the
task is very difficult (i.e. the probability of success is
low) the incentive, or kudos, attached to succeeding is
correspondingly high. Now if we look at how the theory works
in principle we find that it gives rise to some quite specific predictions. Consider first a person whose need to
achieve (nAch) is dominant over their fear of failure. Their
tendency to approach a task or strive at it is going to be
maximized when the probability of success MULTIPLIES with
the incentive value to give the highest overall result. If,
as we have said, probability of success and incentive are
intrinsically related and therefore:

Incentive value = (1) - (probability of success)

then it is clear that the multiplicative product of the two
variables is at its greatest when probability of success is
0.5 and the incentive is also therefore 0.5 (i.e. 1 - 0.5).
All that really needs to be understood is that high nAch

subjects, relatively speaking, are predicted to show a real preference for middlingly difficult tasks. Now let us consider the person whose dominating motive is to avoid failure. Where the probability of success is 0.5, so obviously is the probability of failure. Also, if the probability of failure is 0.5, the negative incentive or shame of failing is 0.5 (i.e. 1 minus the probability of failure). Thus the person's avoidance tendency is maximally aroused in exactly the same situation as that which attracted the more nAch-orientated person. Once again, regardless of the mathematics, the prediction is that a person whose fear of failure is stronger than their level of nAch will show a preference for either very easy tasks or very difficult ones, but definitely avoid middlingly difficult ones. If the prediction that such a person may seek out very difficult tasks seems to you paradoxical, then just remember that in such tasks the negative incentive or shame of failing is very low; such a person may be considered to have a 'get-out' clause which allows people to say, 'He didn't succeed, but it was very difficult and at least he tried.'

So much for the theory. Are its predictions borne out? In the laboratory, a simple test is to ask subjects to play a hoop-la game of throwing a ring over a peg. In such a situation, the probability of success is clearly largely influenced by how closely one stands to the peg. When given a free choice, dominant nAch subjects showed a much greater propensity to stand a middling distance from the peg than did dominant fear-of-failure subjects. However, Atkinson's theory stands up to examination not just in the laboratory but in the world outside.

Achievement motivation in classroom and college
One of the perennial discussions in education is whether to 'stream' or not. Is mixed ability teaching to be recommended or not? Well, it is not our intention here to give any full answer to the question but it can be shown that Atkinson's theory is of relevance. Let us assume that a child very reasonably gauges his probability of success in academic matters by reference to his classroom peers. This means that a child who is in a class with his own ability range is more likely to put his probability of success not far from 0.5 and similarly therefore his probability of failure. Our theory predicts that this is ideally motivating for a child whose motivation towards achievement is greater than any fear of failure, but is the worst situation for a child whose two compelling motivations are balanced the other way. In fact, a psychologist called O'Connor tested out the theoretical predictions and largely verified them, both with respect to interest in school work and measures in academic improvement. It should be said that motivational effects of the type of classroom situation are not the only variables which may be important when this controversy is debated; however, anyone's performance is a mixture of ability and motivation, so such motivational factors deserve attention.

Atkinson's theory has also been applied in higher education. Researchers have examined the choice of options that students take in college. Options were first of all classed as easy, middling, or difficult. Students were then measured both in terms of nAch and fear of failure motivation. Once again the predictions were upheld. Students who were relatively high in nAch tended to go for middlingly difficult options, whilst this tendency was not pronounced in the students who were relatively strong on fear-of-failure motivation.

Lastly, some research has been done into how achieveme motivation and fear-of-failure motivation influence career choice. Mahone has shown that students whose dominant motivation is nAch are more realistic in their career choices (we can define 'realistic' as choosing middlingly difficult careers) whilst those students higher in fear-of-failure tend to be unrealistic by going for too easy and unchallenging careers or, alternatively, aiming too high for their abilities.

Can we talk of achieving societies?

The originator of nAch research, McClelland, has tried to investigate this question by examining the literature of different societies and societies at different times with a view to measuring the amount of achievement themes shown, just as for an individual his fantasy stories are examined. Some fascinating results have been reported. Measures of nAch taken from literary sources do predict economic performance. For example, nAch themes in English literature from 1500 to 1800 correspond in their ups and downs very well with economic performance as measured by coal imports into the port of London. In the USA, nAch between 1810 and 1950 rises and falls in tune with the number of patents issued per million of population. Even non-literate societies have been measured for nAch by analysing achievement themes in vase paintings and orally-transmitted folk tales!

The really interesting finding to come out of this work is that changes in nAch typically occur some years before the subsequent change in economic performance. Hence it is possible to make some predictions for the future. According to nAch measures the USA, for example, peaked in nAch aro 1945, so the outlook is pretty gloomy for subsequent economic performance! However, all this work is extremely tenuous. The studies are all correlational in nature and difficult to interpret without a degree of arbitrariness. They are crucially dependent on measurement which is difficult to assess in terms of its reliability. And yet it must be said that McClelland's recent work is nothing if not stimulating, and his statement that scientists should turn away from: 'an exclusive concern with the external events of history to the internal psychological concerns that in the long run determine what happens in history' is a statement worthy of consideration.

nxiety as a motive

We all know individuals who claim to act better when goaded with a bit of 'adrenalin', as the saying goes. Actors claim to give their peak performances when anxiety is there to give them a helping hand. Equally there are many (students taking exams, for example) who claim that anxiety is responsible for poor performance. What then is the truth? To predict the effects of anxiety we have to specify more variables. First, we obviously must take into account the level of anxiety experienced. Second, we must expect that the type of task being considered is important as a variable. Third, whatever the level of anxiety likely in the situation, we should expect some difference in the level experienced by different people: that is, it is to be expected that people have different capacities for being aroused in an anxious way by identical situations.

Let us deal with the simple relationship first between level of anxiety and performance. If we think back to Hull's force of drive, it is clear that we can consider anxiety a source of drive or, some might say, general arousal of the organism. Now there is a long-standing law in psychology which relates drive to performance by a so-called 'inverted-U function'. This is simply illustrated in figure 1.

Figure 1
_____

The inverted-U function relating drive to performance

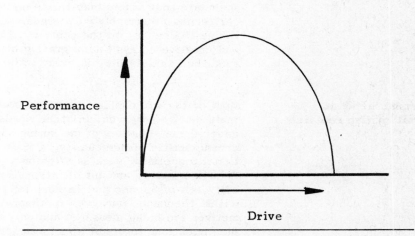

The predictions that this law makes are equally simple. Other things being equal, performance will be enhanced by increasing drive, but only up to a certain point. Beyond this, further increases in drive will lead to poorer and poorer performance. We can assume anxiety, then, acts broadly in this fashion. However, we should still like to know a bit more. When, for example, is the peak of the inverted U likely to be met? This is where it is important to consider our other factors, such as the nature of the task and the nature of the person. One of the major ways tasks differ is in their difficulty. Spence and Taylor, two psychologists who may be described as latter-day Hullians, did a series of experiments to shed light on how high-anxiety and low-anxiety persons were differentially affected by tasks which were either easy or difficult. Without going into too much theoretical detail, let us say something more about drive. Drive is taken to be a non-directive general pushing force and hence is taken to energize incorrect performance as much as correct performance. The prediction was made, therefore, that in an easy task, where incorrect responses are not much in evidence, high anxiety serves mainly to energize just the correct responses. Therefore Spence and Taylor predicted that high-anxiety subjects would perform such tasks better than low-anxiety subjects. In the case of a difficult task we can assume that incorrect responses are constantly competing with correct ones and that high levels of drive are counter-productive in the sense that they serve only to energize further such incorrect responses. The prediction, therefore, was that low-anxiety subjects would outperform high-anxiety subjects in such tasks. These predictions were in fact upheld in the laboratory tests. Moving outside the laboratory, then, we may speculate that actors may thrive on anxiety because they are performing presumably well-rehearsed material; our exam-taking student is, on the contrary, having to create novel and creative essays by integrating his knowledge on the spot, and anxiety here is likely to be disruptive.

Recent trends in 'trait' motive research

Most of the work so far described could be classified as 'trait' motive research. In other words, psychologists have adopted the approach of measuring some assumed stable characteristic of personality, a trait which has motivational properties, such as nAch or anxiety. Within this tradition a large amount of integration is now under way. The work of Spence and Taylor, for example, is considered within the same framework of theory as that of Atkinson. New motives are being measured and entered into ever more complex equations to predict performance with more accuracy, often with the aid of computers.

There is another aspect to the modern trend, however, which needs to be mentioned, and that is the questioning of the unity of these assumed motives. Nowhere is this more in evidence than in the case of 'fear' or 'anxiety' as assumed single entity motives. Motives are usually felt (it is no accident that motivation and emotion share the same Latin root!) and it is when we try to measure that felt emotion or motive at the individual level that we run into difficulties. Clinical psychologists, for example, have learnt a lot recently about phobic reactions and their treatment; and yet, as they find out more, they have increasingly come to question the traditional view that the motive of fear motivates the avoidance behaviour which is the essence of a clinical phobia. The point is that fear is not a 'lump' (see Rachman, 1978); it is divisible. Some people show fear by reporting that they feel afraid, but show no fear in their behaviour. Others show fear by their physiological reactions, such as a pounding heart and clammy hands, but report that they are not feeling fear. There is, in other words, often a non-correspondence between the different measures that we have traditionally conceived as indicating fear. The message, in the case of individuals at any rate, is that the measurement of an assumed single unitary motivational trait is full of pitfalls. This is to some extent, then, a limitation of the type of research strategy that we have been describing so far. Note, however, that we say limitation rather than criticism. To be capable of reasonable prediction of the behaviour of broad types of people in a reasonable variety of situations is no mean achievement. The work described so far has demonstrated that this is possible.

The reinforcement view of motivation: no hidden motives

We promised at the beginning to return to the animal laboratory for an assessment of the relevance of that work to motivational questions. We mentioned then that one of the embarrassing findings for Hull's early theory was that the incentive or reinforcement which followed a response had motivational properties in its own right. The way in which different patterns of responding in an organism can be motivated and maintained by different patterns of reinforcement has been of central interest to that body of researchers who, broadly speaking, have followed in the footsteps of the celebrated psychologist B. F. Skinner. The literature which has accumulated is so vast that we can here do no more than give one or two examples and refer the interested reader elsewhere, if he likes the flavour of what he reads.

Let us delve straight in with an example of a problem which might be faced by any marketing man. You have a product called 'Superchoc' which you want to push. You devise a traditional promotion campaign which requires your young consumers to collect 20 wrappers, send them in, and be reinforced by the gift of a Superchoc plastic space-ship. Can this basic strategy be improved upon? Let us look at the animal laboratory. Your technique so far resembles that in which a rat is trained to press a bar 20 times for one sugar-pellet reward. The ratio of responses to reinforcement is fixed at 20 to 1; that is, in psychologists' terms the rat is on a fixed-ratio 20 schedule of reinforcement. Now we know that all organisms respond in the same sort of way on a fixed-ratio schedule. The pattern of cumulative responding is given below in figure 2.

Figure 2

The typical scalloped record of cumulative responding obtained on a fixed-ratio schedule. The schedule is FR20, and instances of reinforcement are shown by slashes.

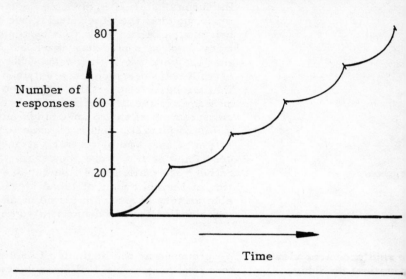

Note that after each reinforcement the organism takes a break; there is a lull in responding shown by a scallop on the graph. In terms of your marketing problem, these scallops represent unprofitable periods which you could do without. Now there are easy ways of removing scallops by making the reinforcement come after a varying amount of responses, but this method is not applicable in this case, nor would it motivate more vigorous (buying) behaviour overall. Let us then adopt a different method. Let us redefine the problem by considering it in terms of two schedules, one superimposed on the other. First we say that one response is going to be made up of five of our previous responses, and that the organism has to make four of these larger unit responses in order to get the reinforcement. In terms of the rat in the laboratory, what we do is to give it some sort of signal, perhaps a tone or a light, after each five bar-presses which signals that it has made one composite response; when it has made four composite responses it gets its food pellet. In the case of the marketing problem, we say that five wrappers get a certificate and that four certificates earn a space-ship. Well, you might say, nothing has really been changed: the same number of wrappers are finally exchanged for the same amount of reinforcement. Tha

may be so, but the two methods of going about the exercise
motivate very different patterns of performance and in the
case of the second method, the lull that we talked about is
shortened and performance as a whole is more vigorous; a
worth-while thing to know in applied contexts.

Note that this area of research is not interested in
'hidden motives'. It is solely interested in how behaviour
patterns can be predicted from a knowledge of the way
behaviour is externally reinforced. It must be said that
individual differences are largely ignored, which is the
very opposite of the 'trait' motive research that we have
previously dealt with. On the other hand, when one is
interested in motivating behaviour of large numbers of
people, on the average so to speak, it is perfectly possible
to ignore individual differences in the certain knowledge
that one's reinforcement contingencies will by and large
have the predicted results.

The reader who wishes to explore further this entire
area, known as the experimental analysis of behaviour,
should consult any major text such as Rachlin (1976).

nclusions   Let us try now to pull some theoretical strands together.
Motivation is a potentially vast and wide-ranging area of
psychology. Traditionally it has been about the causes of
action. There are two traditions which have defined the
major approaches to the study of motivation. One sees action
as a result of an interaction between current environmental
variables – the context of the act if you like – and a
motivational tendency within the organism. Such a tendency
may be considered a convenient fiction since no one supposes
that motives are real things like tables and chairs; to talk
of a motive is to use a kind of shorthand for referring to a
relatively stable propensity for engaging in certain acts.

The other broad tradition is the Skinnerian approach
mentioned latterly and perforce briefly since it takes
motivation into almost a new field altogether. If we think
of behaviour as output, the Skinnerian would have us believe
that all output can in principle be predicted from a knowledge of input in terms of environmental observables, with
no necessity to ask what goes on inside the organism. Motivation as traditionally conceived is rather redundant.
Motivation becomes at once everything and nothing.

The former approach which does allow for the term
'motive' stems directly from the Hullian tradition. Note
how similar Atkinson's theory is to Hull's. Probability of
success is like habit strength and both reflect the capability of the organism; nAch is like drive and reflects the
motivational push to perform; finally, both admit an incentive variable which also motivates the organism towards a
goal. All three variables interact in both systems in a
broadly multiplicative fashion.

Both approaches have proven to be useful and lastly we
should perhaps point out that in certain areas, notably

choice of behaviour where an organism has a choice of activities, it is becoming evident that their predictions are essentially the same (see Atkinson and Birch, 1979). Perhaps, like so many differences of approach and theory, eventually our two traditions described here will be seen to differ solely in their vocabulary, terms, and ways of putting the argument.

References

Atkinson, J.W. and Birch, D. (1979)
An Introduction to Motivation. Princeton, NJ: Van Nostrand.
Murrell, H. (1976)
Motivation at Work. London: Methuen.
Rachlin, H. (1976)
Introduction to Modern Behaviorism. San Francisco: Freeman.
Rachman, S.J. (1978)
Fear and Courage. San Francisco: Freeman.

Questions

1. What do you understand by the term 'drive' as used by psychologists? Discuss its merits and demerits.
2. Write a short essay examining the proposition that we avoid things because we fear them.
3. We have to 'interpret' a stimulus before we react to it as that particular stimulus. Do we have to interpret our motives before we act on the basis of that particular motive?
4. Discuss the contribution of one of the following to our understanding of motivation: (i) Hull; (ii) Maslow; (iii) McClelland.
5. How do nAch and fear of failure work together in determining the extent to which different people approach achievement-orientated situations?
6. Outline and illustrate with experimental evidence Atkinson's theory of achievement-related behaviour.
7. Write an essay on the topic of unconscious motivation.
8. Compare and contrast the ideas of Hull and Freud on motivation.
9. 'Reinforcement equals motivation.' Discuss.
10. Write an essay on the motivational properties of reinforcers and 'secondary' reinforcers.
11. What can psychologists working in the animal behaviour laboratory tell us about motivating changes in behaviour patterns in individuals and groups of individuals by the operation of reinforcement principles?
12. Are some societies more 'motivated' to achieve than others?
13. Examine the proposition that motives can be measured by looking at fantasy themes.
14. To what extent are TAT measures of nAch reliable and valid?

15. Why might anxiety give the edge to one person's performance and take the edge off another's?
16. What human needs may underlie the motivation of human behaviour?
17. Is fear a unitary motive?

annotated reading

Atkinson, J.W. and Birch, D. (1979) Introduction to Motivation. Princeton, NJ: Van Nostrand.
    This book covers the area of human motivation well from the point of view of internal trait motives interacting with environmental contingencies. It fills in the details of recent research in achievement motivation and allied topics. At times the mathematical statements of theory might be too much for certain arts-biassed students, but the essential logic - all that is needed for an introductory appreciation - is usually clear.

Evans, P. (1975) Motivation. London: Methuen.
    This is a short book which should not present the reader with any difficulty. It is very much a theoretical-cum-historical overview of approaches to the study of motivation, leaving it to other texts, such as the one above, to fill in details of particular approaches. It also has chapters on instinct and on biologically based motivations such as hunger, thirst, sex, and sleep. This might interest a student who wishes to extend the chapter's coverage at a still introductory level.

Rachlin, H. (1976) Introduction to Modern Behaviourism. San Francisco: Freeman.
    This is the best introductory book for the student who is interested in following up the idea mentioned in the chapter that 'Motivation = Reinforcement'. In line with that view, it is no surprise that the word 'motivation' does not occur in the index! (Reinforcement, however, does.)

4

Learning and Teaching
David Fontana

Learning can be defined as a 'relatively persistent change
in an individual's possible behaviour due to experience'. It
is thus clearly distinguished from those changes in behaviour which come about as a consequence of maturation
(i.e. as a consequence of the individual's physical growth
and development). Learning can take place either as a result
of informal circumstances (e.g. parent-child relationships,
interaction with friends and with the mass media), or as a
result of the formal efforts of society to educate its
members through schools and academic institutions. Though
both are important our main concern is with the latter: that
is, with the ways in which the teacher or the tutor can best
monitor and assist learning within the class or lecture
room.

Bruner (1973) considers that in dealing with learning
activities the teacher must take account of three important
variables, namely the nature of the learner, the nature of
the knowledge to be learned and the nature of the learning
process. Accordingly we adopt this threefold division as a
way of structuring the present chapter, taking each of the
variables in turn and examining the major factors associated
with them.

**The nature of the
learner**

There are a number of factors within the learner himself
that influence his ability to learn. Best known of these are
cognitive factors such as intelligence and creativity, but
there are many others of equal relevance. These include
affective factors, motivation, age and sex, study habits
and, above all perhaps, memory.

Affective factors
Psychologists take the term 'affective' to cover all aspects
of personality. One of these aspects which has particular
importance for learning is anxiety. From general experience
the teacher soon discovers that a mild degree of anxiety in
a pupil can be a useful aid to learning, but that too much
anxiety has an inhibiting effect (particularly if the
learning task is a complex one). We see this particularly in
a student preparing for an important examination, or in a
student fearful of the anger or ridicule that failure in a

particular task may invite from unsympathetic tutors or classmates. The anxiety consequent upon these stressful situations interferes with both learning and performance, and the individual concerned produces results way below his potential. Closely linked to anxiety as an affective factor is the individual's self-esteem. Research studies show that individuals with low self-esteem (that is, with a low regard for their personal worth and abilities) consistently set themselves artificially depressed learning and attainment goals, and consistently perform less well than individuals of similar intelligence and background who enjoy high levels of self-esteem. It appears that low self-esteem subjects are so fearful of further blows to their self-regard that they set themselves low goals in order to avoid the chances of failure.

High and low self-esteem can be referred to as a dimension of personality. Another such dimension that has implications for learning is that of extraversion-introversion. Typically the extravert is an individual who enjoys change and variety and is orientated towards the external world of people and experiences, while the introvert is more concerned with stability and the inner world of thoughts and feelings. All of us find our place at some point on this dimension, and the evidence suggests that those who incline towards the two extremes learn best in different kinds of learning environments. The extravert tends to favour groups and social activities, with plenty of variety and fresh stimuli, while the introvert generally prefers more ordered individual activity. Thus a particular learning failure may be due less to any lack of ability on the part of the learner than to the fact that his working environment is not really suited to relevant aspects of his personality. On occasions the teacher or tutor may also tend to favour pupils whose personalities approximate to his own, with the extravert complaining that an introverted pupil is too quiet, and the introvert complaining that an extraverted pupil is too noisy.

Motivation
Satisfactory learning is unlikely to take place in the absence of sufficient motivation to learn. We have already mentioned one possible source of motivation, namely a degree of anxiety, but there are many others. For convenience we can divide these into intrinsic forms of motivation, which come from the individual himself, and extrinsic which are imposed upon him by the environment. Taking intrinsic first, it is axiomatic that people work generally harder at learning tasks that interest them than at those that do not. If we had to say why a particular thing captures a person's interest we would probably argue that it has some direct relevance to his daily life. It either diverts or amuses him in some way (and thus makes him feel better) or it enables him to cope more effectively with the problems and achieve the ambitions in his daily life. No matter what

the subject, however, there is often the danger that the
learner is asked to tackle theoretical issues whose practical application escapes him, or to work towards goals that
are too remote or not of his own choosing. Whilst of course
the student cannot be the arbiter of what he should or
should not learn, it is important that the tutor who wishes
to appeal to intrinsic motivation should be fully aware of
the concerns and aspirations of his students, and should
demonstrate clearly the way in which the proposed learning
relates to them.

Nevertheless, however stimulating the teacher, there
will always be occasions when intrinsic motivation is in-
sufficient and recourse has to be made to motivation of an
extrinsic kind. Such motivation usually consists of marks,
grades, examinations, and of course tutor praise and
approval. Success in these areas builds up prestige in the
student's own eyes and enhances his standing in the eyes of
others. The student finds success to be rewarding, and
builds up expectations which he has to work harder and more
purposefully to fulfil. Thus extrinsic motivation can be
highly effective, but it raises a number of important
considerations (quite apart from the obvious fear that it
may raise anxiety to an inhibiting level).

* Instead of success, some individuals experience only
  failure. This tends to produce either the low self-
  esteem to which we have already made reference, or a
  rejection of everything to do with the formal learning
  tasks offered through educational institutions. Such
  rejection is a defensive attempt to protect self-esteem
  by insisting that it is these tasks that are at fault
  rather than the individual himself (i.e. it is a way of
  saying 'I COULD do it if it was worth doing'). To combat
  the harmful effects of consistent failure the wise tutor
  provides the student with opportunities for success at
  however low a level. Through such opportunities the
  student gradually builds up a new self-image and a new
  attitude to work, and is encouraged progressively to set
  his sights higher.
* Sometimes motivation suffers because the student is not
  supplied with prompt knowledge of results. The longer
  the gap between performance and the provision of this
  knowledge, the greater the chance that the student will
  lose interest in the whole exercise.
* Competition between students is a useful extrinsic
  motivator provided they are all of a similar level of
  ability and can all experience a fair degree of success.
  Co-operation, where students adopt group norms and wor
  together to achieve them, can be of even more benefit.
* Wherever the pressures of extrinsic motivation are too
  strong students may resort to strategies like feigned
  illness (or even cheating) to avoid the consequences of
  failure.

Age and sex

The ability to tackle complex learning tasks increases
throughout childhood. Both Piaget (cf. Inhelder and Piaget,
1958) and Bruner (1966) have demonstrated that children
appear to go through a number of stages in the development
of their powers of thinking, and that unless learning tasks
are presented to them in the form appropriate to their
particular stage they may be unable to understand what is
required of them. For example, before children reach what
Piaget calls the stage of formal operations (usually at
approximately age 12) they are strictly limited in their
ability to engage in abstract thinking, and can only handle
concepts when they have experienced them in some practical
sense (e.g. they can deal with weight and number, which can
be practically experienced, but not with density and volume,
which require to be defined more theoretically). On the
basis of this kind of evidence it seems that the individual's powers of thinking reach maturity during adolescence,
and we know that measured intelligence and memorizing abilities also appear to have reached their peak by the end of
this period. Much less is known about the subsequent decline
of these powers and therefore of the ability to learn. There
certainly appears to be a general slowing of the rate at
which the individual can learn many mental and physical
skills throughout adult life, and this decline may have
reached significant proportions in people not involved in
academic work by the mid- and late-twenties. In those constantly using academic skills, however, the decline may be
more gradual, and may be amply offset by greater self-
discipline, higher motivation, and the increased ability to
organize learning that comes through experience.

Just as the ability to learn is influenced by age
variables, so is it influenced by sex. Girls are generally
more verbal than boys at school age, and have fewer reading,
speech, and general behaviour problems (Davie et al, 1972),
while boys are more advanced in number skills. These differences tend to disappear by age 16, however, and boys
between five and ten years old appear twice as likely to
show an increase in measured intelligence as girls (Kagan et
al, 1958). Throughout school life, however, girls tend to be
better all-rounders, while boys are better at the subjects
they enjoy and spurn those they do not. These sex-related
differences could be in part genetic and in part related to
the home (where girls are generally taught to be more
dependent and more concerned for adult approval), but recent
research in the USA suggests that they could also be due to
the fact that most early school teaching is done by women,
and boys therefore come to associate school with feminine
values. Where such teaching is done by men, the higher rate
of backwardness and school rejection shown by boys tends to
disappear. Sadly, at all ages, girls tend to show lower self-
esteem than boys, and may artificially depress their level
of performance in conformity with an outmoded and
unfortunate social conception of the inferiority of the
female role.

Memory

Clearly, learning depends intimately on memory. At the
practical level psychologists recognize the existence of two
main kinds of memory, short-term and long-term. All information received by the senses and to which we pay attention
seems to enter short-term memory, but it can be held there
briefly and is either then forgotten (as when we look up a
telephone number and forget it the moment we have dialled
it) or translated to long-term memory where it can be held
more permanently (though it is still, of course, subject to
forgetting). Obviously this transfer is vital for effective
learning. Available evidence suggests it involves some form
of consolidation, typically a short pause during which the
information is held consciously in the mind. Even after an
interesting lesson or lecture students often remember
little, probably because each piece of information is so
quickly followed by the next that there is no time for
consolidation. However, a number of strategies exist for
helping consolidation and for increasing the efficiency of
long-term memory generally.

* By pausing, repeating and questioning, the lecturer can
  prompt students to dwell sufficiently upon material for
  transfer from short- to long-term to take place.
* By putting material to immediate practical use consolidation is also greatly helped. Material that is interesting, and that is properly understood, is also more
  likely to be remembered than is material which is
  perceived as dull or irrelevant.
* By practising OVERLEARNING, material is made particularly resistant to forgetting. Overlearning implies
  the continued revision of a learning task even after it
  appears to have been perfected, and is particularly
  valuable where the material has to be remembered in a
  stressful situation (e.g. in the examination room or on
  the concert platform).
* By associating new material with something that is
  already familiar, or with something that is particularly
  striking or novel in itself, the chances of its being
  remembered are greatly improved. Through the association
  with something that is already familiar the material is
  placed within context, and can be recalled readily when
  cued in by this material in future; through the association with something striking the material tends to be
  remembered when this striking stimulus is called to
  mind. This is particularly true if the stimulus is a
  visual one: hence the importance of visual aids. Such
  aids need not necessarily be closely linked in terms of
  meaning with the material to be learned (witness the
  highly successful advertisements on commercial television), but they must be presented concurrently with
  this material so that a strong association is built up.

In discussing memory, it is important to stress that there

appears to be a functional difference between recognition (where we spot as familiar some stimulus physically presented to us) and recall (where we have to retrieve some word or fact from memory itself). Recognition appears to come more readily than recall (e.g. it is easier to recognize a face than to recall a name, to recognize a work in a foreign language than to recall it from memory), and in consequence, unless we are deliberately setting out to test recall, it is of value to provide appropriate cues that bring recognition to the aid of recall.

So much for the factors that aid long-term memory. Now for those that appear to interfere with it. One of these, anxiety, has already been touched upon. Material that can readily be recalled in a relaxed state may prove elusive when one is under stress. Two others of importance are known as retroactive and proactive interference respectively. Retroactive interference occurs when recently learned material appears to inhibit the recall of that learned earlier. The phenomenon appears to take place at all levels of learning, and is apparent, for example, in the student who crams for an examination and finds that the facts he learned the night before keep coming back when attempts are made to recall those studied earlier in the week. Proactive interference, on the other hand, occurs when earlier learning seems to block the recall of later, as when a student starts learning a second foreign language and finds himself unable to remember the word he wants because the equivalent in the first language keeps coming to mind. We discuss ways of minimizing retroactive inhibition when we deal with study habits below, but proactive inhibition is only likely to be a problem when the two subjects being studied share certain similarities, and it tends to disappear as the new material becomes more familiar and overlearning takes place.

Finally, we come to the subject of memory training. It is often assumed that the memory can be trained, like a muscle, if we exercise it (e.g. by learning large chunks of poetry). There is no evidence, however, that this assumption is correct. The memory is improved by learning how to memorize rather than by the simple act of memorizing itself. We have already listed some of the skills relevant to this task, and reference is made to others in the next section, but we should perhaps mention here the value of mnemonic devices. These are devices created specifically to aid recall, and range from simple tricks like tying a knot in a handkerchief and short jingles like 'thirty days hath September ...' to the elaborate devices used by stage 'memory men'. One such device is the so-called peg-word system, where the digits 1-10 (or more) are each associated with a rhyming word (e.g. 1 is bun, 2 is shoe, 3 is a tree, etc.). These simple associations are learned, and then the facts to be memorized are associated with them in turn, preferably using visual imagery. Thus, for example, if we wished to learn the agricultural produce exported by New Zealand we could visualize first butter spread on a bun, second a lamb wearing shoes and so on. Such devices are remarkably effective in the learning of long lists of facts, though their use beyond this is limited.

Study habits

Much of the effectiveness of learning depends upon good study habits, particularly in older students who have to take more responsiblity for their own work. Some of these habits, like working in an environment free from distraction, are obvious while others, like overlearning, have already been covered. We can summarize the remainder as outlined below.

* REALISTIC WORK TARGETS. Realistic work targets, which the student plans in detail, are far more effective than impossibly ambitious or vague commitments. Ideally these targets should be expressed publicly (so that the student's prestige is at stake if he fails to stick to them!).

* REWARDS. Small rewards, built into the student's work schedule, can be very effective in helping sustain effort. These can take the form of a cup of coffee, for example, or a five-minute break at the end of each hour of solid work, with the purchase perhaps of an inexpensive though coveted treat each time weekly or monthly targets are met.

* PUNCTUALITY. Work should be started promptly at the appointed hour. This forestalls the elaborate (and plausible) strategies we each develop to delay actually sitting down at our desks and getting on with it.

* WHOLE AND PART LEARNING. A new learning task should be read through first in its entirety to get the general drift of it before being broken down into small units and learned methodically.

* ORGANIZING MATERIAL. Often textbooks (and lectures do not present material in a way which accords best with the learner's own experience and understanding. Time spent reorganizing the material into notes that render it generally more comprehensible and assimilable is time well spent.

* REVISION. A programme of phased revision throughout the duration of a course is of far more value than an attempt to cram everything in during the final weeks before an exam. Retroactive inhibition (and increased anxiety) are the almost inevitable consequences of such cramming. Phased revision, however, leads to a growing mastery of the whole course as the student works his way through it, with each new piece of knowledge being placed in its proper context. When it comes to final examination preparation the student is therefore looking back over material that has already been overlearned. Revision is best done before material has actually been forgotten. This is known as maintenance revison.

e nature of knowledge be learned

Obviously in any learning activity we have to consider not only the abilities of the learner but the nature of the material he is to learn. Equally obviously, this material must be organized in such a way that learning is facilitated, and in such a way that we can assess afterwards whether the desired learning has taken place or not. In considering such matters we have first of all to decide the level at which we wish learning to take place. Do we want the learner simply to learn facts, or do we want him to operate at higher levels and understand these facts, and be able to put them to use? Bloom (1956) has presented us with a comprehensive list of the various levels at which learning can take place, and this list is an indispensable aid in all matters relating to the planning and assessment of learning. The list arranges the various levels in hierarchical order, from the simplest to the most complex. Each of the higher levels subsumes those inferior to it (e.g. learning at level 3 involves learning at level 1 and 2 as well), and we can summarize them in ascending order. It will be noted that this taxonomy, as it is called, relates only to thinking skills (or skills in the cognitive domain). Other taxonomies exist which cover aspects of personality (the affective domain: see Krathwohl et al, 1964) and physical skills (the psychomotor domain: see Simpson, 1972), but these are of less immediate relevance for our purpose.

vels of learning in the gnitive domain (after om et al, 1956)

* Knowledge (i.e. simple knowledge of facts, of terms, of theories, etc.).
* Comprehension (i.e. an understanding of the meaning of this knowledge).
* Application (i.e. the ability to apply this knowledge and comprehension in new and concrete situations).
* Analysis (i.e. the ability to break material down into its constituent parts and to see the relationship between them).
* Synthesis (i.e. the ability to re-assemble these parts into a new and meaningful relationship, thus forming a new whole).
* Evaluation (i.e. the ability to judge the value of material using explicit and coherent criteria, either of one's own devising or derived from the work of others).

Having decided the level at which we intend to work, the next step (both for the tutor and for the student planning his own study programme) is to define the precise outcomes (or objectives) that our learning is intended to achieve. This is often one of the hardest parts of the exercise. Frequently learning objectives make the mistake of simply outlining what is to be done rather than concentrating upon why it is done. The best way to avoid this error is to remember that a learning objective should state the behaviour expected from a student as the result of a lesson. Thus, for example, we would not write that our objective is 'to demonstrate a particular skill (whatever it may happen to be) to the class', but rather that at the end of the lesson the students should be able to do one or more of the following (depending upon the level at which we intend learning to take place):

* to recognize and identify the elements involved in the skill (these elements would then be specified - this is an objective at the KNOWLEDGE level);
* to define these elements and to know the part they play in the skill (an objective at the COMPREHENSION level)
* to practise the skill itself (an objective at the APPLICATION level);
* to describe what is happening - and why - during this practice (an objective at the ANALYSIS level);
* to utilize elements of this skill in solving a particular novel problem (an objective at the SYNTHESIS level);
* to assess the degree of success achieved in this solution and to propose improvements (an objective at the EVALUATION level).

It can be readily appreciated that, once he has stated a clear objective (or objectives) at the beginning of his lesson plan, the tutor is in a much better position to determine his lesson content and to keep it practical and relevant. He is also better able to assess whether learning has taken place or not at the end of the lesson, since he specified in advance the student behaviour that will provide evidence of that learning. An assessment is a major topic in itself; we can now turn to it in more detail.

Assessment

Much assessment takes place simply observing student behaviours, or by directing questions at students, but often the tutor wishes to provide his class with specially devised opportunities to demonstrate whether their behaviour has changed in the desired direction or not. The tutor's choice of which opportunities to offer (i.e. of which assessment techniques to use) will be influenced by the level (in terms of the taxonomy discussed above) at which he intends learning to take place. All too frequently, particularly in arts and social science subjects, assessment simply takes the form of a written essay, which may be appropriate for gauging progress at the more complex cognitive levels but which samples only a very limited range of knowledge and comprehension. The main alternative to the essay is the so-called objective test, each of whose items carries only a single right answer. Such items are usually of the multiple choice variety, with the student being asked which of a range of possible answers is the correct one: for example, 'The Theory of Association was first advanced by; Herbart/ William James/Francis Galton/none of these'. It will be noted that multiple choice questions test recognition; if it was desired to test recall, the question would be allowed to stand on its own without the addition of the possible answers.

It is often claimed that objective tests take the tutor longer to construct than tests of the essay type. There is no gainsaying this, but on the other hand they are quicker to mark, and the teacher is left with the satisfaction of knowing that he has adequately tested the knowledge that he set out to test. Further, the student is motivated to acquire this knowledge since he knows that it is to be comprehensively tested, rather than fractionally sampled as in an essay. He is also left with the reassurance that good marks really do mean that he knows the field and is equipped with the basic grammar of his subject.

e nature of the arning process

Having looked at the learner and at the knowledge to be learned we now come to the last major variable, namely the process (or methods or techniques) by means of which learning actually takes place. Gagné (1974) suggests that the learning act involves a chain of eight events, some internal to the learner and others external. These events are, in their usual order of occurrence:

* motivation (or expectancy);
* apprehending (the subject perceives the material and distinguishes it from the other stimuli competing for his attention);
* acquisition (the subject codes the knowledge - i.e. makes sense of it, relates it to what he already knows);
* retention (the subject stores the knowledge in short- or long-term memory);
* recall (the subject retrieves the material from memory);
* generalization (the material is transferred to new situations, thus allowing the subject to develop strategies for dealing with them);
* performance (these strategies are put into practice);
* feedback (the subject obtains knowledge of results).

Where there is a failure to learn, Gagné argues, it will take place at one of these eight levels, and it is thus the task of the tutor to ascertain which. It may be that the learning has failed to capture the pupil's attention, or it makes no sense to him, or he has failed to transfer it to long-term memory, or he is unable to recall it from his memory. Analysing learning failure in this way renders the tutor much better able to help the pupil since it enables him to concentrate upon the specific point at which the pupil appears to be going wrong. Frequently, too, he may discover that the fault lies not simply with the pupil himself but with the way in which the learning task has been presented - and explained - to him.

The manner in which this presentation should be effected depends again upon the level (in terms of Bloom's taxonomy)

at which we intend learning to take place. Where we are
concerned with levels 1-3 (knowledge, comprehension, and
application) then the strategy derived from the experimental
findings of Skinner (e.g. Skinner, 1969) is of most help.
Skinner's work indicates that factual knowledge and its
comprehension and application is normally absorbed most
efficiently if it is presented to the learner in small
steps, each of them within his competence; if he is then
required to demonstrate this learning in some way; and if he
is given immediate knowledge of results on whether his
demonstration was correct or not. In the event of failure,
the whole procedure is repeated. This strategy cannot only
be put to efficient use by the teacher in his direct dealings with his pupils, it also lies at the heart of what has
come to be known as programmed learning. Programmed
learning uses either specially written textbooks or rolls
of paper mounted in simple learning devices to present each
unit of learning in turn to the learner, to question him on
it, and to inform him whether or not his answer to the
question is correct. An example of an item from a programme
on electrical wiring illustrates this clearly.

Stage 1 (information): In wiring a 13 amp plug the brown
            wire is connected to the live terminal.
Stage 2 (question): Which colour wire is connected to the
            live terminal of a 13 amp plug?
Stage 3 (answer): A. the blue; B. the brown; C. the green
            and yellow.
Stage 4 (results): The brown wire is connected to the live
            terminal of a 13 amp plug.

This example tests recognition in Stage 3 by offering the
three possible right answers, but of course these could be
omitted if we wished to test recall.
      This learning procedure involves what Skinner calls
operant conditioning in that at each point it involves,
after the presentation of the information to be learned, a
stimulus (the question), an item of behaviour (the student's
answer), and a reward or reinforcement (the knowledge of
results). This operant conditioning (or S-B-R) model lies
behind all learning, claims Skinner, and where there is
learning failure this is normally because we have omitted to
present the appropriate stimulus or, more frequently, the
appropriate reinforcement. For many pupils immediate and
accurate knowledge of successful results (remember that
Skinner advocates presenting material to pupils in small
steps, each one within their competence) is sufficient
reinforcement, but for others teacher approval, good marks
and grades, and even small physical rewards (e.g. where the
child is retarded or handicapped and cannot understand the
significance of marks and grades) may have to be used.
Similarly, where incorrect learning has taken place, Skinner
claims this can also be due to misapplied reinforcement. The
parent or teacher, for example, fails to realize that the

very fact of his attention (whether angry or not) is a powerful reinforcement for some children. Thus the more scolding the adult directs at the child's misbehaviour the more persistent it may tend to become. The correct procedure would be to ignore the child when he produces this behaviour and reward him with attention when he shows behaviour of the opposite, desirable kind. This approach is part of a range of strategies based upon conditioning theories (and known collectively as behaviour modification techniques) which are attracting increasing attention in educational and clinical circles.

Many psychologists, however, though granting the effectiveness of Skinner's approach at the first three levels in Bloom's taxonomy, consider it an inadequate basis for prompting learning at the higher levels. Learning at these levels involves more than a mere knowledge of the facts and formulae produced by other people (the so-called middle language of the subject); it involves the ability to discover the fundamental logic underlying the subject. Bruner (1966) argues that to help students achieve such discovery we must present them with problems and challenges, with questions that contain an element of controversy and contradiction. Such questions, known as springboard questions, introduce material which does not quite fit in with the student's accepted knowledge and beliefs. A 'level 1' question, such as 'What is the population of Britain?' or 'What is the formula for water?' demands nothing from the student beyond a single answer delivered in the form in which he first heard it. A springboard question, on the other hand, such as 'The poles are equidistant from the equator, yet the south is colder than the north; why?' or 'Christianity teaches you that you should love your enemies, yet men have committed terrible massacres in its name; why?' prompts the student to reflect on the subtle ways in which his subject works, on the relationship between cause and effect, on methods of procedure and enquiry. The same is true of simulation exercises, which present the learner with imaginary problems designed to mimic those faced in real life by social workers, nurses and economists, for example, and ask him to produce solutions. These solutions are then compared with genuine case histories, and comparisons and contrasts are drawn which promote debate, understanding, and the efficient workings of memory.

ferences

Bloom, B.S. et al (1956)
Taxonomy of Educational Objectives. Handbook 1: The cognitive domain. London: Longmans Green.

Bruner, J.S. (1966)
Towards a Theory of Instruction. Cambridge, Mass.: Harvard University Press.

Bruner, J.S. (1973)
The Relevance of Education. New York: Norton.

Davie, R., Butler, N. and Goldsmith, H. (1972)
From Birth to Seven. London: Longmans.

Gagné, R.M. (1974)
   Essentials of Learning for Instruction. Hinsdale, Ill.:
   Dryden Press.
Inhelder, B. and Piaget, J. (1958)
   The Growth of Logical Thinking from Childhood to
   Adolescence. London: Routledge & Kegan Paul.
Kagan, J., Sontag, L., Baker, C. and Nelson, V. (1958)
   Personality and IQ change. Journal of Abnormal and
   Social Psychology, 56, 261-266.
Krathwohl, D.R. et al (1964)
   Taxonomy of Educational Objectives. Handbook II: The
   affective domain. New York: David McKay.
Simpson, E.J. (1972)
   The classification of educational objectives in the
   psychomotor domain. The Psychomotor Domain, Volume D
   Washington: Gryphon House.
Skinner, B.F. (1969)
   Contingencies of Reinforcement: A theoretical analysis.
   New York: Appleton-Century-Crofts.

Questions

1. Think about the definition of learning offered in the text. Can you suggest ways in which it could be made more satisfactory?
2. Sometimes anxiety is an aid to learning and sometimes the reverse. Why is this? Do we think we are ever right to encourage even mild anxiety?
3. Outline the kinds of learning environment likely to appeal to the marked extravert. How does this environment differ from that suitable for the marked introvert?
4. Make lists of the intrinsic and extrinsic motivators which have respectively been of most importance to you in your own learning experiences.
5. Why is it that the experience of consistent failure is so damaging to a person's readiness to learn?
6. What action do you think should be taken against a student who cheats in their academic work? What does such cheating tell us about the student concerned?
7. List some of the factors both in the home and in the school which you feel may influence the respective rates at which boys and girls learn.
8. Define short- and long-term memory respectively. What are some of the strategies that aid transfer from one to the other?
9. What is meant by overlearning and why is it a valuable strategy?
10. Write short descriptions of three television advertisements that you have seen recently and that appear to apply ASSOCIATION as an effective aid to memory. Consider ways in which similar techniques can be used as an aid to formal learning.
11. Define the difference between recognition and recall. How can a recognition task be converted into a recall task (and vice versa)?

12. When and in what circumstances must we be alert to possible interference with the process of remembering?
13. Write down as many examples as you can of well-known mnemonics. Construct a mnemonic for aiding memory in an important area of your own subject.
14. List the six suggested ways in which study habits can be improved. Can you think of any further ways of your own?
15. Write out the six categories in Bloom's taxonomy of educational objectives.
16. Discuss the respective functions of the essay and of the objective test.
17. Construct a simple multiple choice test designed to establish whether a student has correctly learned the principles and/or the facts behind one or more of the following: (i) propagating plants by means of softwood cuttings; (ii) starting a motor car and drawing safely away from the kerb; (iii) swimming the crawl; (iv) the symbols on a map (or on a weather map).
18. What are the eight events in a learning chain according to Gagné?
19. Design a simple programme to teach a student an important aspect of your own subject.
20. What are the principles that underlie good springboard questions? Give some examples of such questions drawn from your own subject.
21. Construct a simulation designed to help students face common problems in their practical work. Suggest ways of evaluating their responses.

notated reading

Bigge, L. (1976) Learning Theories for Teachers (3rd edn). New York: Harper & Row.
>One of the best and most comprehensive surveys of learning theories and their application to teaching.

Hintzman, L. (1978) The Psychology of Learning and Memory. San Francisco: Freeman.
>A good choice for those who want to take their study of learning theories rather further, and examine their relationship to memory.

Marjoribanks, K. (1979) Families and Their Learning Environments. London: Routledge & Kegan Paul.
>A thorough and scholarly survey of the research into the relationship between intelligence, personality, family variables and learning.

Fontana, D. (1977) Personality and Education. London: Open Books.
>A more general discussion, with an examination of the implications for the teacher.

Hunter, I. M. L. (1964), 'Memory' (rev. edn), Harmondswort
Pelican.
 Difficult to beat as an examination of all aspects of
 memory.

Klatsky, R.L. (1975) Human Memory. San Francisco: Freema
 Gives a more up-to-date picture than Hunter's book.

Rowntree, D. (1976) Learn How to Study. Harmondsworth:
Pelican.

Mace, C.A. (1968) The Psychology of Study (rev. edn).
London: MacDonald.
 Both of these are among the good books currently
 available on study habits, and are highly recommended.

Gronlund, N.E. (1978). Stating Objectives of Classroom
Instruction (2nd edn). London: Collier Macmillan.
 One of the best short books on the writing of educational objectives. It also has something useful to say
 on the construction of objective tests.

Vernon, P.E. (1964) An Introduction to Objective-type
Examinations. London: Schools Council Examinations Bulletin
No. 4.
 One of the most valuable short introductions to the
 subject.

Gagné, R.M. (1975) Essentials of Learning for Instruction.
Hinsdale, Illinois: Dryden Press.

Gagné, R. M. (1977) The Conditions of Learning (3rd edn).
London: Holt, Rinehart & Winston.
 Good introductions to Gagné's work.

Jones, R.M. (1972) Fantasy and Feeling in Education.
Harmondsworth: Penguin.
 A good discussion of Bruner's ideas within the practical
 classroom context.

Taylor, J.L. and Walford, R. (1972) Simulation in the
Classroom. Harmondsworth: Penguin.
 Simulation exercises are comprehensively explained, with
 examples.

Rowntree, D. (1974) Educational Technology in Curriculum
Development. London: Harper & Row.
 The best approach to programmed learning and the whole
 field of educational technology.

Part two

Interpersonal and Social Behaviour

5

Interviewing
Russell P. Wicks

If there is one universally applied technique to be found
in behavioural research it is 'interviewing'. If there is
one technique basic to all professional practice it is the
interaction between people that is called 'interviewing'. It
is the nature of this interaction between people which is
the concern of this chapter. It is to be hoped that what
is said can be applied not simply to 'the interview' in
'an interview situation' but to all purposive contacts
between individuals, the critical feature, it is claimed,
being the purposive nature of the encounter. The participants bring hopes, fears, expectations, misconceptions and
many other cognitions to the situation most times in the
hope that their wishes will be met, fears reduced and so on.
Customarily this view is found in the characterization of an
interview as a 'conversation with a purpose'. So it is, but
ALL those participating in an interview have their purposes
and not simply, for example, the interviewer. In the complex
transactions of getting and giving information we observe
effort aimed at achieving purposes. Thus the psychologist
testing a client by means of, say, the Wechsler Adult
Intelligence Scale is conducting an interview as defined.
The purpose from one point of view is to help the client in
some way, from the other to be helped. In the exchange of
information each has purposes and expectations that they
hope will be met. Each may be optimizing their strategies
towards fulfilling these purposes. Roles will be assumed
constraining and shaping behaviour. If participants in
interviews can become more skilful and aware of the processes involved there is some hope of raising levels of
satisfaction. It is, therefore, the aim of this chapter to
examine such interview processes with this goal in mind. For
this purpose a simple model of an interview will be described (see figure 1) and for illustrative purposes reference made to three particular interview situations;
occupational counselling, job interviews and research
interviewing.

iation

The view that it is the purposive nature of the interview that is crucial leads us to consider the motives of the
participants. An individual approaching a counselling

81

Figure 1

Model of an interview

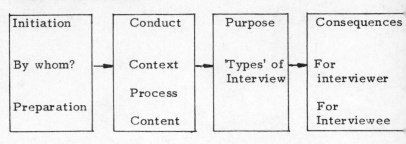

Initiation	Conduct	Purpose	Consequences
By whom?	Context	'Types' of Interview	For interviewer
	Process		
Preparation	Content		For Interviewee

situation may be motivated by a complex of needs and voluntary or compulsory attendance may be crucial in structuring these needs. Whether these needs are shared and whether the can be fulfilled is another matter. It may well be the case that some frequently voiced criticisms of interviews arise, in part, from a failure to make explicit the needs and expectations of the parties involved. Nowhere is this more important than in those situations with a high level of emotional involvement. Two people may look back on an interview as a total failure because each had different expectations which unfortunately were not fulfilled. We all, interviewers and interviewees, bring hopes and fears to the task. Just as Orne (1962) draws our attention to the 'demand characteristics' of the experimental situation as a result of which subjects perform as they believe they are expected so to do, so participants in interviews will seek a role that they perceive as being appropriate. Not always, unfortunately, do they choose correctly.

In analysing an interview it follows, therefore, that attention to preliminaries and preparation is vital. Many writers on interviewing stress the physical preparations needed, literally setting the scene. Here, 'cognitive' scene setting is judged to be more important; for example, in employment interviewing paying attention to providing information about the organization, or providing an adequate job description. Considering the contribution of application forms and references, together with other 'scene setting' activities, will go a long way towards minimizing the cognitive gap that may occur. Furthermore, such preparations are in fact part of the information exchange that lies at the heart of an interview. In general, preparation from the interviewer's point of view means careful planning of all aspects of the situation. Briefing oneself, rehearsing the interview, anticipating needs; all contribute to an efficiently managed, worth-while encounter.

Recently, increasing attention has been given to preparation on the part of the interviewee, especially for those about to be interviewed for a job. For example, a great deal of work stemming from careers work with young people has resulted in programmes aimed at developing 'life

skills'. There is clear evidence that all can profit from
paying attention to the activities and skills involved in
job seeking. The material included in such programmes varies
widely but may cover:

* where to get job information;
* work experience;
* how to reply to advertisements;
* how to become more self-aware;
* how to be interviewed.

The techniques employed range from self-instructional
material to the use of video-recording of role-play situations. In general, however, the emphasis is on providing
guidelines, improving social skills, self-presentation and
making people more aware of the processes of social
interaction.

Context

What effect on the behaviour of the participants in an
interview might the following environments have: a police
station; a doctor's surgery; a street corner; a psychology
laboratory? Clearly the effect can be dramatic. We have
the clearest evidence here for the importance of the frame
of reference, role expectations and construal of the situation upon behaviour in an interview. Indeed, the subtlety
of the rules of the 'games' played out in different contexts
is such that we spend our lives refining and editing our
private rule books. Within each context there may be a range
of indicators signalling to us how to behave, how to address
people, what to say and what not to say, an obvious example
being dress, particularly a uniform which may be anything
from a pin-stripe suit to a white coat. What is the experience of people who customarily wear a 'uniform' when they
discard it? What might people say to a priest in mufti that
they would not say if he donned his clerical garb? Thus our
perception of the interview context is an essential part of
the scene setting previously discussed. Most interviewers,
being aware of this, go to some trouble to ensure that the
physical setting signals what they wish it to: they dress in
a particular style, arrange the seats appropriately, adjust
the lighting, ensure that interruptions do or do not occur.
They try to ensure that the interview is conducted in a
'good mannered' way.

A further aspect is that participants bring substantial
resources to the task: their background knowledge, and
skills expectations. Whilst these resources may bring
benefits to an interview, they sometimes create problems.
Such difficulties have been extensively investigated by
Rosenthal (1969) and his co-workers in studies of the
characteristics of 'volunteers' in research and studies of
the expectations of subjects in experiments, as well as the
experimenters. Avoiding bias and error arising from these

factors is a major concern of investigators; thus one should be aware that volunteers for survey research tend to be better educated, if male score higher on IQ tests, and are better adjusted than non-volunteers. Such factors should be taken into account in evaluating data. Similarly, the survey interviewer asked to find a sample of five people, even though certain characteristics of the sample are specified, may unwittingly choose those they feel it would be 'nice' to interview.

Process

A great deal of what we know about interpersonal communication has been learnt by systematic study of interviews, especially the face-to-face two-person encounter. What is offered here, however, is a general communication model which may be used to analyse an interview (see figure 2). The utility of this model as a tool for examining inter-personal behaviour rests upon the conceptualization of communication as a system; the model is dynamic because it has independent parts with provision for feedback.

Figure 2

A communication model

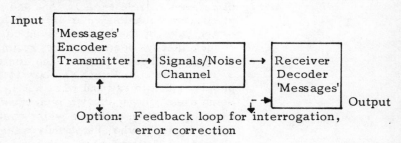

Such a model could stand for many communication systems; radio or television tranmission, a nervous system or, in this case, an interview. A useful procedure arising from the 'system' model is that we can examine its integrity. In other words, we can see what happens when one part of the system is distorted or eliminated. Examples of this approach are given in the exercises included in the teaching material for this volume.

In this model, 'message' is taken to stand for that which we wish to transmit. Embedded in this is the difficult problem of meaning and an obvious use of the model is to compare inputs and outputs according to some criterion of meaningfulness. Such a comparison is the basis of an often hilarious game in which the distortion occurring when a 'message' is passed along a line of people by word of mouth is examined. Bartlett (1972) showed in his method of serial reproduction the simplifications and intrusions which occur in this process.

Within the interview, 'meaning' arises at a number of levels. First, at the level of verbal content. What was the question and what is the answer? Much has been written about asking the right sort of question in an interview, whether to use direct or indirect questions, the appropriate form of words, and the dangers of certain questions such as leading or multiple forms. Skilful interviewers do not seem to be constrained by rigid rules but show flexibility, constantly probing and following up interesting leads. They tend to ask: 'Tell me', 'When was that?', 'How was that?', 'What did you do?' and perhaps the most difficult question of all, 'Why?'

Second, the question of meaning arises at the level of recording the interview material. What gets lost or distorted when an interviewer distils a reply into notes or makes a decision? Third, a consideration arising especially in the research interview is: what has happened to the original meaning when a response is coded, probably into a pre-determined category, and is lumped together with others when the study is reported?

However, the verbal content of the message is only a small part of the signal. Many researchers assert that the non-verbal component of a signal is of greater importance. Argyle (1973, 1975) in particular has drawn our attention to the role of non-verbal communication factors such as:

* bodily movements: body language: gestures;
* facial expression;
* eye movements and eye contact;
* personal space: proximity.

The socially skilled performer is simultaneously transmitting signals using all these components together with verbal material whilst reacting to similar signals constituting feedback from their partner.

Utilizing and decoding this complex of information involves us in consideration of interpersonal perception, a key area in the analysis of interviewing. How we form judgements about other people is at the heart of interview decisions: the substantial literature on this topic, for example Cook (1979), suggests that the information we use includes:

* a person's actions;
* the situation in which the person is observed;
* appearance - including facial expression, physique, speech characteristics and dress style;
* non-verbal cues mentioned previously.

The powerful influence of some cues is seen most clearly in the study of stereotypes. Picking up one piece of information and building often unwarranted assumptions upon it is the classic error in judging others. Reacting to a regional accent, to hair colour, to ethnic origin or any other isolated item is all too common. Such a reaction, especially to irrelevant information, is usually dubbed the 'halo effect'. Since the judge or interviewer is striving for cognitive consistency, information is often interpreted in such a way that it fits this single judgement. Thus favourable material or even attributions will be ascribed to a liked person. Contrariwise, undue weight may be given to negative indications in the case of dislike. Clearly, interviewers must be constantly on their guard against introducing bias of this kind. Awareness of their prejudices and the sorts of errors we make in judging others will help.

It is the process component of interviewing which has received most attention in the training of interviewers. Such training commonly takes the form of general social skills training together with exercises directed at the specialization of the interviewer; for example, obtaining clinically relevant material in the hospital setting. Just how effective training may be is not easy to assess. Largely this is so because published studies of interview training tend to use different criteria, thus making comparisons difficult. The benefits to the trainee probably come from receiving informed feedback in role-playing or group tasks about their performance together with enhanced self-awareness.

Content

The point has been made that the absence of a shared common aim or lack of a clear plan in an interview leads to many difficulties. Specifically, criticisms in terms of interview decisions tend to the view that they may leave much to be desired. It is claimed, for example, that the research literature points overwhelmingly in this direction. Without wishing to dismiss the many studies leading to this conclusion, it must be pointed out that they cover a wide range of interview outcomes made by many interviewers at different levels of experience and training with their decisions based on imprecise criteria. The message of these studies seems to be that all concerned with interviews should be aware of the shortcomings and take steps to overcome them. Apart from errors arising from factors already mentioned in describing context and process aspects at an interview, the principal source is often the lack of a clear plan for an interview; in other words, content must be tailored to the particular aim in mind, each interview requiring careful planning with preparation related to a desired outcome. By way of illustration let us consider the content of interviews within the three professional contexts of counselling, job interviews and research interviewing.

Counselling: occupational guidance

What is the aim of an occupational guidance procedure? At one time the approach was modelled upon the notion of talent matching. Specify the job, specify the man and attempt to

match the two. On the job side of the equation, techniques
of task analysis, job description and content specification
were developed whilst evidence of congruent relevant behaviour was sought from the interviewee. It is no coincidence
that the heyday of this approach coincided with the early
boom in psychological test production. Aptitude tests,
occupational interest guides, and tests of specific skills
were all produced to aid the matching. Today, with the
application of computer-based matching procedures, the
approach is enjoying a revival. The role of the interview in
this model was largely to establish the congruence of job
and applicant profiles by comparison through discussion.
From this approach evolved the contemporary developmental
model, with an emphasis on career decision making as a
process over time, starting in the early years with educational counselling, proceeding to occupational counselling and then to career development counselling, with
perhaps counselling for retirement in later years. Thus
there may be many interviews within this model each with a
specific aim, the sum aimed at the overall development of
the individual. Among the sub-goals of this process we can
recognize the following:

* self-appraisal: equipping the client to achieve
  realistic self-assessment;
* self-perception: providing frames of reference,
  categories of occupationally significant behaviours;
* job perception: acquiring the skills required to assess
  the world of work in terms of job content, values, roles
  and life style;
* reality testing: matching aspirations and goals with
  opportunities within one's limitations;
* setting goals and objectives: specifying attainable
  goals and precise objectives;
* hypothesis generation: helping the client to generate
  occupational 'theories';
* interaction of the person and the job environment:
  examining the complexities of the person/work situation
  interaction;
* sharing information: providing the client with educational and occupational information, and providing the
  counsellor with perceptions of the client;
* task setting: translating immediate goals into discrete
  tasks, such as finding an address, seeking information,
  reading a pamphlet, etc.

The task of the interviewer/counsellor therefore becomes
that of achieving these goals at the appropriate time and in
a manner which meets the client's needs. Flexibility, wide
background knowledge and the ability to relate to the client
are clearly prerequisites on the part of the counsellor.
Similar goals are shared by modern staff appraisal schemes
and staff development procedures.

Job interviews

Being interviewed for a job, for promotion or for annual
assessment is probably the most commonly experienced form
of interview. It has certainly attracted a substantial body
of folk-lore, myth, jokes and hard-luck stories. That this
is so is, in itself, of considerable psychological significance. The job interview comes in many varieties, not least
the panel interview. Here especially the crucial importance
of planning an interview is seen. The justifiable criticism
of such encounters is frequently due first to poor interviewing skills on the part of the individual board members,
and second to the lack of an agreed role for each.

Whilst not normally included under the heading of
interviews, such behavioural observation techniques as role-
playing by candidates, group discussions, problem-solving
exercises and others raise the same problems previously
mentioned of reliable and valid judgements about other
people.

Two examples of interview plans used in job interviews
will be presented here: one is a general approach commonly
employed, namely, the biography; the second a well-known
technique called the Seven-Point Plan.

THE BIOGRAPHY: the majority of job interviews employ this
approach, often, however, in an undisciplined fashion,
hunting and pecking at a person's history. However, a simple
structure which can be readily shared consists of establishing landmarks within relevant areas; commonly times of
change such as leaving school. Bearing in mind the selec-
tivity of recall, in itself an important indicator within an
interview, and that the recent past may be more accessible,
one should not expect uniform coverage of a life history.
This raises the problem of breadth and depth within the
interview in relation to the relevance of the information.
Too often an interviewer will spend time on an irrelevant
area, missing the opportunity to explore a significant point
in detail.

However, a plan such as that shown in figure 3 provides
a secure frame of reference for interviewer and interviewee.
Not least, the interviewee can be assembling information and
anticipating questions; the task is not unlike talking
through a curriculum vitae. A final benefit of this approach
is that it enables the interviewer to check dates, spot gaps
in the account and draw out the inter-relationships between

Figure 3

	Education	Interests	Home	Work
The past Landmarks The present	Dates			

events. This approach is underpinned by application forms and curricula vitae, which are customarily set out in biographical order.

THE SEVEN-POINT PLAN: probably the best known of all assessment and interview formats, the plan was originally developed by Alec Rodger within the framework of the talent matching approach to occupational guidance. It was intended to apply to both candidates and jobs, to obtain relevant information about people and by asking the same questions of a job to facilitate matching.

The plan was rapidly adopted for job interviewing and has undoubtedly been highly influential insofar as it provides the unskilled interviewer with a robust, easily understood framework within which to work. Over the years, a number of modifications have been suggested to the original plan. Similarly based schemes have been published, but what is essentially the original is presented here (Rodger, 1974).

1. Physical characteristics:
   Physical abilities of occupational importance.
   State of health. Vision, hearing. Appearance. Speech.
2. Attainments (and previous experience):
   Educational background, achievements. Occupational and professional training. Experience. How well has this person done? Personal achievements in any area: sports, pursuits, etc.
3. General ability:
   Especially general intelligence and cognitive skills - words, numbers, relationships.
4. Special aptitudes:
   Particularly occupationally applicable talents - scientific, mechanical, mathematical, practical, literary, artistic, social skills.
5. Interests:
   Often the core information: type of interests, how they are pursued, to what effect. Intellectual, practical, physical, social and artistic interests may be occupationally significant.
6. Personality:
   What is this person like? Especially in terms of self-perception. Social relationships, behaviour indicative of self-reliance, dependability.
7. Circumstances:
   The context of the person's life insofar as it affects his aspirations. Family circumstances, financial background, current problems.

The first six points apply particularly to the study of jobs. What physical characteristics, what attainments and so on are required for this job? It should be added that Rodger emphasized the importance of paying attention to individual likes and dislikes, to difficulties or distastes mentioned by people, and to the individual's strengths and weaknesses when applying the plan; in particular, stressing the importance of negative information in making selection decisions and the noting of danger signs.

Finally, in considering job interviews it should be noted that advice and preparation for interviewees is widely available in relation to the job interview. Social skills training, and self-presentation courses are examples.

Research interviews
The place of the interview in social research is central. Its contribution ranges from preliminary information gathering to a place as the principal research tool. Clearly it takes many forms but the main dimension along which it varies is that of being unstructured/structured, from free to semi to structured. Here, the highly structured form typically found in market research and surveys will be considered, the characteristics of the unstructured form being similar to counselling interviews. For the structured approach a unique feature is the use of an interview schedule: in effect, a carefully prepared script meticulously adhered to by the interviewer. A great deal of thought is put into preparing the schedule in order that question form and content, question order, response mode, use of response aids and other factors can be taken into account.

Customarily these factors are checked by conducting pilot studies. Another feature of research interviewing is the attention paid to teaching interviewers how to present a particular schedule, together with supervision of their work in the field. Finally, since it is often the case that large numbers of respondents are involved, it is usual to design the schedules with data analysis in mind. For example, the coding of responses by interviewers for data entry.

As an example of research interviewing the approach of the Government Social Survey is now described. The Social Survey began work dealing with wartime problems of the 1940s. It is now a Division of the Office of Population Censuses and Surveys carrying out a wide range of studies of social and economic interest for public departments. A detailed description of the practices and procedures it employs is to be found in the handbook for interviewers (Atkinson, 1971).

Steps in producing such surveys include:

* identifying research question: decide on form and content of survey, consider costs;
* draft proposals: content of schedule, sampling of respondents;
* pilot stage: explore degree of structure appropriate, such as free to highly. Coding of replies. Analyse pilot material;
* brief and train interviewers: careful training including practice on schedule. How to contact the public.

Identifying the person to be interviewed (e.g. by age, sex, role). Putting over the purpose of the survey; problem of refusals or non-co-operation. Conducting the interview: defining the roles of interviewer and informant;

* timetable: prepare addresses, number of interviewees, target dates;
* carry out field survey: interviewers adhere to research officers' instructions on each question. Comprehend the purpose of each question: (i) factual information; (ii) expression of opinion; (iii) attitude measures.
  Deploy response modes without distortion: open questions with free response, closed/forward choice questions with pre-coded or scaled responses. Interviewers practise use of response aids: prompt cards for scaled responses, self-completion scales, repertory grids, examples of products in market research.
  Interviewers pay particular attention to prompting and probing. Guard against distortion in recording data: both precoded and open response items are susceptible;
* coding: check schedules and categorize response;
* computing: produce tables, analyse data;
* conclusion: write report.

rpose

At this stage in the discussion of our model of an interview it must be clear that so many varieties exist as to demand careful consideration of each in terms of purpose. The variety of purposes has been mentioned, and also that the approach may vary from structured to unstructured according to purpose. Thus a number of recognizable forms of interview have emerged to meet particular needs. Examples include:

* non-directive counselling, client-centred therapy;
* psychotherapeutic encounters of many kinds;
* depth interviews emphasizing motivational factors;
* group interviews involving a number of respondents in a discussion group type format;
* psychological testing, especially individual tests such as WAIS (Wechsler Adult Intelligence Scale);
* problem-solving interviews such as individual role-playing for a variety of purposes.

nsequences

Accepting the purposive nature of the interview implies that outcomes are important for all concerned and that their nature depends on the situation, and not least how the situation is perceived. For the interviewer, this will involve achieving the particular aims which have been identified together with maintenance of professional competence; for example, in the research interview maintaining the validity, reliability and precision of data with errors eliminated as far as possible.

For the interviewee or respondent one might ask: what do they get out of the experience? All too often what might be called the public relations aspect of interviewing is ignored. Symptoms of this include fears on the part of correspondents regarding the confidentiality of data, or that in some way they are being threatened. Such considerations appear to bring us full circle, for if attention is paid to the initiation stage of the proceedings by way of setting the scene such alarms can be reduced. Nevertheless, the sometimes necessary use of subterfuge in research needs to be handled with great care, a minimum requirement being the provision of an adequate explanation after the event on an account of the research.

References

Argyle, M. (1973)
Social Interaction. London: Tavistock.
Argyle, M. (1975)
Bodily Communication. London: Methuen.
Atkinson, J. (1971)
A Handbook for Interviewers (2nd edn). London: HMSO.
Bartlett, F.C. (1932)
Remembering. Cambridge: Cambridge University Press.
Cook, M. (1979)
Perceiving Others. London: Methuen.
Orne, M.T. (1962)
On the social psychology of the psychological experiment. American Psychologist, 17, 776-783.
Rodger, A. (1974)
Seven Point Plan. London: NFER.
Rosenthal, R. and Rosnow, R.L. (1969)
The volunteer subject. In R. Rosenthal and R.L. Rosnow (eds), Artifact in Behavioral Research. New York: Academic Press.

Questions

1. 'The interview is a wide-band procedure with low fidelity'. Discuss.
2. Assess the contribution of the study of social skills to the improvement of job selection interviewing.
3. 'Interviewing is the most commonly used selection tool'. Why do you think this is and what else are its strengths and weaknesses?
4. What future do you see for the interview?
5. Discuss the significance of role expectations for the conduct of an interview.
6. Write an account of the function of non-verbal communication in the interview.
7. Critically assess the form of an interview in a counselling situation with which you are familiar.
8. What are the advantages and disadvantages of using a scheme such as the Seven Point Plan for job interviewing?

9. Identify common sources of error in research interviewing. How might these be eliminated?
10. Choose a particular type of interview and design an appropriate interviewer training course.

annotated reading

Anstey, E. (1976) An Introduction to Selection Interviewing. London: HMSO.
> Originally prepared for staff training in the Civil Service, this practical guide is useful for the advice it gives on general preparation for selection interviewing as well as the conduct of interviews.

Bingham, W.V. and Moore, B.V. (1959) How to Interview (4th edn). New York: Harper & Row.
> A classic work. An early attempt to offer general guidance for those engaged in selection, survey interviews and counselling. Rather general in its approach.

Cannel, C.F. and Kahn, R.L. (1968) Interviewing. In G. Lindzey and E. Aronson (eds), The Handbook of Social Psychology, Volume II: Research methods (2nd edn). London: Addison-Wesley.
> A systematic account of the research interview. Tends towards a theoretical presentation, problems of reliability and validity and measurement using interview data being examples. Includes discussion of interview technique, question form and the training of interviewers.

Cross, C.P. (1974) Interviewing and Communication in Social Work. London: Routledge & Kegan Paul.
> A useful guide to the 'helping' interview. Represents the movement towards enhancing social skills of all involved in such encounters.

Sidney, E. and Brown, M. (1973) The skills of Interviewing. London: Tavistock.
> Aimed at managers, especially personnel staff. A generally acclaimed book, based on the extensive experience of the authors, it offers a very practical guide to the selection interview.

Sidney, E., Brown, M. and Argyle, M. (1973) Skills with People. London: Hutchinson.
> A guide for managers. Concerns itself with a wide range of topics: communication in general, social skills, interviews, meetings and committees, interpersonal skills and training in social skills.

Ungerson, B. (ed.) (1975) Recruitment Handbook (2nd edn).
London: Gower Press.
   Very useful guide to the context of job interviewing,
   preparing job specifications, advertising, references;
   all the supporting activities of selection are covered.

6

Bargaining and Negotiation
Ian E. Morley

We expect that most of the people who read this chapter
have some experience of industrial relations. Some will, no
doubt, be engaged in the 'art of negotiation' themselves.
Others may be contemplating the possibility of 'collective
bargaining' with a certain amount of apprehension. Others
still may simply be intrigued that 'problem-solving' groups
or committees to which they belong turned into negotiation
groups, and failed to solve the problems they were assigned.
But very few people will require a definition of negotiation
of the kind to be found in academic texts. Quite simply,
negotiation occurs whenever people confer, or exchange
ideas, to define or redefine the terms of their
relationship.

In contrast, many readers may be unsure what psychology
is all about. And to be frank, there are probably as many
definitions as there are psychologists. However, broadly
speaking, the subject is concerned with activity of individuals or small groups, and the reasons why they behave as
they do. As part of this general enterprise we believe that
psychologists can contribute to our understanding of the
ways negotiators prepare for bargaining and negotiate their
case. In particular, we argue that:

* to understand the process of negotiation we need to
  combine models of the task with models of the negotiators. We need 'models of negotiation' as well as 'models
  of man';
* planning and process may be regarded as the intra-group
  and inter-group aspects of a task which engages the
  'core' processes of information interpretation, influence and decision-making;
* structure in the process of negotiation is determined by
  the working out of the core processes which are
  involved;
* attempts to influence the other depend upon the ways in
  which negotiators resolve 'dilemmas' built into the
  negotiation task;
* an understanding of the effects of uncertainty, complexity and stress is central to the psychology of
  bargaining and negotiation;
* negotiation is a skill. More precisely:

95

the skilful negotiator is one who, through an
understanding of the risks and opportunities
associated with negotiation, and of the resources he
can bring to bear, is able to take active and
effective measures to protect or pursue the values
and interests he has at stake (Morley, 1980).

Let us say a little more about the kinds of move which
we intend to make. First, note that the fifth element requires consideration of the ways in which individuals, or
groups of individuals, adapt to various kinds of stress.
Recent work on the psychology of conflict, commitment and
choice is considered in some detail. Psychology has always
had a good deal to say about the flaws and limitations
evident in the performance of complex cognitive tasks. The
model of man which has emerged emphasizes:

Man's vulnerability to gross errors in arriving at a
decision through superficial search and biased
information processing ... we see man not as a cold fish
but as a warm-blooded mammal, not as a rational
calculator always ready to work out the best solution
but as a reluctant decision-maker - beset by conflicts,
doubts, and worry, struggling with incongruous longings,
antipathies and loyalties, and seeking relief by
procrastinating, rationalizing or denying responsibility
for his own choices (Janis and Mann, 1977).

We shall discuss psychology's view of 'rational man' and
present evidence that 'skilled' negotiators bargain in ways
which help others to manage the uncertainties and
complexities of the negotiation task.
    Second, note that 'skill' requires that actions be
selected and organized in the pursuit of more or less
explicit goals. In general, 'risks and opportunities' have
to be perceived in the political context of which the
negotiations form a part. The actions taken will reflect
attempts to exploit asymmetries in the situation, generated
by unequal resources and unequal stakes in the issues. We
may expect, therefore, that the outcome will roughly reflect
the relative costs incurred in rejecting rather than accepting a given demand. We may also expect that 'the weak' and
'the strong' will tend to bargain in rather different ways.
That is, negotiation as a process cannot be understood
without an appreciation of bargaining styles, values and
power.
    Third, we adopt the kind of approach which has been
advocated by Strauss in considering the question, 'Can
psychology contribute to industrial relations?' From this
point of view industrial relations is to be

approached as one of a family of institutionalized
(regularized) relationships in which various elements of
co-operation and competition co-exist ... Thus if ...

psychology is to make a contribution it is through providing an understanding of human behaviour in such institutions generally. Thus psychological insights derived from industrial relations studies, if they are to be useful to either IR or psychology, should take a form that has meaning in other institutional contexts (Strauss, 1979).

The chapter is divided into six main parts.

* We begin by considering four models of negotiation, each containing some of the elements which are important from a psychological point of view.
* Negotiation is conceptualized as a 'system' of inputs, transformation elements, memory element, and outputs. This model, proposed by Allen (1971), is used to illustrate how psychologists have approached the study of negotiation, using the methods of experimental research.
* We begin to consider structure in the process of negotiation, paying particular attention to Walton and McKersie's statement of 'A Behavioral Theory of Labor Negotiations'. In their view, labour negotiations involve four 'sub-systems' of activity, 'each with its own function for the interacting parties, its own internal logics, and its own identifiable set of instrumental acts or tactics' (Walton and McKersie, 1965).
* Negotiation is described in terms of the 'core processes' of information interpretation, influence, and decision making. Particular attention is paid to factors which promote task 'success'.
* We outline and discuss Janis and Mann's (1977) theory of 'decisional conflict', with its implication that, under certain circumstances, members of policy-making groups will 'use their collective cognitive resources to develop rationalizations supporting shared illusions about the invulnerability of their organizations'.
* Finally, we outline and discuss some of the ways in which psychological research may be applied.

sons, parties and lels of negotiation

Students of industrial relations who have studied the institutional arrangements, or 'bargaining structures', which make collective bargaining possible, tend to talk about 'the system of industrial relations' in Great Britain. There is, of course, no great harm in this, as long as the phrase is taken simply as a shorthand way of indicating a general area of study. But we should realize:

There is no such thing as a system of industrial relations in Great Britain. If we think of industrial relations as concerned with the determination of terms and conditions of employment and the rules of work, then the manner in which they are settled moves through an almost infinite number of variations between unilateral determination by employers to unilateral determination by workers (Anthony, 1977).

And since it is difficult to contemplate the infinite, to study collective bargaining at all we shall have to simplify what is going on.

Clegg (1979), for example, is able to describe collective bargaining structures in terms of three models, a 'statute law model', a 'common law model', and a 'primitive bargaining model'. He recognizes that actual cases may approximate one model rather more closely than another, or contain elements of more than one type. Nevertheless, he provides a framework which is both simple to use and helps to show how negotiation works, from a systemic point of view. Here, the task is to show how negotiation works, from a psychological point of view. Let us, therefore, introduce five models in the spirit of the analysis outlined by Clegg. Each provides reference points with which to begin an analysis and helps to identify the skills which negotiators employ.

Model 1: Negotiation as a game of strategy

Negotiation is sometimes regarded as a game of strategy, analogous to games such as poker or chess. Furthermore, like chess, it is sometimes compared to an exercise in war in which moves are visible to each of the sides. It is, however, probably a mistake to think of negotiation in this latter way. Despite the fact that certain aspects of industrial relations resemble guerilla warfare at times, the object of the exercise is always co-operation. Therefore, rather than study poker or chess, psychologists have utilized abstract games of a kind thought to reveal the logical structure of certain of the bargaining problems negotiators face.

For example, the well-known 'Prisoner's Dilemma Game' attempts to represent the essential psychological aspects of a deadlock in which negotiators are unable to co-operate for want of mutual trust. Research suggests that those who show dissimilar behaviour in one game may appear almost indistinguishably alike in another. What is important is the reward structure of the game, the way that structure is displayed, and the social meaning participants read into the game.

The process of negotiation is analysed in terms of a sequence of behavioural dilemmas inherent in the nature of the task: for example, shall I stand firm or risk signalling flexibility? Negotiators make choices guided by expectations about the others' response. Outcomes depend upon the accuracy of their diagnoses and the skill with which they construct appropriate moves.

Model 2: Negotiation as struggle

'Pressure bargaining' or 'dispute settlement' models
preserve the flavour of strategic thinking by emphasizing
'concealment' and 'competitive' strategies (Winham, 1977a).
They recognize the truth in the common-sense view that
negotiators only modify their positions when they have
fought to the limit. Negotiation is seen as a struggle in
which negotiators move stepwise toward an agreement which
will be acceptable to both. It is a struggle which in itself
validates the final terms, demonstrating that participants
have done the best they can.

It is tempting to say that negotiators are seen as
treating 'agenda items' rather like legal issues. Like John
Foster Dulles they will not do their opponents' work, and
will not 'go down' unless they have to. Furthermore, like
Dulles they may set out to look for evidence to support
their case, ignoring evidence on the other side (here we
have relied upon Goold-Adams, 1962). They may appear inconsistent, ignoring connections between one dispute and
another. Above all they will concentrate single-mindedly on
the interests of those they represent, at times regardless
of cost.

Model 3: Negotiation as collaboration

Common sense would suggest that in some cases negotiators
are more willing to work towards agreement than in others.
Negotiation may, therefore, be viewed in terms of a 'collaborative model' in which parties make sacrifices, rather
than concessions, in the pursuit of some overriding goal.
For example, Strauss' description of the negotiations to
achieve economic union between Belgium, the Netherlands,
and Luxembourg shows the parties 'kept major focus on the
shared benefits of economic union' (Strauss, 1978). Elements of threat and manipulation were still there but
negotiators did not, in general, openly exploit asymmetries
in the balance of power. In Winham's terms, strategy was
more a matter of forestalling the consideration of certain
unattractive solutions than a matter of extracting change of
position from an adversary (Winham, 1977a).

Model 4: The 'two-track' or 'boundary role' model

Negotiation in industry is concerned to define or re-define
the terms upon which employee and employer will 'do
business', so to speak. The participants may be employers,
managers, trade union officials, or workers themselves. By
and large, however, negotiation is conducted between REP-
RESENTATIVES of groups. This is one of the things implied
when we say that, in negotiation, one bureaucracy is opposed
to another. However, we should note that:

> The positions which each organization brings to the
> negotiating table have been formulated and changed by
> a process of internal adjustment ... Neither union nor

management is a simple, monolithic structure with clear
and distinct objectives which it wishes to impose upon
the other (Anthony, 1977).

In practice the relationships involved may be extremely
complex, particularly on the union side.

Daniel (1976) reported that, in his study, trade union
involvement was 'very frequently an amateur affair'. When
union negotiators referred to someone outside the negotiating team the people concerned were most likely to be
full-time officers, brought in to solve problems rather than
involved from the start. When officers were involved from
the start the incidence of strikes or other withdrawals of
labour dropped, as it happens, to zero.

In contrast, the incidence of industrial action was more
than twice as frequent when management's initial offer was
approved by someone outside the establishment concerned.
Apparently, management is a rather loose coalition of
interests in which those remote from negotiation generate
far too optimistic expectations of what can be achieved.
Surveys of personnel specialists reveal: 'a penumbra of
imprecison in objectives, a grey area in which negotiators
(are) guided by tacit expectations of what the Board would
accept' (Anthony and Crichton, 1969).

To sum up, negotiators belong to, and work for, organizations. They negotiate rules or interpret the manner in
which they are to be applied. The attitude they adopt is
determined by internal negotiations which place various
kinds of restriction on their autonomy at the negotiation
table. In some cases the restriction applies to 'latitude of
decision'. In others it comes from uncertainty about the
policy the organization wishes to pursue. Negotiators
therefore monitor their constituents (where should we be?)
as well as their opponents (where are they?) (Druckman,
1977), and the process of negotiation may be charted by
mapping the extent to which they are responsive to the one
or the other. Following Druckman, we call this the 'two-
track' or 'boundary role' model of negotiation.

Model 5: Negotiation as interpersonal and interparty exchange

The work of Douglas (1962) may be used to elaborate the
nature of the two tracks which follow from negotiators'
boundary roles. Let us say, rather, that negotiators operate
at two levels; that it is possible to distinguish interpersonal and interparty forces which act on the members of
negotiation groups. Party forces operate insofar as negotiators are representatives of groups. Personal forces
derive from relationships built up at the bargaining table.
The former (party) relationship is the superordinate (or
dominant) one; the main struggle. The latter (personal)
relationship is the subordinate (or diplomatic) one, which
'tidies up the battle'. The relative emphasis upon the one
or the other changes as negotiation proceeds.

Later we argue that it is functional to separate personal and party aspects of negotiation, but that is another matter. The more general point is that the style of negotiation, and the kinds of agreement obtained, are affected by the general form of the relationship between the parties as well as the nature of the bargaining relationship 'at the table'.

Studies of bargaining relationships have recently come to the fore in industrial relations research. 'Strong' relationships have important cognitive, affective, and motivational elements. They allow negotiators to exchange information freely, indicating (say) the likely reaction of one organization to proposals from the other. They are affectively positive in terms of trust, respect, liking, and so on. They are 'co-operative', rather than 'individualistic' or 'competitive'.

systems view of
ustrial negotiations

Each of the models we have outlined draws our attention to certain aspects of negotiation which may be more or less important in any actual case. The models suggest the kinds of description psychologists are likely to give of the process of negotiation. What is not yet clear is how descriptions of process are to be linked to descriptions of the environment of which the negotiation forms a part. Once again we have to simplify what is going on. A 'systems model', adapted from Allen, is shown in figure 1.

Conflict begins when some change in existing circumstances, sometimes inadvertent, sometimes deliberate, creates a situation in which one party feels it must confront another. That is, conflict starts with some input from the environment. We do not mean that the historical relationship is unimportant. We are simply establishing some initial conditions from which to construct an analysis.

The 'working core' of the model is, however, the transformation element, the process of negotiation. Input is coded, summarized and sorted and a decision made to act. The activity is activity of information search and influence. The 'core processes' of the model are the processes of information interpretation (including the search for information), influence, and decision making.

The control element in a 'basic' systems model contains policies, decision rules, and goals. In negotiation, policies and decision rules (themselves the product of social action) operate upon the process of intra-organizational bargaining to produce a more detailed specification of goals. Controls are also imposed by various background factors and negotiating conditions.

The memory element contains the data storage facilities of the management and union organizations.

The output element contains the product of the negotiation including effects on the attitudes of the negotiators, and members of the domestic groups (constituencies) which they represent.

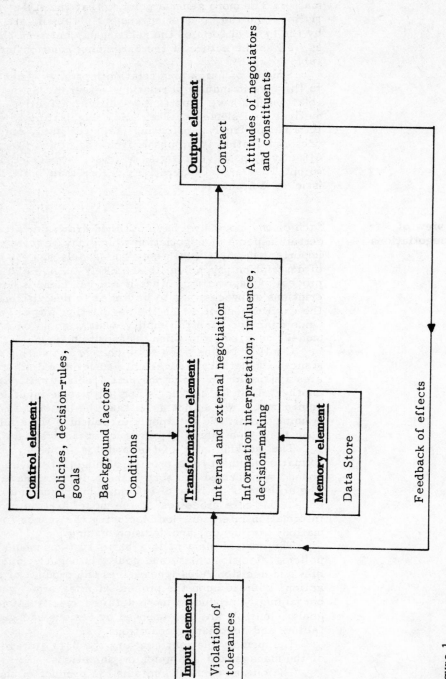

Figure 1

A 'systems model'
From Allen, 1971.

Finally, the model contains a loop for feedback of effects, emphasizing once again the importance of continuity in the relationships between the sides. The inclusion of explicit feedback loop also reminds us that negotiations are part of a more general process in which practitioners LEARN about the methods and expectations of the other side. Models represent the key variables involved in a complex setting and provide a language, a set of conventions, for describing what is going on. Allen (1971) has argued that a systems model can help practitioners to identify interrelationships between basic variables, forecast changes in the environment, and make bargaining decisions. For our present purposes, however, it is sufficient to note that the model underlines the importance for practitioners of working out what their opponents are trying to do.

First, negotiation is described as a transformation element. That is, input requires interpretation (diagnosis) as well as action (treatment). It is all too easy to think of negotiation in terms of strategy, tactics, and struggle without considering why the struggle is perceived in this or that kind of way. The systems model reminds us that negotiators are operating in an uncertain, threatening environment in which they use their mental resources to make sense of what is going on.

Second, the language of control suggests that negotiators operate within a system of constraints. To understand an opponent's behaviour it may be necessary to identify the constraints, perceived from his point of view. Strong bargaining relationships help negotiators do this kind of job.

We can now begin to characterize the kind of research psychologists have conducted to study the control and transformation elements which link inputs to outputs. Most of the research uses laboratory simulations of the negotiation task; some uses material collected on site, from industry, or more often from negotiations between nations.

We take the existence of an input for granted and turn to consideration of the elements of transformation and control.

The control element

To begin with, let us consider two elements of control which make negotiations psychologically more difficult than they need be. The first element, issue emphasis, has been manipulated by Bonham (1971) in a laboratory simulation of some of the disarmament negotiations which took place between 1946 and 1961. The experiment consisted of 11 four-hour sessions, each with an internal (intra-group) and an external (inter-group) phase. Negotiators were assigned roles as representatives of the United States, the Soviet Union, or the United Kingdom. The inter-group phase involved conferences with an 'Agency Director' responsible for formulating and implementing 'national' policy. Written messages were exchanged between the three negotiators concerned.

At the beginning of each session negotiators received sealed instructions from the leaders of their nations. In some cases one negotiator was instructed to give priority to reducing arms and another instructed to give priority to problems of inspection. Otherwise, negotiators were given instructions neutral in these respects. Differences in issue emphasis led to two rather different patterns of behaviour. Either participants exchanged fewer messages and tried to 'avoid the problem'; or they increased their activity, partly to make more attacks on the motives of the others. (Not surprisingly, concessions were less likely to be exchanged.) All in all, Bonham felt it legitimate to conclude that differences in the relative saliency of the issues produce misunderstanding, negative attitudes, hostile interaction, fewer concessions and a lower probability of eventual agreement (Bonham, 1971).

The second element, identified by Hammond and his associates, may mean that negotiators following the same general policy nevertheless judge possible outcomes in very different ways. Balke, Hammond and Meyer (1973) asked three union and three management negotiators to 're-enact' certain aspects of the negotiations they had conducted at the Dow Chemical Company, in the United States. The participants agreed that there had been four main issues: duration of contract in years; percentage increase in wages per annum; number and use of machine operators; and number of strikers to be recalled.

Five levels were assigned to each issue so that the final agreement represented a choice of one contract from 625 possibilities. Negotiators judged 25 contracts, drawn at random from the larger set. Each person indicated the acceptability of the contract to his own side, estimated the weight (importance) he attached to each issue, and forecast the response of his opposite number on the other side.

Surprisingly, only two of the issues thought to be significant actually were significant. Furthermore union negotiators found that they had three management policies, rather than one, with which to cope.

This study forms part of a much larger programme of research dealing with 'cognitive conflict' and 'interpersonal learning'. The general message from this kind of research may be summarized by saying:

the inability to describe judgement policies accurately and completely is one of the major reasons why cognitive conflict between persons is so hard to resolve and successful negotiation is so elusive. For while the student of human judgement will realize that the descriptions of judgement policies produced by introspection are likely to be inaccurate and incomplete because of human INABILITY to be otherwise, the lay person will attribute inconsistencies, inaccuracies, and incompleteness to an INTENTION TO BE DEVIOUS; current folklore suggests that it is naïve to do otherwise.

Failure to acknowledge the limitations of human judgement results in the attribution of evil intent to the other person (Brehmer and Hammond, 1977).

To understand negotiation we need models of man as well as models of the negotiation task.

Psychologists have sometimes given the impression that all elements of control make negotiations more difficult, psychologically, than they need to be. But this is to treat negotiation as if it were, essentially, an interpersonal task, made more difficult by the constraints of the representative role. It is to mistake the subordinate relationship for the superordinate one. It would be more sensible to say that the task of representing an organization, one business relationship, is made more difficult psychologically by the constraints of maintaining another, a bargaining relationship with someone on the other side. However, given this shift in emphasis it is important to note that negotiators 'define' their representative task in different ways depending on control elements which, in a sense, 'link' them to their constituency groups.

Attention has been given to variables such as latitude of decision (e.g. leader versus delegate role); mode of selection (e.g. assigned to role versus elected to role); attitude of constituency towards its spokesman (e.g. constituent trust versus constituent distrust); method of monitoring performance (e.g. continuous versus intermittent review); and the background of the negotiators concerned (e.g. representative from inside the constituency versus representative from outside the constituency).

Most of the research has concentrated on forces acting on the representative. Broadly speaking, the greater the 'pressure' on the representative the greater his concern explicitly to demonstrate his commitment to group positions, and to 'confirm and validate' the final settlement by his behaviour at the negotiation table. For example, it has been found that negotiation takes longer when representatives face post-negotiation evaluation by members of a cohesive group.

A few studies have investigated the ways in which a constituency looks at its spokesman. For example, Klimoski and Breaugh (1977) have argued that, in some cases, 'performance doesn't count'. In their study the 'behaviour of outsiders was censured and their agreements rejected', despite a level of performance comparable to representatives who came from inside the group.

It is not just that negotiation takes longer in certain circumstances than others. Settlements may exhibit greater variability, reflecting unilateral domination by one of the sides, depending (say) upon perceptions of the 'win-lose' character of the conflict, or its links with more ideological disputes. This may imply that, in some cases, 'the success of collective bargaining as a control process may require that it never has to come to terms with real differences of value' (Anthony, 1977).

This is one of the reasons why collective bargaining has been described as a conservative process. To some extent its rules and procedures reflect 'a perceived need to respect differences in outlook by preventing the confrontation of quite different value systems' (Anthony, 1977). According to Anthony, when ideological attacks do occur in negotiation there is a sense in which the negotiation simply stops: 'the attack tends to be treated as ritual and the opponent waits for it to subside before "getting back to business" ' (Anthony, 1977).

Negotiators are, of course, linked to their groups and to the wider social context by shared attitudes and values. Early research was guided by the assumption that negotiators' attitudinal commitments to party positions produced conflicts which prevented them working out the problems posed by the negotiation task. However, it is now clear that this need not be the case. Attention has shifted to an analysis of the ways in which attitudes help individuals categorize, simplify, and make sense of the complex political environment in which they operate. Despite this, it must be admitted that we know very little about the processes which go on when a negotiator makes statements of the kind, 'when they say this, what they really mean is ...'.

To conclude our discussion of the control element, let us say a little about some of the conditions which may be important. We have two lines of research in mind.

The first is geared to Douglas' model of negotiation. It has investigated the proposition that formal systems of communication (which restrict the cues one person can transmit to another) affect the balance between interpersonal and interparty forces. Morley and Stephenson (1977) have argued that elements such as seating arrangements, size of group, medium of communication, etc., may act to depersonalize negotiation so that interparty considerations come to the fore. Evidence has been obtained to show that negotiators given the stronger case drive harder bargains when formal rather than informal systems of communication are used.

The second line of research deals with some of the effects of 'situational complexity'. Put simply, negotiations become complex:

> when there are a lot of 'things' to be kept in mind, either issues being debated or positions taken by different parties, or implications that the negotiation might have for the environment. Complexity is created also under conditions of uncertainty, when information that is needed is difficult or costly to obtain or is simply unavailable (Winham, 1977b).

Following Winham we refer to the 'size' of the negotiation situation when there are lots of things to be kept in mind. We use the term uncertainty when information is difficult to obtain or is ambiguous once it is obtained. As the size of the negotiation situation is increased:

* negotiators may not have time to study important documents and work out what is going on. Considerations of this kind may be particularly important with respect to productivity bargaining, or any kind of exercise in which wholesale job evaluation is involved. This may be one of the reasons why Daniel (1976) found that only one-fifth of the establishments included in his survey, 'Wage Determination in Industry', attempted to cost how long they could afford any interruption to work. More generally, increasing the size of negotiation may lead to uncertainty about value judgements of one's own;
* parties are less likely to agree on the nature of concessions, or even that concessions have been made. The more complex the negotiation (particularly if it is multilateral rather than bilateral), the harder it will be to establish that a breakthrough has been made;
* uncertainty will increase. It will be harder to estimate what opponents are likely to accept. Note that the negotiators questioned by Balke, Hammond and Meyer (1973) were confident they understood their counterpart's policies, a belief based on years of association and negotiation. Yet they were wrong.

Accordingly, it will be more difficult for each party to assess the other's resolve and to assess its relative bargaining; but more of this later.

The transformation element
In Allen's framework the transformation element contains the process of negotiation, both internal (within parties) and external (between parties). It also contains the processes of conciliation, mediation, or arbitration. We are not sure what Allen intended but, except for arbitration, psychologists have emphasized the similarities between what might seem like disparate elements in the process of transformation.

Here, we want to emphasize that preparation and process are linked by virtue of the fact that they are intra-group and inter-group phases of a complex task. The output of one is input to the other which provides input in its turn: and so on. Both involve the core processes of information interpretation, influence, and decision making. We are not sure that the internal process can 'be explained in precisely the same terms as the external process' (Anthony, 1977) but we do think that the similarities are more important than the differences.

1. THE PROCESS OF INTERNAL ADJUSTMENT: the ways in which negotiators prepare, in groups, for negotiation between groups are little understood, surprisingly. By and large the process of internal adjustment has been taken for granted, rather than studied in detail. So far as laboratory research is concerned there have been studies of the effects of role reversal; preparation in strategy versus study groups; the effects of linking conflicts to more basic

values (system maintenance versus system change); and the effects of preparation for negotiation in a group.

Much the most important research, however, has been conducted by Rackham and Carlisle (1978b), who compared the planning techniques used by 'effective' and 'average' negotiators. By 'effective', Rackham and Carlisle meant a negotiator (i) rated as such by both sides, union and management, supplier and purchaser; (ii) with a good 'track record' in terms of reaching agreements; and (iii) able to reach agreements which 'stick'. 'Average' negotiators were those who failed with respect to (i) or (ii) or (iii), or negotiators for whom no criterion data were available.

Briefly, the 'effective' negotiators considered a wider range of 'options for action' than 'average' negotiators, and were more likely to identify a range of possible outcomes than think in terms of fixed objectives. In short, they recognized that what can be achieved is partly a function of what is available. An 'effective' plan is a plan which survives contact with the opposition and does not require a 'mental change of gear' when they fail to react as they should. It is, for example, a mistake to rely on verbalizations such as, 'First I'll bring up A, then B, then C, then D'. Effective negotiators used plans which were independent of sequence: 'issue planning' rather than 'sequence planning', as Rackham and Carlisle say.

2. THE PROCESS OF EXTERNAL ADJUSTMENT: STAGES IN NEGOTIATION. Two of the models outlined earlier (model 4 and model 5) emphasize that negotiation is as it is because negotiators act as representatives of groups. Model 5, however, derives from research (by Douglas) which implies that, to be successful, negotiators must separate in time the interpersonal and inter-party demands of their task.

Douglas has argued that 'movement, orderly and progressive in nature, stands out as a staid property of the collective bargaining situation which terminates in agreement' (Douglas, 1957). More precisely, negotiations which end in agreement go through stages, so that: 'changes in overt behavior come as spurts, often rather abrupt ones, following periods of prolonged circular activity which appear to accomplish remarkably little in a forward direction' (Douglas, 1962).

Indeed, Douglas goes so far as to say that, during the first stage of negotiation, it is precisely 'to the extent that the contenders can intrench their seeming disparity' that they 'enhance their chances for a GOOD AND STABLE SETTLEMENT (our emphasis) in the end' (Douglas, 1957). That is, in some sense, not to disagree means not to solve the problem.

Initially (stage I) the negotiators observed by Douglas showed 'prodigious zeal' for discrediting their opponents. Speeches were exceptionally long and emphasized the representative role participants had to play. Apparently the activity functioned to provide 'a thorough and exhaustive

determination of the range within which the parties will
have to do business' (Douglas, 1957). Presumably this helped
participants to avoid positions which were non-starters. It
may also have forced negotiators to look beyond the easy,
obvious solutions.

Subsequently (stage II) negotiators subordinated their
representative roles whilst engaging in unofficial behaviours designed to reconnoitre the bargaining range and give
a more precise idea of the settlements which might be
obtained. Finally (stage III) negotiators returned to an
emphasis upon their representative roles, as they moved to
commit their parties to an agreement and 'precipitate a
decision-making crisis'.

Douglas analysed cases submitted to a United States
Mediation Agency. Morley and Stephenson (1977) have shown
that her model applies to British cases conducted without
third-party help. In addition, they have extended Douglas'
treatment in a number of ways.

* They have argued that stage I (as well as stage II)
  allows negotiators to assess the 'strength of position'
  of the parties concerned by considering the merits of
  the arguments ('strength of case') and the power of
  parties to inflict damage on opponents in the event of
  failure to agree. Let us repeat, uncertainty is the link
  between bargaining power and bargaining process.

  What is implied here is that bargaining power is
  situation specific. In some cases, participants delay
  issues, waiting for the balance of power to shift in
  their favour. One 'leader' steward, interviewed by
  Batstone, Boraston and Frankel, commented: 'Management
  aren't giving anything away at the moment ... and we're
  in no position to fight ... We'll hold back, and then
  when management are crying out for production we'll hit
  them with this and they'll give it' (Batstone et al,
  1977).

  More generally, we may say that bargaining power
  has something to do with bargaining costs. Different
  writers give different definitions, but what is important here is that the costs are discovered through
  an exploratory process of negotiation. That is to say,
  initially

  > the parties are either uncertain or mistaken about
  > relative bargaining power, primarily because they
  > cannot know the value of each other's interests at
  > stake and HOW FIRM THE OTHER ULTIMATELY WILL
  > BE (our emphasis). Toward the end of the con-
  > frontation stage, the parties develop fairly clear,
  > if not correct, pictures of mutual resolve and hence
  > relative bargaining power, and then a process of
  > resolution occurs - either compromise or one-sided
  > capitulation depending on the revealed power
  > relations. PROCESS IS THEREFORE PRACTICALLY

INSEPARABLE FROM POWER SINCE IT IS THROUG
PROCESS THAT THE TRUE POWER RELATIONS
BECOME MANIFEST IN THE PARTIES' VALUES AN
PERCEPTIONS (our emphasis) (Snyder and Diesing,
1977).

Snyder and Diesing were talking about conflict between
governments but, in these respects, we believe their
account would apply to conflict between other organizations, such as trade unions and management.

* Morley and Stephenson have argued that what is important
about stage II is that it allows the bargaining relationship between the negotiators to come to the fore.
Party and opposition roles are still salient in the
negotiation. But, to quote Douglas (1962), 'the acute
observer can detect soft spots as the negotiating opens
a second front and the institutional actors undergo re-
casting for another set of roles'.

If the first stage of negotiation allows negotiators to 'get
on the record a turgid edition of what they wish to say
about themselves and their postions', the second stage
allows the argument to get truly under way. There are more
explicit statements to people on the other side: 'what
you're really saying, Brian, is that it's not a bank holiday
when you're on standby'; 'you have circumscribed me to such
an extent that I can't find a solution', and so on (Morley
and Stephenson, 1977).

In this respect it is interesting to note that 'the
systems of argument employed tend to differ between steward
who have a strong bargaining relationship and those who do
not' (Batstone et al, 1977). When stewards enjoyed a strong
bargaining relationship with an opponent they were more
likely (i) to emphasize their 'leader' role within the
workforce; (ii) stress 'the men are on my back' rather than
'the men have instructed me'; (iii) demonstrate their
understanding of management politics; and (iv) attempt to
work out how particular goals could be achieved.

Accordingly, there is an important sense in which stage
II can be regarded as a 'problem-solving' stage, but it is
problem-solving with an irreducibly political component. The
behaviour followed by the negotiators follows from and
functions to develop or maintain the bargaining relationship
between the negotiators 'at the table'.

* The stages in Douglas' account are almost certainly
notional. Recent research suggests that negotiators
learn rapidly to switch roles from inter-group anta-
gonist to group problem-solver. For this to occur it is
essential that disagreement between the negotiators as
representatives is not interpreted as dislike or
antagonism between the negotiators as persons. There is
anecdotal evidence that those unable to maintain the
distinction are not highly regarded as negotiators.

A second account of stages in negotiation
(mediation) is also supported by American research.
Landsberger (1955) has argued that negotiation is
successful to the extent that it follows a phase-
sequence identified in laboratory problem-solving
groups. Apparently, the more closely negotiation
conformed to this sequence the greater the extent to
which 'specific items in dispute ... were resolved'
(Landsberger, 1955).

At the moment it is not possible to say which account
applies when. Several authors have argued that negotiation
groups resemble problem-solving groups in some more general
sense. However, here we are getting close to the level at
which all groups have something in common precisely because
they are groups.

3. THE PROCESS OF EXTERNAL ADJUSTMENT: BID AND
COUNTERBID: social scientists have assumed (frequently) that
negotiation involves little more than a process of bid and
counterbid. Douglas' analysis does not necessarily diminish
the importance of bid and counterbid but makes it clear that
any concession-convergence process is likely to occur late
in the day, once the participants have established an
'exchange rate' determining what sized concession from A is
equivalent to what sized concession from B.

Psychologists have studied the process of bid and
counterbid in some detail, not always after a careful
analysis of how the concession-convergence process is to be
fitted into the wider context of negotiation as a whole. Two
rather different accounts have been given of the kind of
analysis which is required.

First, Magenau and Pruitt (1979) have made an impressive
attempt to build on what has gone before. In their view
negotiating positions, or rather current levels of demand,
are to be understood in terms of negotiators' levels of
aspiration (LOA) and the minimum necessary share (MNS) each
deems he has to obtain with respect to the distribution of
valued 'goods'. Thus, if negotiator A were asking for an
increase of 25 per cent as part of a strategy designed to
secure 15 per cent, A's LOA is defined by the value to A
of achieving a settlement on those terms: that is, at 15 per
cent. A's MNS, if he has one, is defined by 'the smallest
level of value acceptable in the foreseeable future' or the
'level below which he would rather break off negotiation
than reach agreement' (Magenau and Pruitt, 1979). Consequently, the term 'limit' is used interchangeably with the
term 'minimum necessary share'.

What is important is the suggestion that the nature of
the concession-convergence process depends upon the presence
or absence of a solution that is above the negotiators'
minimum necessary shares (i.e. can be sold to domestic
organizations), is perceptually prominent (to emphasize this
really is the end), and is supported by one or more moral
rules.

Given such a solution it seems that negotiators are inclined to match the other's offers. That is, 'the more he demands initially, the more they will demand ... The more rapidly he concedes, the faster are their concessions' (Magenau and Pruitt, 1979). Otherwise, a mismatch occurs. That is, 'If he makes a large initial demand, they make a small one ... If he makes a large concession they make small ones' (Magenau and Pruitt, 1979). Almost certainly, a detailed analysis has to be more complicated than this to take account of deadlines, time cost, and so on, but we hope that enough has been said to indicate some of the moves which might be made.

In contrast, Zartman (1977) has argued, that models of concession-making in negotiation are grounded in experiments in which

> there is no substance to the negotiations to impose a
> more realistic pattern; the reports of caucus and
> negotiating sessions show an absence of coherence and
> reasons for action. When experimental subjects are given
> a chance to define their own stakes and control their
> value rather than accept fixed, externally determined
> values ... they tend (1) to invent a formula first to
> cover their own positions and then to provide a basis
> for a mutually satisfactory agreement, and (2) increase
> their satisfaction with the results to the extent that
> they do develop such a formula.

From this point of view, what looks like an 'exchange' of concessions is really the negotiation of 'detail' within the framework of a 'formula' which helps negotiators define issues in the same kind of way.

According to Zartman, experimental work should be directed toward helping participants structure negotiations so that they can find a formula (if one exists), rather than towards explication of concession-convergence phenomena which give a quite misleading view of what is going on.

Zartman's analysis was based on cases such as the Paris Peace Negotiations to end the Vietnam War. However, certa aspects of Walton and McKersie's (1965) treatment of 'integrative bargaining' suggest a concern with similar kinds of theme. In some cases, as they say, negotiators tend

> to disagree about how the problem should be defined, to
> disagree about what criteria for settlement will be
> considered and what weight will be given to these
> criteria, to suppress or disregard certain alternatives
> which might be considered, and to withhold certain facts
> relevant to understanding the consequences which will
> flow from certain alternatives under consideration
> (Walton and McKersie, 1965).

At the very least, psychologists are likely to pay increasing attention to questions of the kind, which model when?

Walton and McKersie (1965) have provided the 'classic'
statement of certain psychological aspects of the process of
collective bargaining. Labour negotiations are treated as
one example of the more general class of 'social negotiations' which occur whenever 'two or more complex social
units ... are attempting to define or re-define the terms of
their inter-dependence' (Walton and McKersie, 1965). More
precisely, their theory contains five main elements.

The elements of the theory
First, Walton and McKersie identify four 'sub-processes'
which serve different goals and operate according to different internal dynamics: distributive bargaining, in which
negotiators settle the issues which divide them; integrative
bargaining, in which they work through problem areas of
joint concern; attitudinal structuring, by which they modify
or maintain the bargaining relationships they have built up;
and intra-organizational bargaining, the process of internal
adjustment in which negotiators influence, and respond to,
the demands of the domestic organizations they represent.
    Second, there is a theory of individual choice behaviour
in distributive bargaining, namely maximization of
'subjectively expected utility' or SEU.
    Third, there is a theory of individual choice behaviour
in integrative bargaining, namely 'utility matching'.
    Fourth, there is a discussion of the tactical possi-
bilities that negotiators can exploit, with tactics classified according to the 'internal logic' of the sub-processes
they are designed to serve.
    Fifth, there is a discussion of the ways in which the
'sub-processes' place conflicting demands upon the participants. For example, Walton and McKersie argue that: 'the
techniques for fostering the integrative process are generally the reverse of the techniques for implementing the
distributive process' (Walton and McKersie, 1965).

The distribution between the sub-processes of distributive
and integrative bargaining
What is immediately apparent is the contrast between distributive and integrative bargaining which Walton and
McKersie's theory contains. However, the nature of this
distinction is not at all clear (Anthony, 1977; Snyder and
Diesing, 1977; Morley, 1979). It is important to remember,
therefore, that bargaining is a process in which 'the
parties start with differences in view-points, perceptions,
and tentatively preferred solutions' (Walton and McKersie,
1965).
    Anthony (1977) has developed the point in the following
way:

> Bargaining IMPLIES a difference in interests and
> objectives. Collective bargaining is concerned to reach
> accommodations, often of a temporary nature, between
> different interests and expectations. In this sense

collective bargaining is ALMOST ALWAYS (our emphasis) what Walton and McKersie define merely as a subprocess; it is always distributive bargaining in which the parties are negotiating over the distribution of scarce resources, money, status, or power.

From this point of view 'integrative bargaining' is simply distributive bargaining in which participants adopt a collaborative rather than a competitive approach to the problems of distribution which are involved (Anthony, 1977).

A more radical approach is, perhaps, to distinguish distributive bargaining and integrative bargaining in terms of a direct versus an indirect approach to change (Morley, 1979).

The direct approach (distributive bargaining) consists of two elements, an agenda specified in advance of the negotiation and a process of pressure bargaining.

The indirect approach (integrative bargaining) also consists of two elements, an agenda and a process of distributive bargaining, but the agenda items arise only after an exercise in problem-definition and problem-solving jointly undertaken by the two sides. Because of this the bargaining may take on a different character from that involved in the direct approach.

What is clear in all of this is that 'integrative' bargaining cannot be identified simply by looking at the content of the agenda negotiators use. Given (say) that formal and informal Works Conferences contain different types of reference, we need to go on and ask whether different kinds of approach are adopted, 'competitive' in the former and 'collaborative' in the latter. We should not conclude automatically that this will be the case. Similarly, given that productivity bargaining permits solutions which benefit both sides, we should not assume that productivity bargaining automatically means integrative bargaining in any of the senses identified so far.

As a matter of fact, examples of the indirect approach are extremely rare, not least because the bargaining relationship is 'set' to revert to the direct approach when 'difficulties' occur. The distributive process is, after all, subordinated only temporarily to the search for joint gain.

These points are not just of academic interest. The way we think about bargaining processes is likely to influence the way we behave. It is perfectly in order to talk about 'problem-solving' in collective bargaining. But the problem-solving is problem-solving which helps each side get what it wants with respect to the problems of distribution which jointly they face. Once an agenda has been drawn up it must be recognized that bargaining, by which we mean distributive bargaining, is well and truly under way.

Research on integrative bargaining
Before moving on to the other aspects of Walton and

McKersie's theory it is, perhaps, worth considering the kind of research psychologists have conducted under the heading of 'integrative' bargaining. To do so, we should note that some laboratory tasks, often those which simulate negotiation between buyer and seller, allow one negotiator to increase the profit obtained by the other at little or no cost to himself. In other words, one negotiator (say A) may be able to maintain a given level of profit whilst maximizing the joint gain (A's profit plus B's profit). Some writers use the term 'integrative' to refer to distributive bargaining which is efficient in this kind of way.

To give some idea of the kinds of result which have been obtained let us cite two pieces of research which are of interest. The first, by Kelley and Schenitzki (1972), shows that under some circumstances joint profit is maximized provided only that 'one individual behaves systematically and that the other one terminates the process by accepting the highest offer available to him'. The second, by Pruitt and Lewis (1975), shows that 'a period of conflict is often necessary before people look beyond the easy obvious options in search of those that provide more joint profit'. The conflict which was productive was, however, conflict guided by a co-operative rather than a competitive 'mode of thought'.

The sub-processes of attitudinal structuring and intra-organizational bargaining

Attitudinal structuring and intra-organizational bargaining may be described as 'sub-processes' in ways distributive bargaining and integrative bargaining may not. Nevertheless, their status is not entirely clear. Anthony (1977) has argued that attitudinal structuring is best regarded as identifying tactics which may be selected as part of an overall co-operative or collaborative approach. He has added that 'There is a further confusion over the sub-process "intra-organizational" bargaining because this represents neither strategic nor tactical concerns but rather an environmental characteristic of the total field within which bargaining takes place' (Anthony, 1977).

Evaluation

Despite this, 'A Behavioral Theory of Labor Negotiations' remains a valuable work, and for several reasons. First, the discussion of strategy and tactics is extremely thorough and remains a useful supplement to work written from a British point of view. Second, the discussion of attitudinal structuring reminds us that negotiation skill is not just a matter of learning which tactical opportunities are available. Rather, the bargaining process is 'constrained' by continuities in the relationships between the persons and parties involved: tactics must be seen to follow naturally from that process as it 'unfolds'. Negotiation which ends in agreement is negotiation structured in a series of smooth steps. Third, Walton and McKersie have demonstrated the multiplicity of outputs from the process of collective bargaining: obtaining favourable agreements, avoiding disasters, maintaining goodwill, improving bargaining relationships, educating constituents and the like. To the extent that negotiators seek different outputs, and establish different objectives, we may say that their choice of strategy is 'constrained' in various ways. Finally, Walton and McKersie have demonstrated the importance of a theory of individual decision-making, or choice, one of the 'core' processes which we now consider in rather more detail.

Information interpretation, influence and decision making

Walton and McKersie predicated their account of distributive bargaining upon a prescriptive theory which says that the rational thing for negotiators to do is to choose that outcome which maximizes subjectively expected utility, SEU. Details of the theory are given in Walton and McKersie (1965) but what is important here is that SEU theory is one example of a more general class of theories which define rational behaviour in 'analytic' terms (Steinbruner, 1974).

Analytic theories derive from attempts to provide formal criteria which would define rational choice. However, in complex cases, such as negotiation, it is clear that we should look at the spirit, rather than the letter, of the laws. Bearing this in mind we can say that the 'analytic' decision maker recognizes that different policies lead to different benefits and carry different costs. As information comes in, the decison maker is able to spell out the implications of different choices in more and more detail. The 'optimal' choice is identified by comparing, however roughly, the costs and benefits attached to each option, explicitly identifying the trade-off relationships which are involved. The decision-maker confronts the uncertainties in his environment and does his best to work out the most sensible policy, all things considered.

There are good reasons, however, to suppose that, in many cases, people have neither the time, the energy, nor the ability to carry out the mental operations required by analytic theories of choice. As negotiations become more complex settlements may be accumulated 'from the bottom up' rather than conceptualized in advance. Thus, negotiators SATISFICE rather than maximize; they control uncertainty by looking for a settlement which is 'good enough' in terms of a few key variables such as domestic support, precedent, and so on. The risk is, of course, that they will fail to appreciate important implications of the agreements which are reached.

A negotiator is likely to use different strategies, maximizing or satisficing, at different times and in different circumstances (Janis and Mann, 1977). Broadly speaking, the more complex the negotiation the lower the probability that negotiators will proceed according to the analytic paradigm which has been outlined. However, the mo general point is that to understand the process of negotiation it is important to ask whether, and if so how, negotiators cope with the information processing demands of their task.

Essentially, given input ('violation of tolerances'), negotiators must first define the nature of the 'challenge' and work out what is going on. Second, they must decide what they will try to do; consider means to achieve those ends; take note of likely reactions from the other side; and decide on a strategy for 'sorting things out'. Third, they must revise their policies in the light of information obtained once bargaining is under way.

Information interpretation and rationality in negotiation
Negotiation is one example of decision making under uncertainty, not least because values, interests, and power relations have to be worked out as arguments are presented and moves are made. Negotiators cannot escape questions about the validity of information presented by the other side. Negotiation as a process includes negotiators' attempts to impose order and certainty, and work out what is going on. However, there is a sense in which negotiators may exercise too much ingenuity in sorting what is essential from what is not.

Let me explain. The interpretation of input, 'violations of tolerances', requires an assessment of the intentions of the other side. As argued elsewhere (Morley, 1980), people look for some kind of 'master script' which defines in ordinary language the threats and opportunities which they are likely to face. Similarly, Winkler (1974) has suggested that 'directors activated those interpretations of workers' behaviour which, in varying concrete contexts, best furthered their long-term interests'.

In one case, this might be 'what they need is discipline', in another 'what they need is motivation'. Alternatively, a director may argue 'The old loyalties are dead; they don't give a damn about the company'; and later that 'They'll pitch in if you let them know what the score is' (Winkler, 1974).

Initially, it is inevitable that messages will be interpreted in the light of scripts formulated at a very high level of generality, in terms of 'images' of the other. However, following Snyder and Diesing (1977) we may then distinguish two kinds of development. The 'rational' bargainer is one who learns from the process of negotiation so that his image of the other is corrected or updated by what happens 'at the table'. Once negotiation is under way interpretation of new messages

is based on the developing pattern of information itself. It is based, not on what we 'know' the opponent's fundamental characteristics and ultimate aims are, but on the specific pattern of his overt statements and actions THIS TIME (our emphasis). New information is, as always, interpreted by its fit with what we 'know', but what we know comes from the bargaining process rather than from the image (Snyder and Diesing, 1977).

In contrast, the 'irrational' bargainer is one whose perceptions, from first to last, are dominated by the general characteristics of his image of the other. In some cases of 'endemic conflict' the image of the other appears more like the image of an 'enemy' and it is, perhaps, appropriate to say 'the bargainer "knows" what is going on and is not going to be fooled by any new information' (Snyder and Diesing, 1977).

The 'irrational' bargainer is 'irrational' in two kinds of way (Morley, 1980). He holds a rigid system of beliefs, retains and defends images and policies even when, to the outsider, they are clearly 'out of date'. Furthermore, his beliefs are organized so that all considerations point to the same strategic choice. This policy is seen as superior to others in all important respects. Jervis (1976) argues that this is a kind of 'overkill' in which the belief system minimizes the conflict between different kinds of constraint. It is 'irrational' because we can be fairly sure that the world is not so benign; negotiation is complex because it requires one kind of constraint to be balanced, or traded-off, against another.

It is in recognition of this that Drucker (1970) describes 'The Effective Executive' as one who understands 'the need for organized disagreement'.

Decisions of the kind the executive has to make are made well only if based on the clash of conflicting views, the dialogue between different points of view, the choice between different judgments. The first rule in decision-making is that one does not make a decision unless there is disagreement (Drucker, 1970).

The 'rational' bargainer described by Snyder and Diesing is rather like the 'effective executive' described by Drucker. Each begins with tentative judgements and initiates an active search for new information. The search is designed to root out ideas which are plausible, but false or incomplete. It is designed to test hypotheses so that conclusions follow from, rather than precede, the 'facts' which are obtained. Each attempts to understand the problem from the perspectiv of the other side, and makes moves designed to reduce ambiguity, clarify communications, and slow negotiation dow (Rackham and Carlisle, 1978a; Morley, 1980).

Three aspects of this treatment deserve further comment First, the search for information involves elements such as diagnosing the basic cause of a given demand; looking for alternative means to achieve the same ends; determining which aspects of the other's position are flexible, and by how much; and so on. If the negotiator is to do these jobs he must attempt a realistic assessment of the bargaining power he has relative to his opponent. That is to say, he must make estimates of the kind: how do the costs to the other of rejecting my proposals compare with his costs if he accepts my proposal? If costs are identified, rated according to importance and perceived probability, the negotiator may put his analysis to work, to assess the probability of a stoppage at work, to decide whether the other is bluffing, or whatever. Atkinson's 'The Effective Negotiator' (1975) contains some very interesting examples of this kind of analysis and will, we think, repay further study. Once strengths and weaknesses have been determined, the negotiator can move on to seek 'links' between issues so that an exchange of concessions can be made. Again, Atkinson gives some useful examples of the techniques which might be used.

Second, the rational bargainer concentrates his effort in an attempt to work out the strategy of the other, since to ask, 'Is my strategy working?', is to invite wishful thinking of one kind or another (Snyder and Diesing, 1977). Furthermore, although Snyder and Diesing do not make this explicit, I am tempted to extend the analogy with the effective executive and argue that the rational bargainer asks, 'What does this fellow have to see if his position were, after all, tenable, rational, intelligent?' (Drucker, 1970).

Third, the rational bargainer appreciates that signals clear to him may be interpreted differently by others. Accordingly, he

> builds redundancy into his ... messages ... He does not assume that the opponent 'must know' what he is doing, but rather assumes the situation is pretty confused. Consequently he tries to send a message several different ways, always through a different channel, AND KEEPS REPEATING THE SAME THEME (our emphasis). The purpose is to break through the resistance set up by the opponent's mistaken expectations AND ALSO TO GIVE HIM TIME TO TEST, RETEST, AND ADJUST HIS EXPECTATIONS (our emphasis) (Snyder and Diesing, 1977).

The reader should note that this is not just a theoretical analysis. Snyder and Diesing's account is derived from the empirical study of documents describing crisis bargaining between nations. It is consistent with other work.

For example, the 'effective' negotiators studied by Rackham and Carlisle (1978a) tended to label messages as questions, suggestions, warnings (rather than threats) and so on; they were less likely to respond immediately to proposals with counter-proposals of their own, possibly because they recognized the proposal might not be perceived as a proposal at all (but as 'blocking' or 'disagreement'); they made frequent attempts to summarize positions and test the other's understanding of what was going on; they organized disagreement so that ambiguities were cleared up and each gained an understanding of how the other would proceed; and they showed a proper respect for difficulties likely to arise when agreements were put into effect.

Power and influence
It is often said that psychology is strong on influence but weak on power. Broadly speaking, however, psychologists ha taken the view that power is to be analysed in terms of potential for influence: that there is a kind of 'negotiation power' deriving from the personal resources of the negotiators, from 'facility and shrewdness in the execution of negotiation tactics' (Stevens, 1963). The power is power in the sense that it 'determines the final result': without it negotiation would not be the same.

From one point of view the power derives from negotiators' ability to choose an appropriate strategy, meaning a set of tactics ordered in a certain kind of way. Here I shall argue that the selection and sequencing depends on the way negotiators view certain 'behavioural dilemmas' (model 1) inherent in their task. Some of the dilemmas are linked to questions of information interpretation which have already been raised. For example, should an issue be treated on its merits or as a symptom of a more basic conflict which happens to have been expressed in this particular way? Does this clause have to be spelled out in detail? Or will the other keep the spirit of the agreement in areas not explicitly put into words?

Other dilemmas follow from a negotiator's concern to protect his reputation for resolve. Consider the question, 'Shall I make a concession or not?' According to Pruitt (1971), negotiators face costs whichever decision they make. To stand firm may be to nail my colours to a position I cannot possibly maintain, or make it look as if I am not trying to reach an agreement at all. But to move too early may give my opponent the expectation that more will follow if he persists. In detail, Pruitt's analysis is much more complicated. But what is important is the idea that, as time goes by, the decision is harder to make. Costs of both kinds are perceived to increase, and negotiators may fail to agree even when they have compatible goals. Some ways of dealing with the dilemma are outlined in Morley (1980).

Strategies are, of course, designed to influence others' behaviour. Consequently, it is important to realize that negotiation is not the same as other forms of debate. 'Effective' negotiators tend 'to advance single reasons insistently' rather than provide mutually supporting reasons to back up proposals they have made. Apparently, a negotiating position is only as credible as the weakest argument in the chain, but to influence the other it is necessary to know what counts as a strong argument from his point of view.

Negotiation as decision making
In one sense negotiators continually face a threefold

choice: to accept the offer on the table, to continue in the hope of negotiating better terms, or to break off nego- tiation, for the time being at any rate. However, it is perhaps more useful, analytically, to identify major choice points in terms of the decision whether to negotiate or not; the decision to pursue these objectives rather than those; the choice of this strategy rather than that; the decision to stay with this strategy rather than that; and, finally, the decision whether or not to accept the 'final' offer which has been made.

We have said quite a lot about these processes already; we say more later. Here we want to emphasize that

> WITHOUT CLEAR-CUT GOALS, THE SELECTION OF
> MEANS CANNOT BE ACCOMPLISHED IN ANY RELIABLE
> FASHION (our emphasis). When the goals are vague
> enough it becomes nearly impossible to rule out any
> proposed policy as being incompatible with the end which
> is sought (O'Leary, 1973).

There are, however, cases in which goals are clear-cut, and strategies maintained despite warning signs that things are going wrong.

cisional conflicts as
rces of stress

The negotiators studied by Douglas were not only experi- enced, but had a good deal of third-party help. Douglas described one mediator as 'a perceptualizer of each to the other',

> and in the course of fashioning READY-MADE
> PERCEPTIONS (our emphasis) about each for the other,
> he appended his own embellishments in such a manner as,
> not to deceive, but to highlight, intensify, or other-
> wise single out certain elements for special attention
> ... Such tactics would unquestionably influence a
> party's estimate of the status of the conflict (Douglas,
> 1962).

Without such help it is not too difficult to believe that the concession dilemma identified by Pruitt may have deepened to the point where negotiators felt whatever they did was likely to be wrong. Under such circumstances, particularly when issues are complex, or there is a feeling that the environment cannot be controlled at all, nego- tiators may 'short circuit' the activities of information interpretation and information search, ignoring authentic warnings that things are going wrong.

Essentially, we propose to treat the concession dilemma as one example of a 'decisional conflict' in which there are 'simultaneous opposing tendencies within the individual to accept and reject a given course of action' (Janis and Mann, 1977). According to Janis and Mann, decisional conflicts produce intense stress when the individual faces a 'crisis situation' in which each course of action carries serious risks and he sees little hope of obtaining new information to reduce some of the uncertainty.

They argue, further, that the individual seeks forms of 'defensive avoidance' which enable him 'to escape from worrying about the decision by not exposing himself to cues that evoke awareness of anticipated losses' (Janis and Mann, 1977). If the decision can be postponed or delayed the individual will procrastinate; if the deadline is tight the individual will try to shift the responsibility to someone else, or 'bolster' the decision in various ways.

If the former, he directs his thoughts and actions towards getting others involved, rationalizing why they, not he, should make the decision and why they, not he, should take the blame if it turns out badly. If defensive avoidance takes the form of bolstering, the decision maker will continue to think and talk about the conflictful issue but will ward off stress by selective attention and distorted information processing (Janis and Mann, 1977).

Finally, Janis and Mann argue that their analysis applies not only to individuals but also to groups, to teams. In their view, being in a group amplifies the tendency of individuals to avoid raising controversial issues or confront difficulties head on. Apparently, group members are motivated (i) to shift responsibility, by seeking out the policy alternative favoured by the leader, or the most esteemed person, and (ii) to pool their resources collectively to bolster (rationalize) the choice he would like to make.

Janis and Mann refer to this collective tendency as 'group-think' and argue that it is fostered when members belong to a cohesive group, 'insulated' from others in the organization; when the leader directs attention to the policy he would prefer; and when the group lacks systematic procedures for information appraisal and search. They argue, also, that the way to reduce tendencies towards group-think is not to change the composition of the group. Rather, it is to ensure that the group devotes its energies to the right kinds of task.

Essentially, Janis and Mann have extended work on emergency decision making to cover all cases of decision making in which participants are concerned or anxious about the possibility that they may not attain the objectives which they seek. Details of the analysis are still being worked out, but one thing is clear; not to disagree, not to express 'organized dissent', means not to solve the problem. Dissent, properly conducted, is essential to clarify one's own position, and the position of the other side.

aat can psychology
ntribute from a
actical point of
ew?

1. We have argued that to understand the process of negotiation we require models of the negotiation task and
models of the people who carry out that task. Psychologists
have provided simple models of the negotiation task which
identify elements important from a psychological point of
view. They have also provided models of man which identify
limitations in the capability of negotiators to process
information and engage in complex acts of choice. Research
and theory of this kind provides people with a set of
concepts they can use to think about the process of negotiation. At a fairly general level psychologists are able to
offer advice of the kind: do not expect to reach agreement
too soon. Do not give up because your opponent keeps on
rejecting the proposals you have to make. The disagreement
may enhance the possibility that you will obtain a stable
settlement in the end. Try to work out how your opponent
analyses negotiation in terms of the threats and opportunities which it represents. Ask yourself whether his options
are really more open than yours. Is he not a representative
faced with role obligations of a similar kind to your own?
And so on.

2. Psychologists have attempted to analyse the nature of
negotiation as a social skill. In part this derives from
analyses of the nature of the negotiation task, and of the
'core processes' involved. In part it derives from detailed
observations, such as those of Douglas (1962), Morley and
Stephenson (1977), and Rackham and Carlisle (1978a and b).
We are impressed by convergences between the two lines of
research. The negotiators observed by Rackham and Carlisle,
and others, are rational in an information-processing sense:
they learn from negotiation themselves and they help opponents to come to grips with the complexities of their task.
Others may be less impressed, but the reader should note
that psychologists can offer some practical advice, based
upon the results of empirical research.

This is an important contribution, for two main reasons.
First, 'there is a growing literature on practically every
aspect of industrial relations except the actual conduct of
negotiations' (Anthony and Crichton, 1969). To be sure,
there is a certain amount of literature dealing with kinds
of arguments which are used (comparability, profitability of
the company, custom and practice, and so on) but there is
very little detailed study of the ways in which negotiators
select tactics and sequence behaviour in an organized and
coherent way. When textbooks of industrial relations
include chapters on the conduct of negotiation they more
often reflect the viewpoint of the author than report what
has been learned from systematic research.

Second, it is possible that information of this kind may
be important. Karrass, for example, has argued that

Negotiation training is a high-return business investment. It takes but a simple success at the bargaining

table to more than recover the entire cost of training a man. There is probably no other activity in which improved skill can be so quickly converted to profit (Karrass, 1970).

Similarly, Rackham and Carlisle (1978b) have said that they

are dismayed at the number of times ... industrial buyers are so constrained in their negotiations by production deadlines and engineering preferences as to become mere stock order clerks. The resultant loss of bargaining power must cost some large companies literally millions of pounds.

In contrast, effective negotiators somehow find the time to do their homework and prepare well. Let me repeat, the skill of the negotiators is, in itself, a form of 'negotiation power'.

Writers on industrial relations have tended to neglect the importance of the negotiators' skills. There is, no doubt, a feeling that 'effectiveness' depends so much on the perspective of the judge (one man's meat is another man's poison) that any kind of generalization must be ruled completely out of court. However, progress can be made if it is assumed that the parties are negotiating genuinely to reach an agreement, and that the issues are agreed to be, in some sense, matters appropriate for joint regulation (Morley, 1980).

3. Research dealing with social judgement has shown that judgement processes are simple, inconsistent (i.e. only partly regular), and that experts (even) may have little idea how their judgements are made. Psychologists may be able to provide techniques which help negotiators come to grips with certain key components of their task. It is possible, for example, that third parties may be able to adapt the techniques of decision counselling outlined by Janis and Mann (1977), or use computer aids of the kind described by Balke, Hammond and Meyer (1973).

4. Psychologists have devoted some attention to the ways and means by which negotiation skills are to be taught. In particular, they have considered the effectiveness of different forms of feedback, the use of controlled pace negotiation and the advantages/disadvantages of negotiation in 'reversed role' rather than 'standard' groups.

5. Finally, the reader may like to note that what has been said has implications which go far beyond the context of formal negotiation over the table, so to speak. Organizations are arenas of repeated conflict, if we may borrow Dubin's (1979) phrase. Furthermore, to quote Dubin, the conflict

is conflict that arises from differential points of view and differential objectives of those who collectively engage in a complex division of labor ... what is most important in the resolution is that the losing party be willing to return to the battle the very next time with the same vigour in pursuing its functional objectives. Leadership skills are required in resolving such functional conflicts so that the losers do not feel permanently defeated, and can therefore, retain their belief in their own special functional perspective.

We submit that the study of a topic such as negotiation has implications for the study of organizational behaviour in general, and leadership in particular.

References

Allen, A.D. Jr (1971)
A systems view of labor negotiations. Personnel Journal, 50, 103-114.
Anthony, P.D. (1977)
The Conduct of Industrial Relations. London: Institute of Personnel Management.
Anthony, P.D. and Crichton, A. (1969)
Industrial Relations and the Personnel Specialists. London: Batsford.
Atkinson, G.N. (1975)
The Effective Negotiator. London: Quest.
Balke, W.M., Hammond, K.R. and Meyer, G.D. (1973)
An alternative approach to labor-management relations. Administrative Science Quarterly, 18, 311-327.
Batstone, E., Boraston, I. and Frenkel, S. (1977)
Shop Stewards in Action: The organization of workplace conflict and accommodation. Oxford: Blackwell.
Bonham, M.G. (1971)
Simulating international disarmament negotiations. Journal of Conflict Resolution, 15, 299-315.
Brehmer, B. and Hammond, K.R. (1977)
Cognitive factors in interpersonal conflict. In D. Druckman (ed.), Negotiations: Social psychological perspectives. Beverly Hills: Sage.
Clegg, H.A. (1979)
The Changing System of Industrial Relations in Great Britain. Oxford: Blackwell.
Daniel, W.W. (1976)
Wage Determination in Industry. London: Policy Studies Institute.
Douglas, A. (1957)
The peaceful settlement of industrial and inter-group disputes. Journal of Conflict Resolution, 1, 69-81.
Douglas, A. (1962)
Industrial Peacemaking. New York: Columbia University Press.

Drucker, P.F. (1970)
The Effective Executive. London: Pan Business
Management.
Druckman, D. (1977)
Boundary role conflict: negotiation as dual
responsiveness. In I.W. Zartman (ed.), The Negotiation
Process: Theories and applications. Beverly Hills:
Sage.
Dubin, R. (1979)
Metaphors of leadership: an overview. In J.G. Hunt and
L.L. Larson, Crosscurrents in Leadership. Carbondale:
Southern Illinois University Press.
Goold-Adams, R. (1962)
The Time of Power: A reappraisal of John Foster Dulles.
London: Weidenfeld & Nicolson.
Janis, I.L. and Mann, L. (1977)
Decision Making: A psychological analysis of conflict,
choice and commitment. London: Collier Macmillan.
Jervis, R. (1976)
Perception and Misperception in International Politics.
Princeton, NJ: Princeton University Press.
Karrass, C.L. (1970)
The Negotiating Game. New York: World Publishing.
Kelley, H.H. and Schenitzki, D.P. (1972)
Bargaining. In C.G. McClintock (ed.), Experimental
Social Psychology. New York: Holt, Rinehart & Winston.
Klimoski, R.J. and Breaugh, J.A. (1977)
When performance doesn't count: a constituency looks at
its spokesman. Organizational Behavior and Human
Performance, 20, 301-311.
Landsberger, H.A. (1955)
Interaction process analysis of mediation of labour-
management disputes. Journal of Abnormal and Social
Psychology, 57, 522-528.
Magenau, J.A. and Pruitt, D.G. (1979)
The social psychology of bargaining: a theoretical
synthesis 1. In G.M. Stephenson and C.J. Brotherton
(eds), Industrial Relations: A social psychological
approach. Chichester: Wiley.
Morley, I.E. (1979)
Behavioural studies of industrial bargaining. In G.M.
Stephenson, and C.J. Brotherton (eds), Industrial
Relations: A social psychological approach. Chichester:
Wiley.
Morley, I.E. (1980)
Negotiation and bargaining. In M. Argyle (ed.), Handbook
of Social Skills, Volume 2. London: Methuen.
Morley, I.E. and Stephenson, G.M. (1977)
The Social Psychology of Bargaining. London: George
Allen & Unwin.
O'Leary, M.K.O. (1973)
Policy formulation and planning. In R.J. Boardman and
A.J.R. Groom (eds), The Management of Britain's Exter
Relations. London: Macmillan.

Pruitt, D.G. (1971)
Indirect communication and the search for agreement in negotiation. Journal of Applied Social Psychology, 1, 205-239.

Pruitt, D.G. and Lewis, S.A. (1975)
Development of integrative solutions in bi-lateral negotiation. Journal of Personality and Social Psychology, 31, 621-633.

Rackham, N. and Carlisle, J. (1978a)
The effective negotiator - Part 1: the behaviour of successful negotiators. Journal of European Industrial Training, 2, 6-11.

Rackham, N. and Carlisle, J. (1978b)
The effective negotiator - Part 2: planning for negotiations. Journal of European Industrial Training, 2, 2-5.

Snyder, G.H. and Diesing, P. (1977)
Conflict Among Nations: Bargaining decision making and system structure in international crises. Princeton, NJ: Princeton University Press.

Steinbruner, J.D. (1974)
The Cybernetic Theory of Decision. Princeton, NJ: Princeton University Press.

Stevens, C.M. (1963)
Strategy and Collective Bargaining Negotiation. New York: McGraw-Hill.

Strauss, A. (1978)
Negotiations: Varieties, contexts, processes, and social order. London: Jossey-Bass.

Strauss, G. (1979)
Can social psychology contribute to industrial relations? In G.M. Stephenson and C.J. Brotherton (eds), Industrial Relations: A social psychological approach. Chichester: Wiley.

Walton, R.E. and McKersie, R.B. (1965)
A Behavioral Theory of Labor Negotiations: An analysis of a social interaction system. New York: McGraw-Hill.

Winham, G.R. (1977a)
Negotiation as a management process. World Politics, 30, 97-114.

Winham, G.R. (1977b)
Complexity in international negotiation. In D. Druckman (ed.), Negotiations: Social psychological perspectives. Beverly Hills: Sage.

Winkler, J.T. (1974)
The ghost at the bargaining table: directors and industrial relations. British Journal of Industrial Relations, 12, 191-212.

Zartman, I.W. (1977)
Negotiation as a joint decision making process. In I.W. Zartman (ed.), The Negotiation Process: Theories and applications. Beverly Hills: Sage.

Questions

1. Discuss the view that the skilful negotiator is one who, through an understanding of the risks and opportunities associated with negotiation, and of the resources he can bring to bear, is able to take active and effective measures to protect or pursue the values and interests he has at stake.
2. Compare and contrast the effective negotiators described by Rackham and Carlisle with the effective executives described by Drucker.
3. Why might collective bargaining be described as a rather conservative exercise?
4. Outline Janis and Mann's model of decisional conflict and evaluate its significance for the study of negotiation.
5. Discuss Clegg's view that negotiation as a process cannot be understood without an appreciation of bargaining styles, values and power.
6. Can psychology contribute to industrial relations?
7. Outline and discuss Allen's 'systems model' of negotiation. Is it advantageous to think about negotiation in this kind of way?
8. Outline and discuss Douglas' model of successful negotation.
9. Write an essay on social psychology's view of rational man.
10. Discuss the effects of complexity in industrial relations.
11. Why are negotiations sometimes more difficult than they need to be?
12. Critically evaluate experimental studies of industrial bargaining.
13. Discuss Warr's view that 'decisions made by negotiators are similar in all essential ways to perceptions, judgements and conclusions drawn in any other setting'.
14. 'The basic operation of interests which exists within negotiation is mediated by personal relationships which facilitate the constructive resolution of problems' (Batstone, Boraston and Frenkel, 1978). Discuss.
15. Compare and contrast processes of internal and external negotiation.
16. What do effective negotiators do?
17. Discuss the view that uncertainty is the link between bargaining power and bargaining process.
18. Evaluate Walton and McKersie's 'behavioural theory'.
19. Outline and discuss the distinction between rational and irrational kinds of bargaining.
20. Outline and discuss some of the 'behavioural dilemmas' inherent in the negotiation task.

Annotated reading

Atkinson, G.M. (1975) The Effective Negotiator. London: Quest.

   One of the best of the 'how to do it' books. Atkinson introduces theoretical ideas in a clear, concise way. He also makes a number of extremely interesting suggestions designed to help negotiators set objectives based firmly on the realities of the power position between the sides.

Batstone, E., Boraston, E. and Frenkel, S. (1978) Shop Stewards in Action: The organization of workplace conflict and accommodation.
Emphasizes the importance of continuity in industrial relations. Batstone et al provide an excellent account of the nature of bargaining relationships. Further, they argue that one class of shop stewards, 'leader stewards', are particularly likely to establish strong bargaining relationships with members of management. For more on the organization of conflict see Batstone's chapter in Stephenson and Brotherton (1979).

Druckman, D. (ed.) (1977) Negotiations: Social psychological perspectives. Beverly Hills: Sage.
Contains 13 chapters illustrating the kinds of problems psychologists take to be important in the study of negotiation. Some of the chapters are technical and require a background in psychology. Others may be read without detailed preparation. Overall the book gives a good idea of the 'state of the art' with respect to the 'social psychology of negotiation'.

Elcock, H. (1972) Portrait of a Decision. London: Eyre Methuen.
It is a good idea to read a detailed case study of a negotiation, or a biography of a skilled negotiator. There are very few studies of industrial negotiation which provide detailed accounts of the ways in which decisions were made. Elcock provides an account of the Paris Peace Conference which led up to the Treaty of Versailles, since roundly condemned. A very interesting account, full of psychological insight, discussed in detail in my paper, 'Preparation for negotiation: conflict, commitment and choice' (in press).

Lockhart, C. (1979) Bargaining in International Conflicts. New York: Columbia University Press.
A very clear and well-written statement of the processes of information interpretation, influence and decision-making as they occur in negotiation groups. Lockhart emphasizes decisions which shape the general form negotiation will take.

Miron, M.S. and Goldstein, A.P. (1979) Hostage. Oxford: Pergamon Press.
An extremely interesting account of the skills involved in 'hostage negotiations'. In many respects the book is a manual to be used in training the police. Readers may find it useful to compare and contrast hostage

negotiation procedures with the conduct of industrial negotiation.

Morley, I.E. (1980) Negotiation and Bargaining. In M. Argyle (ed.), Handbook of Social Skills, Volume 2. London: Methuen.
    Provides an account of negotiation skill. The chapter is organized around Snyder and Diesing's model of negotiation. Examines processes of information interpretation, influence strategy and tactics, and decision making. Discusses some of the psychological factors which promote success in negotiation. Readers may be interested in some of the other social skills outlined in Argyle's book.

Morley, I.E. and Stephenson, G.M. (1977) The Social Psychology of Bargaining. London: George Allen & Unwin.
    Reviews the psychological factors which influence bargaining, defined as negotiation for agreement. There is a detailed review of laboratory research and a report of a programme of research designed to investigate Ann Douglas' ideas. Includes transcripts of actual cases.

Stephenson, G.M. (1978) Negotiation and collective bargaining. In P.B. Warr (ed.), Psychology at Work (2nd edn). Harmondsworth: Penguin.
    A concise, well-written account which places negotiation agreement in the context of a more general treatment of relations between groups.

Stephenson, G.M. and Brotherton, C.J. (eds) (1979) Industrial Relations: A social psychological approach. Chichester: Wiley.
    A collection of 16 chapters reviewing the contribution of psychology to various aspects of industrial relations. Attempts to show that psychology is applicable to all levels of the 'industrial relations system'. There are several general discussions of psychology and industrial relations, as well as chapters dealing with intergroup relations, the organization of conflict, pay comparisons, analyses of processes of bargaining and mediation, participation, and government psychologists and industrial relations specialists.

Warr, P.B. (1973) Psychology and Collective Bargaining. London: Hutchinson.
    Provides an introduction to some of the general areas of psychology relevant to the study of industrial relations. The book is aimed at managers and trade union officials and is written in a straightforward, non-technical style. Warr includes an interesting case study of pay and productivity negotiation covering a new wages structure in two industrial plants.

7

Social Behaviour
Michael Argyle

We start by presenting the social skill model of social
behaviour, and an account of sequences of social interaction. This model is very relevant to our later discussion
of social skills and how these can be trained. The chapter
then goes on to discuss the elements of social behaviour,
both verbal and non-verbal, and emphasize the importance and
different functions of non-verbal signals. The receivers of
these signals have to decode them, and do so in terms of
emotions and impressions of personality; we discuss some of
the processes and some of the main errors of person perception. The sender can manipulate the impression he creates
by means of 'self-presentation'. The processes of social
behaviour, and the skills involved, are quite different in
different social situations, and we discuss recent attempts
to analyse these situations in terms of their main features,
such as rules and goals.

We move on to a number of specific social skills.
Research on the processes leading to friendship and love
makes it possible to train and advise people who have difficulty with these relationships. Research on persuasion
shows how people can be trained to be more assertive. And
research on small social groups and leadership of these
groups makes it possible to give an account of the most
successful skills for handling social groups.

Social competence is defined in terms of the successful
attainment of goals, and it can be assessed by a variety of
techniques such as self-rating and observation of role-
played performance. The most successful method of social
skills is role-playing, combined with modelling, coaching,
videotape recorder (VTR) playback, and 'homework'. Results
of follow-up studies with a variety of populations show that
this form of social skills training (SST) is very
successful.

Harré and Secord (1972) have argued persuasively that
much human social behaviour is the result of conscious
planning, often in words, with full regard for the complex
meanings of behaviour and the rules of the situations. This
is an important correction to earlier social psychological
views, which often failed to recognize the complexity of
individual planning and the different meanings which may be
given to stimuli, for example in laboratory experiments.

However, it must be recognized that much social behaviour is not planned in this way: the smaller elements of behaviour and longer automatic sequences are outside conscious awareness, though it is possible to attend, for example, to patterns of gaze, shifts of orientation, or the latent meanings of utterances. The social skills model, in emphasizing the hierarchical structure of social performance, can incorporate both kinds of behaviour.

The social skills model also emphasizes feedback processes. A person driving a car sees at once when it is going in the wrong direction, and takes corrective action with the steering wheel. Social interactors do likewise; if another person is talking too much they interrupt, ask closed questions or no questions, and look less interested in what he has to say. Feedback requires perception, looking at and listening to the other person. Skilled performance requires the ability to take the appropriate corrective action referred to as 'translation' in the model: not everyone knows that open-ended questions make people talk more and closed questions make them talk less. And it depends on a number of two-step sequences of social behaviour whereby certain social acts have reliable effects on another. Let us look at social behaviour as a skilled performance similar to motor skills like driving a car (see figure 1).

Figure 1

The motor skill model (from Argyle, 1969)

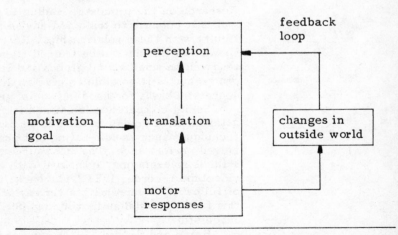

In each case the performer is pursuing certain goals, makes continuous response to feedback, and emits hierarchically-organized motor responses. This model has been heuristically very useful in drawing attention to the importance of feedback, and hence to gaze; it also suggests a number of different ways in which social performances can fail, and suggests the training procedures that may be effective, through analogy with motor skills training (Argyle and Kendon, 1967; Argyle, 1969).

The model emphasizes the motivation, goals and plans of interactors. It is postulated that every interactor is trying to achieve some goal, whether he is aware of it or not. These goals may be, for example, to get another person to like him, to obtain or convey information, to modify the other's emotional state, and so on. Such goals may be linked to more basic motivational systems. Goals have sub-goals; for example, a doctor must diagnose the patient before he can treat him. Patterns of response are directed towards goals and sub-goals, and have a hierarchical structure: large units of behaviour are composed of smaller ones, and at the lowest levels these are habitual and automatic.

The role of reinforcement
This is one of the key processes in social skills sequences. When interactor A does what B wants him to do, B is pleased and sends immediate and spontaneous reinforcements: smile, gaze, approving noises, etc., and modifies A's behaviour, probably by operant conditioning; for example, modifying the content of his utterances. At the same time A is modifying B's behaviour in exactly the same way. These effects appear to be mainly outside the focus of conscious attention, and take place very rapidly. It follows that anyone who gives strong rewards and punishments in the course of interaction will be able to modify the behaviour of others in the desired direction. In addition, the stronger the rewards that A issues, the more strongly other people will be attracted to him.

The role of gaze in social skills
The social skills model suggests that the monitoring of another's reactions is an essential part of social performance. The other's verbal signals are mainly heard, but his non-verbal signals are mainly seen; the exceptions being the non-verbal aspects of speech and touch. It was this implication of the social skills model which directed us towards the study of gaze in social interaction. In dyadic interaction each person looks about 50 per cent of the time, mutual gaze occupies 25 per cent of the time, looking while listening is about twice the level of looking while talking, glances are about three seconds, and mutual glances about one second, with wide variations due to distance, sex combination, and personality (Argyle and Cook, 1976). However, there are several important differences between social behaviour and motor skills.

* Rules: the moves which interactors may make are governed by rules; they must respond properly to what has gone before. Similarly, rules govern the other's responses and can be used to influence his behaviour; for example, questions lead to answers.

* Taking the role of the other: it is important to perceive accurately the reactions of others. It is also
necessary to perceive the perceptions of others; that
is, to take account of their points of view. This
appears to be a cognitive ability which develops with
age (Flavell, 1968), but which may fail to develop
properly. Those who are able to do this have been found
to be more effective at a number of social tasks, and
more altruistic. Meldman (1967) found that psychiatric
patients are more egocentric; that is, talked about
themselves more than controls, and it has been our
experience that socially unskilled patients have great
difficulty in taking the role of the other.
* The independent initiative of the other sequences of
interaction: social situations inevitably contain at
least one other person, who will be pursuing his goals
and using his social skills. How can we analyse the
resulting sequences of behaviour? For a sequence to
constitute an acceptable piece of social behaviour, the
moves must fit together in order. Social psychologists
have not yet discovered all the principles or 'grammar'
underlying these sequences, but some of the principles
are known, and can explain common forms of interaction
failure.

Verbal and non-verbal communication

Verbal communication
There are several different kinds of verbal utterance.

* Egocentric speech: this is directed to the self, is
found in infants and has the effect of directing
behaviour.
* Orders, instructions: these are used to influence the
behaviour of others; they can be gently persuasive or
authoritarian.
* Questions: these are intended to elicit verbal
information; they can be open-ended or closed, personal
or impersonal.
* Information: may be given in response to a question, or
as part of a lecture or during problem-solving
discussion.

(The last three points are the basic classes of utterance.)

* Informal speech: consists of casual chat, jokes, gossip,
and contains little information, but helps to establish
and sustain social relationships.
* Expression of emotions and interpersonal attitudes: this
is a special kind of information; however, this
information is usually conveyed, and is conveyed more
effectively, non-verbally.
* Performative utterances: these include 'illocutions'
where saying the utterance performs something (voting,
judging, naming, etc.), and 'perlocutions', where a goal

134

is intended but may not be achieved (persuading, intimidating, etc.).

* Social routines: these include standard sequences like thanking, apologizing, greeting, etc.
* Latent messages: are where the more important meaning is made subordinate ('As I was saying to the Prime Minister ...').

There are many category schemes for reducing utterances to a limited number of classes of social acts. One of the best known is that of Bales (1950), who introduced the 12 classes shown in figure 2.

Non-verbal signals accompanying speech

Non-verbal signals play an important part in speech and conversation. They have three main roles:

* completing and elaborating on verbal utterances: utterances are accompanied by vocal emphasis, gestures and facial expressions, which add to the meaning and indicate whether it is a question, intended to be serious or funny, and so on;
* managing synchronizing: this is achieved by head-nods, gaze-shifts, and other signals. For example, to keep the floor a speaker does not look up at the end of an utterance, keeps a hand in mid-gesture, and increases the volume of his speech if the other interrupts;
* sending feedback signals: listeners keep up a continuous, and mainly unwitting, commentary on the speaker's utterances, showing by mouth and eyebrow positions whether they agree, understand, are surprised, and so on (Argyle, 1975).

Other functions of non-verbal communication (NVC)

NVC consists of facial expression, tone of voice, gaze, gestures, postures, physical proximity and appearance. We have already described how NVC is linked with speech; it also functions in several other ways, especially in the communication of emotions and attitudes to other people.

A sender is in a certain state, or possesses some information; this is encoded into a message which is then decoded by a receiver.

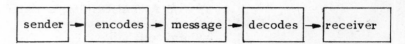

sender → encodes → message → decodes → receiver

Encoding research is done by putting subjects into some state and studying the NV messages which are emitted. For example, Mehrabian (1972) in a role-playing experiment, asked subjects to address a hat-stand, imagining it to be a person. Male subjects who liked the hat-stand looked at it more, did not have hands on hips and stood closer.

Figure 2

The Bales categories (from Bales, 1950)

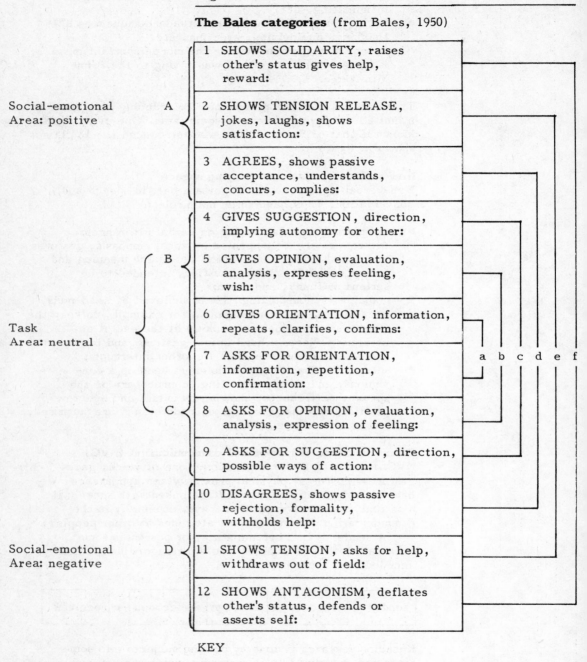

Social-emotional A
Area: positive

1 SHOWS SOLIDARITY, raises other's status gives help, reward:

2 SHOWS TENSION RELEASE, jokes, laughs, shows satisfaction:

3 AGREES, shows passive acceptance, understands, concurs, complies:

B

4 GIVES SUGGESTION, direction, implying autonomy for other:

5 GIVES OPINION, evaluation, analysis, expresses feeling, wish:

6 GIVES ORIENTATION, information, repeats, clarifies, confirms:

Task
Area: neutral

7 ASKS FOR ORIENTATION, information, repetition, confirmation:

C

8 ASKS FOR OPINION, evaluation, analysis, expression of feeling:

9 ASKS FOR SUGGESTION, direction, possible ways of action:

Social-emotional D
Area: negative

10 DISAGREES, shows passive rejection, formality, withholds help:

11 SHOWS TENSION, asks for help, withdraws out of field:

12 SHOWS ANTAGONISM, deflates other's status, defends or asserts self:

a b c d e f

KEY

a problems of communication
b problems of evaluation
c problems of control
d problems of decision
e problems of tension reduction
f problems of reintegration

A positive reactions
B attempted answers
C questions
D negative reactions

Non-verbal signals are often 'unconscious': that is, they are outside the focus of attention. A few signals are unconsciously sent and received, like dilated pupils, signifying sexual attraction, but there are a number of other possibilities as shown in table 1.

Table 1

Awareness of non-verbal signals

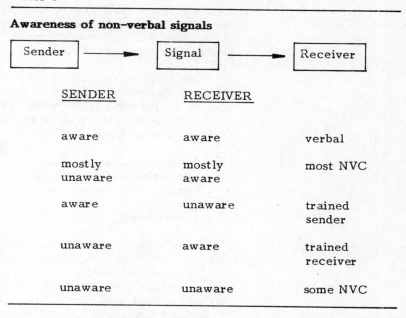

SENDER	RECEIVER	
aware	aware	verbal
mostly unaware	mostly aware	most NVC
aware	unaware	trained sender
unaware	aware	trained receiver
unaware	unaware	some NVC

Strictly speaking pupil dilation is not communication at all, but only a physiological response. 'Communication' is usually taken to imply some intention to affect another; one criterion is that it makes a difference whether the other person is present and in a position to receive the signal; another is that the signal is repeated, varied or amplified if it has no effect. These criteria are independent of conscious intention to communicate, which is often absent.

* Interpersonal attitudes: interactors indicate how much they like or dislike one another, and whether they think they are more or less important, mainly non-verbally. We have compared verbal and non-verbal signals and found that non-verbal cues like facial expression and tone of voice have far more impact than verbal ones (Argyle et al, 1970).
* Emotional states: anger, depression, anxiety, joy, surprise, fear and disgust/contempt, are also communicated more clearly by non-verbal signals, such as facial expression, tone of voice, posture, gestures and gaze. Interactors may try to conceal their true emotions, but these are often revealed by 'leakage' via cues which are difficult to control.

Person perception In order to respond effectively to the behaviour of others
it is necessary to perceive them correctly. The social
skills model emphasizes the importance of perception and
feedback; to drive a car one must watch the traffic outside
and the instruments inside. Such perception involves selecting certain cues, and being able to interpret them correctly. There is evidence of poor person perception in
mental patients and other socially unskilled individuals,
while professional social skills performers need to be
sensitive to special aspects of other people and their
behaviour. For selection interviewers and clinical psychologists the appraisal of others is a central part of the
job.

We form impressions of other people all the time, mainly
in order to predict their future behaviour, and so that we
can deal with them effectively. We categorize others in
terms of our favourite cognitive constructs, of which the
most widely used are:

* extraversion, sociability;
* agreeableness, likeability;
* emotional stability;
* intelligence;
* assertiveness.

There are, however, wide individual differences in the constructs used, and 'complex' people use a larger number of
such dimensions. We have found that the constructs used vary
greatly with the situation: for example, work-related constructs are not used in purely social situations. We also
found that the constructs used vary with the target group,
such as children versus psychologists (Argyle et al, in
press).

A number of widespread errors are made in forming
impressions of others which should be particularly avoided
by those whose job it is to assess people:

* assuming that a person's behaviour is mainly a product
  of his personality, whereas it may be more a function of
  the situation he is in: at a noisy party, in church,
  etc.;
* assuming that his behaviour is due to him rather than
  his role; for example, as a hospital nurse, as a patient
  or as a visitor;
* attaching too much importance to physical cues, like
  beards, clothes, and physical attractiveness;
* being affected by stereotypes about the characteristics
  of members of certain races, social classes, etc.

During social interaction it is also necessary to perceive
the emotional states of others: for example, to tell if they
are depressed or angry. There are wide individual
differences in the ability to judge emotions correctly
(Davitz, 1964). As we have seen, emotions are mainly

conveyed by non-verbal signals, especially by facial expression and tone of voice. The interpretation of emotions is also based on perception of the situation the other person is in. Lalljee at Oxford found that smiles are not necessarily decoded as happy, whereas unhappy faces are usually regarded as authentic.

Similar considerations apply to the perception of interpersonal attitudes, for instance who likes whom, which is also mainly based on non-verbal signals, such as proximity, gaze and facial expression. Again use is made of context to decode these signals: a glance at a stranger may be interpreted as a threat, an appeal for help or a friendly invitation. There are some interesting errors due to pressures towards cognitive consistency: if A likes B, he thinks that B likes him more than B on average actually does: if A likes both B and C, he assumes that they both like each other more than, on average, they do.

It is necessary to perceive the on-going flow of interaction in order to know what is happening and to participate in it effectively. People seem to agree on the main episodes and sub-episodes of an encounter, but they may produce rather different accounts of why those present behaved as they did. One source of variation, and indeed error, is that people attribute the causes of others' behaviour to their personality ('He fell over because he is clumsy'), but their own behaviour to the situation ('I fell over because it was slippery'), whereas both factors operate in each case (Jones and Nisbett, 1972). Interpretations also depend on the ideas and knowledge an individual possesses: just as an expert on cars could understand better why a car was behaving in a peculiar way, so also can an expert on social behaviour understand why patterns of social behaviour occur.

uations, their
les and other
atures

We know that people behave very differently in different situations; in order to predict behaviour, or to advise people on social skills in specific situations, it is necessary to analyse the situations in question. This can be done in terms of a number of fundamental features.

Goals
In all situations there are certain goals which are commonly obtainable. It is often fairly obvious what these are, but socially inadequate people may simply not know what parties are for, for example, or may think that the purpose of a selection interview is vocational guidance.

We have studied the main goals in a number of common situations, by asking samples of people to rate the importance of various goals, and then carrying out factor analysis. The main goals are usually:

* social acceptance, etc.;
* food, drink and other bodily needs;
* task goals specific to the situation.

We have also studied the relations between goals, within and between persons, in terms of conflict and instrumentality. This makes it possible to study the 'goal structure' of situations. An example is given in figure 3, showing that the only conflict between nurses and patients is between the nurses' concern for the bodily well-being of the patients and of themselves (Argyle Furnham and Graham, in press).

Rules

All situations have rules about what may or may not be done in them. Socially inexperienced people are often ignorant or mistaken about the rules. It would obviously be impossible to play a game without knowing the rules and the same applies to social situations.

We have studied the rules of a number of everyday situations. There appear to be several universal rules; to be polite, be friendly, not embarrass people. There are also rules which are specific to situations, or groups of situations, and these can be interpreted as functional, since they enable situational goals to be met. For example, when seeing the doctor one should be clean and tell the truth; when going to a party one should dress smartly and keep to cheerful topics of conversation.

Special skills

Many social situations require special social skills, as in the case of various kinds of public speaking and interviewing, but also such everyday situations as dates and parties. A person with little experience of a particular situation may find that he lacks the special skills needed for it (cf. Argyle et al, in press).

Figure 3

The goal structure for nurse and patient

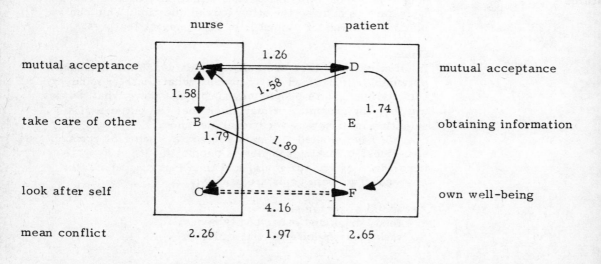

Repertoire of elements
Every situation defines certain moves as relevant. For
example, at a seminar it is relevant to show slides, make
long speeches, draw on the blackboard, etc. If moves
appropriate to a cricket match or a Scottish ball were made,
they would be ignored or regarded as totally bizarre. We
have found 65-90 main elements used in several situations,
like going to the doctor. We have also found that the
semiotic structure varies between situations: we found that
questions about work and about private life were sharply
contrasted in an office situation, but not on a date.

Roles
Every situation has a limited number of roles: for example,
a classroom has the roles of teacher, pupil, janitor, and
school inspector. These roles carry different degrees of
power, and the occupant has goals peculiar to that role.

Cognitive structure
We found that the members of a research group classified
each other in terms of the concepts extraverted and enjoy-
able companion for social occasions, but in terms of dominant, creative and supportive for seminars. There are also
concepts related to the task, such as 'amendment', 'straw
vote' and 'nem con', for committee meetings.

Environmental setting and pieces
Most situations involve special environmental settings and
props. Cricket needs bat, ball, stumps, etc.; a seminar
requires a blackboard, slide projector and lecture notes.
        How do persons fit into situations, conceived in this
way? To begin with, there are certain pervasive aspects of
persons, corresponding to the 20 per cent or so of person
variance found in P x S (personality and situation) studies.
This consists of scores on general dimensions like intelligence, extraversion, neuroticism and so on. In addition,
persons have dispositions to behave in certain ways in
classes of situations; this corresponds to the 50 per cent
or so of the P x S variance in relation to dimensions of
situations like formal-informal, and friendly-hostile.
Third, there are more specific reactions to particular
situations; for example, behaviour in social psychology
seminars depends partly on knowledge of social psychology,
and attitudes to different schools of thought in it. Taken
together these three factors may predict performance in, and
also avoidance of, certain situations - because of lack of
skill, anxiety, etc. - and this will be the main expectation
in such cases.

endship

This is one of the most important social relationships:
failure in it is a source of great distress, and so it is
one of the main areas of social skills training. The
conditions under which people come to like one another have

been the object of extensive research, and are now well understood.

There are several stages of friendship: (i) coming into contact with the other, through proximity at work or elsewhere; (ii) increasing attachment as a result of reinforcement and discovery of similarity; (iii) increasing self-disclosure and commitment; and sometimes (iv) dissolution of the relationship. Friendship is the dominant relationship for adolescents and the unmarried; friends engage in characteristic activities, such as talking, eating, drinking, joint leisure, but not, usually, working.

Frequency of interaction

The more two people meet, the more polarized their attitude to one another become, but usually they like one another more. Frequent interaction can come about from living in adjacent rooms or houses, working in the same office, belonging to the same club, and so on. So interaction leads to liking, and liking leads to more interaction. Only certain kinds of interaction lead to liking. In particular, people should be of similar status. Belonging to a co-operative group, especially under crisis conditions, is particularly effective, as Sherif's 'Robbers' cave' experiment (Sherif et al, 1961) and research on inter-racial attitudes have shown.

Reinforcement

The next general principle governing liking is the extent to which one person satisfies the needs of another. This was shown in a study by Jennings of 400 girls in a reformatory (1950). She found that the popular girls helped and protected others, encouraged, cheered them up, made them feel accepted and wanted, controlled their own moods so as not to inflict anxiety or depression on others, were able to establish rapport quickly, won the confidence of a wide variety of other personalities, and were concerned with the feelings and needs of others. The unpopular girls on the other hand were dominating, aggressive, boastful, demanded attention, and tried to get others to do things for them. This pattern has been generally interpreted in terms of the popular girls providing rewards and minimizing costs, while the unpopular girls tried to get rewards for themselves, and incurred costs for others. It is not necessary for the other person to be the actual source of rewards: Lott and Lott (1960) found that children who were given model cars by the experimenter liked the other children in the experiment more, and several studies have shown that people are liked more in a pleasant environmental setting.

Being liked is a powerful reward, so if A likes B, B will usually like A. This is particularly important for those who have a great need to be liked, such as individuals with low self-esteem. It is signalled, as we showed above, primarily by non-verbal signals.

Similarity
People like others who are similar to themselves, in certain respects. They like those with similar attitudes, beliefs and values, who have a similar regional and social class background, who have similar jobs or leisure interests, but they need not have similar personalities. Again there is a cyclical process, since similarity leads to liking and liking leads to similarity, but effects of similarity on liking have been shown experimentally.

Physical attractiveness
Physical attractiveness (p.a.) is an important source of both same-sex and opposite sex liking, especially in the early stages. Walster et al (1966) arranged a 'computer dance' at which couples were paired at random: the best prediction of how much each person liked their partner was the latter's p.a. as rated by the experimenter. Part of the explanation lies in the 'p.a. stereotype'. Dion et al (1972) found that attractive people were believed to have desirable characteristics of many other kinds. However, people do not seek out the most attractive friends and mates, but compromise by seeking those similar to themselves in attractiveness.

Self-disclosure
This is a signal for intimacy, like bodily contact, because it indicates trust in the other. Self-disclosure can be measured on a scale (1-5) with items like:

> What are your favourite forms of erotic play and sexual lovemaking? (scale value 2.56)

> What are the circumstances under which you become depressed and when your feelings are hurt? (3.51)

> What are your hobbies, how do you best like to spend your spare time? (4.98) (Jourard, 1971).

As people get to know each other better, self-disclosure slowly increases, and is reciprocated, up to a limit.

Commitment
This is a state of mind, an intention to stay in a relationship, and abandon others. This involves a degree of dependence on the other person and trusting them not to leave the relationship. The least committed has the more power.

Social skills training
The most common complaint of those who seek social skills training is difficulty in making friends. Some of them say they have never had a friend in their lives. What advice can we offer, on the basis of research on friendship?

* As we showed earlier, social relations are negotiated mainly by non-verbal signals. Clients for social skills training who cannot make friends are usually found to be very inexpressive, in face and voice.
* Rewardingness is most important. The same clients usually appear to be very unrewarding, and are not really interested in other people.
* Frequent interaction with those of similar interests and attitudes can be found in clubs for professional or leisure activities, in political and religious groups, and so on.
* Physical attractiveness is easier to change than is social behaviour.
* Certain social skills may need to be acquired, such as inviting others to suitable social events, and engaging in self-disclosure at the right speed.

The meaning and assessment of social competence

By social competence we mean the ability, the possession of the necessary skills, to produce the desired effects on other people in social situations. These desired effects may be to persuade the others to buy, to learn, to recover from neurosis, to like or admire the actor, and so on. These results are not necessarily in the public interest: skills may be used for social or antisocial purposes. And there is no evidence that social competence is a general factor: a person may be better at one task than another, for example, parties or committees. Social skills training for students and other more or less normal populations has been directed to the skills of dating, making friends and being assertive. SST for mental patients has been aimed at correcting failures of social competence, and also at relieving subjective distress, such as social anxiety.

To find out who needs training, and in what areas, a detailed descriptive assessment is needed. We want to know, for example, which situations a trainee finds difficult: formal situations, conflicts, meeting strangers, etc., and which situations he is inadequate in, even though he does not report them as difficult. And we want to find out what he is doing wrong: failure to produce the right non-verbal signals, low rewardingness, lack of certain social skills, etc.

Social competence is easier to define and agree upon in the case of professional social skills: an effective therapist cures more patients, an effective teacher teaches better, an effective saleswoman sells more. When we look more closely, it is not quite so simple: examination marks may be one index of a teacher's effectiveness, but usually more is meant than just this. A saleswoman should not simply sell a lot of goods, she should make the customers feel they would like to go to that shop again. So a combination of different skills is required and an overall assessment of effectiveness may involve the combination of a number of different measures or ratings. The range of competence is quite large: the best salesmen and saleswomen regularly sell four times as much as some others behind the same counter; some supervisors of working groups produce twice as much output as others, or have 20-25 per cent of the labour turnover and absenteeism rates (Argyle, 1972).

For everyday social skills it is more difficult to give the criteria of success; lack of competence is easier to spot: failure to make friends, or opposite sex friends, quarrelling and failing to sustain co-operative relationships, finding a number of situations difficult or a source of anxiety, and so on.

Role-playing with coaching

This is now the most widely-used method of SST. There are four stages:

* instruction;
* role-playing with other trainees or other role partners for 5-8 minutes;
* feedback and coaching, in the form of oral comments from the trainer;
* repeated role-playing.

A typical laboratory set-up is shown in figure 4. This also shows the use of an ear-microphone, for instruction while role-playing is taking place. In the case of patients, mere practice does no good: there must be coaching as well.

For an individual or group of patients or other trainees a series of topics, skills or situations is chosen, and introduced by means of short scenarios. Role partners are used, who can be briefed to present carefully graded degrees of difficulty.

It is usual for trainers to be generally encouraging, and also rewarding for specific aspects of behaviour, though there is little experimental evidence for the value of such reinforcement. It is common to combine role-playing with modelling and video playback, both of which are discussed below. Follow-up studies have found that role-playing combined with coaching is successful with many kinds of mental patients, and that it is one of the most successful forms of SST for these groups.

Role-playing usually starts with 'modelling', in which a film is shown or a demonstration given of how to perform the skill being taught. The feedback session usually includes videotape playback and most studies have found that this is advantageous (Bailey and Sowder, 1970). While it often makes trainees self-conscious at first, this wears off after the second session. Skills acquired in the laboratory or class must be transferred to the outside world. This is usually achieved by 'homework': trainees are encouraged to try out the new skills several times before the next session. Most trainers take people in groups which provides a source of role partners, but patients may need individual sessions as well for individual problems.

Figure 4

A social skills training laboratory

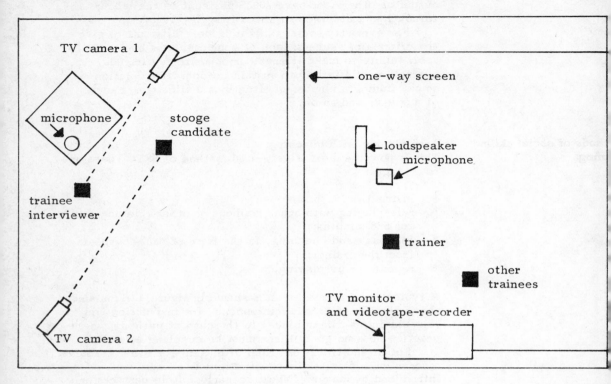

Other methods of training

TRAINING ON THE JOB: this is a widely used traditional
method. Some people improve through experience but others
do not, and some learn the wrong things. The situation can
be improved if there is a trainer who regularly sees the
trainee in action, and is able to hold feedback sessions at
which errors are pointed out and better skills suggested. In
practice this method does not appear to work very well, for
example with trainee teachers (see Argyle, 1969).

GROUP METHODS: these, especially T-groups (T standing for training), are intended to enhance sensitivity and
social skills. Follow-up studies have consistently found
that 30-40 per cent of trainees are improved by group
methods, but up to 10 per cent are worse, sometimes needing
psychological assistance (e.g. Lieberman et al, 1973). It
has been argued that group methods are useful for those who
are resistant to being trained.

EDUCATIONAL METHODS: these, such as lectures and
films, can increase knowledge, but to master social skills
it is necessary to try them out, as is the case with motor
skills. Educational methods can be a useful supplement to
role-playing methods.

Areas of application of SST

NEUROTIC PATIENTS: role-playing and the more specialized methods described above have been found to be slightly more effective than psychotherapy, desensitization, or other alternative treatments, but not much (Trower et al, 1978). Only one study so far has found really substantial differences; Maxwell (1976), in a study of adults reporting social difficulties and seeking treatment for them, in New Zealand, insisted on homework between training sessions. However, SST does produce more improvement in social skills and reduction of social anxiety. A few patients can be cured by SST alone, but most have other problems as well, and may require other forms of treatment in addition.

PSYCHOTIC PATIENTS: these have been treated in the USA by assertiveness training and other forms of role-playing. Follow-up studies have shown greater improvement in social behaviour than from alternative treatments. The most striking results have been obtained with intensive clinical studies of one to four patients, using a 'multiple baseline' design: one symptom is worked on at a time over a total of 20-30 sessions. It is not clear from these follow-up studies to what extent the general condition of patients has been improved, or how well they have been able to function outside the hospital (Hersen and Bellack, 1976). It has been argued by one practitioner that SST is more suitable than psychotherapy for working-class patients in view of their poor verbal skills (Goldstein, 1973).

Other therapeutic uses of SST

ALCOHOLICS have been given SST to improve their assertiveness, for example in refusing drinks, and to enable them to deal better with situations which they find stressful and make them drink. Similar treatment has been given to drug addicts. In both cases treatment has been fairly successful, though the effects have not always been long-lasting; SST is often included in more comprehensive packages.

DELINQUENTS AND PRISONERS have often been given SST with some success, especially in the case of aggressive and sex offenders. SST can also increase their degree of internal control.

TEACHERS, MANAGERS, DOCTORS, etc.: SST is increasingly being included in the training of those whose work involves dealing with people. The most extensive application so far has been in the training of teachers by 'micro-teaching'. The pupil teacher is instructed in one of the component skills of teaching, such as the use of different kinds of question, explanation or the use of examples; he then teaches 5-6 children for 10-15 minutes, followed by a feedback session and 're-teaching'. Follow-up studies show that this is far more effective than a similar amount of teaching practice, and it is much more effective in eradicating bad habits (Brown, 1975). In addition to role-playing, more elaborate forms of simulation are used, for example to train people for administrative positions.

Training on the job is a valuable addition or alternative, provided that the trainer really does his job.

NORMAL ADULTS: students have received a certain amount of SST, especially in North American universities, and follow-up studies have shown that they can be success-fully trained in assertiveness (Rich and Schroeder, 1976), dating behaviour (Curran, 1977), and to reduce anxiety at performing in public (Paul, 1966). Although many normal adults apart from students have social behaviour diffi-culties, very little training is available unless they seek psychiatric help. It would be very desirable for SST to be more widely available, for example in community centres.

SCHOOLCHILDREN: a number of attempts have been made to introduce SST into schools, though there are no follow-up studies on its effectiveness. However, there have been a number of successful follow-up studies of training schemes for children who are withdrawn and unpopular or aggressive, using the usual role-playing methods (Rinn and Markle, 1979).

Conclusion

In this chapter we have tried to give an account of those aspects of social psychology which are most relevant to the work of teachers, social workers and others, both in under-standing the behaviour of their clients and also in helping them with their own performance. We have used various mode of social behaviour such as the social skills model and the model of social behaviour as a game. Some of the phenomena described cannot be fully accounted for in terms of these models: for example, the design of sequences of interaction. A number of practical implications are described; in parti-cular, discussion of the skills which have been demonstrated to be the most effective in a number of situations, and the methods of social skills training which have been found to have most impact. It should be emphasized that much of this research is quite new and it is expected that a great deal more will be found out on these topics in the years to come.

References

Argyle, M. (1969)
  Social Interaction. London: Methuen.
Argyle, M. (1972)
  The Social Psychology of Work. London: Allen Lane and Penguin Books.
Argyle, M. (1975)
  Bodily Communication. London: Methuen.
Argyle, M. and Cook, M. (1976)
  Gaze and Mutual Gaze. London: Cambridge University Press.
Argyle, M., Furnham, A. and Graham, J.A. (in press)
  Social situations. London: Cambridge University Press.
Argyle, M. and Kendon, A. (1967)
  The experimental analysis of social performance.

Advances in Experimental Social Psychology, 3, 55-98.

Argyle, M., Salter V., Nicholson, H., Williams, M. and Burgess, P. (1970)
The communication of inferior and superior attitudes by verbal and non-verbal signals. British Journal of Social and Clinical Psychology, 9, 221-231.

Bailey, K.G. and Sowder, W.T. (1970)
Audiotape and videotape self-confrontation in psychotherapy. Psychological Bulletin, 74, 127-137.

Bales, R.F. (1950)
Interaction Process Analysis. Cambridge, Mass.: Addison-Wesley.

Brown, G.A. (1975)
Microteaching. London: Methuen.

Curran, J.P. (1977)
Skills training as an approach to the treatment of heterosexual-social anxiety. Psychological Bulletin, 84, 140-157.

Davitz, J.R. (1964)
The Communication of Emotional Meaning. New York: McGraw-Hill.

Dion, K., Berscheid, E. and Walster, E. (1972)
What is beautiful is good. Journal of Personality and Social Psychology, 24, 285-290.

Flavell, J.H. (1968)
The Development of Role-taking and Communication Skills in Children. New York: Wiley.

Goldstein, A.J. (1973)
Structured Learning Therapy: Toward a psychotherapy for the poor. New York: Academic Press.

Harré, R. and Secord, P. (1972)
The Explanation of Social Behaviour. Oxford: Blackwell.

Hersen, M. and Bellack, A.S. (1976)
Social skills training for chronic psychiatric patients: rationale, research findings, and future directions. Comprehensive Psychiatry, 17, 559-580.

Jennings, H.H. (1950)
Leadership and Isolation. New York: Longmans Green.

Jones, E.E. and Nisbett, R.E. (1972)
The actor and the observer: divergent perceptions of the causes of behavior. In E.E. Jones et al (eds), Attribution: Perceiving the causes of behavior. Morristown, NJ: General Learning Press.

Jourard, S.M. (1971)
Self Disclosure. New York: Wiley Interscience.

Lieberman, M.A., Yalom, I.D. and Miles, M.R. (1973)
Encounter Groups: First facts. New York: Basic Books.

Lott, A.J. and Lott, B.E. (1960)
The formation of positive attitudes towards group members. Journal of Abnormal and Social Psychology, 61, 297-300.

Maxwell, G.M. (1976)
An evolution of social skills training. (Unpublished, University of Otago, Dunedin, New Zealand.)

Mehrabian, A. (1972)
Nonverbal Communication. New York: Aldine-Atherton.
Meldman, M.J. (1967)
Verbal behavior analysis of self-hyperattentionism.
Diseases of the Nervous System, 28, 469–473.
Paul, G.L. (1966)
Insight v. Desensitization in Psychotherapy. Stanford:
Stanford University Press.
Rich, A.R. and Schroeder, H.E. (1976)
Research issues in assertiveness training. Psychological
Bulletin, 83, 1081-1096.
Rinn, R.C. and Markle, A. (1979)
Modification of social skill deficits in children. In
A.S. Bellack and M. Hersen (eds), Research and Practic
in Social Skills Training. New York: Plenum.
**Sherif, M., Harvey, O.J., White, B.J., Hood, W.R. and
Sherif, C.** (1961)
Intergroup Conflict and Cooperation: The Robbers' Cave
experiment. Norman, Oklahoma: The University of Oklahc
Book Exchange.
Trower, P., Bryant, B. and Argyle, M. (1978)
Social Skills and Mental Health. London: Methuen.
Walster, E., Aronson, V., Abrahams, D. and Rottmann, L.
(1966)
Importance of physical attractiveness in dating
behavior. Journal of Personality and Social Psychology,
5, 508-516.

Questions

1. Is it useful to look at social behaviour as a kind of skill?
2. What do bad conversationalists do wrong?
3. What information is conveyed by non-verbal communication?
4. In what ways do non-verbal signals supplement verbal ones?
5. How is the perception of other people different from the perception of other physical objects?
6. What information about a social situation would a newcomer to it need to know?
7. Do we like other people primarily because they are rewarding?
8. Why do some people have difficulty in making friends?
9. Can social competence be measured?
10. How can the effectiveness of social skills training be assessed?
11. Is social skills training successful with mental patients?
12. If someone has inadequate social behaviour, what else may he require in addition to SST?
13. What criticisms have been made of experiments in social psychology? What other methods are available?
14. Does social behaviour take the same form in other cultures?

15. Are there fundamental differences between social
behaviour in families, work-groups and groups of
friends?

nnotated reading

Argyle, M. (1978) The Psychology of Interpersonal Behaviour
(3rd edn). Harmondsworth: Penguin.
Covers the field of the chapter, and related topics at
Penguin level.

Argyle, M. and Trower, P. (1979). Person to Person. London:
Harper & Row.
A more popular account of the area covered by the
chapter, with numerous coloured illustrations.

Argyle, M. (1975). Bodily Communication. London: Methuen.
Covers the field of non-verbal communication in more
detail, with some illustrations.

Berscheid, E. and Walster, E.H. (1978). Interpersonal
Attraction (2nd edn). Reading, Mass.: Addison-Wesley.
A very readable account of research in this area.

Bower, S.A. and Bower, G.H. (1976). Asserting Yourself.
Reading, Mass.: Addison-Wesley.
An interesting and practical book about assertiveness,
with examples and exercises.

Cook, M. (1979). Perceiving Others. London: Methuen.
A clear account of basic processes in person perception.

Goffman, E. (1956). The Presentation of Self in Everyday
Life. Edinburgh: Edinburgh University Press.
A famous and highly entertaining account of self-
presentation.

Trower, P., Bryant, B. and Argyle, M. (1978). Social Skills
and Mental Health. London: Methuen.
An account of social skills training with neurotics,
with full details of procedures.

Part three

Organizational Behaviour

8

Organizational Behaviour
R. Payne

Organizational behaviour is concerned with refining our
knowledge about the behaviour of individuals and groups in
organizations and their role in the growth, development and
decline of organizations. These various outcomes are also
determined by the financial, political and technical
environment in which the organization functions, so researchers also study these organization-environment relations
and their consequent impact on the behaviour of individuals
and groups. It is a multi-disciplinary enterprise involving
economics, politics, engineering, management science, systems theory, industrial relations, sociology and psychology.
Given this complexity the student will not be surprised to
discover that our ability to predict accurately what will
happen to individuals, groups and organizations is very
limited. In searching to achieve this 'scientist's stone',
however, a variety of frameworks, conceptual schemes and
even a few facts have emerged which can facilitate our
ability to perceive, interpret and organize this social
complexity. This chapter concentrates on presenting some of
these frameworks.

at are organizations
e?
As with men an organization is:

Like all other organizations
Like some other organizations
Like no other organizations.

In your professional work roles you encounter a unique
organization, like no other organization. In this chapter we
deal with the ways in which organizations are the same as
each other and the ways in which groups of organizations are
similar to each other, but different from other types of
organizations. Apart from its intrinsic interest such information should enable you to appreciate the ways in which
your own organization is unique, and also help you
understand something about why it is the way it is.
We are concerned with work organizations so part of our
definition must be that an organization exists in order to
get work done. They differ in the way they achieve this and
two of the major reasons for the differences are (i) the way

the organization divides its work into different tasks and
(ii) how it co-ordinates those tasks. Most organizations
contain several or many people but according to the present
definition an organization could consist of only one person.
Two different silversmiths may divide the different parts of
their work in different ways and co-ordinate the tasks differently. One might choose to design and make one complete
article at a time. Another might make bowls one week,
handles the next week, assemble them the next week and the
polish and finish them.

They represent two different organization structures.
Similarly, seven people may work together and agree that
each is capable of doing all the tasks that are required to
get the work done and the co-ordination of these tasks will
be left to the whim of the individuals on a day-to-day
basis. Another seven people might have six people each
doing different tasks with one person left to co-ordinate
the work they do. One thing that is well proven is that once
the work of the organization requires more than just a
handful of people there is a strong preference for dividing
work into different tasks and giving some people (managers)
responsibility for supervising and co-ordinating them.

Henry Mintzberg (1979) describes five main ways in which
organizations achieve co-ordination amongst people doing
different tasks. They are:

* mutual adjustment which relies on informal, day-to-day
  communication and agreements;
* direct supervision where one person takes the
  responsibility for ensuring that other people
  satisfactorily complete the tasks they have been
  allocated;
* standardization of work processes: this refers to the
  situation where work has been carefully designed from
  the outset so that the system or technology determines
  what work gets done. As they say in the car industry,
  'the track is the boss'. That is, the operator's work is
  so organized that he can only screw nuts on wheels, or
  only place the front seat in the car, or only spray the
  right side, etc.;
* standardization of work outputs achieves co-ordination
  by specifying the nature and quality of the completed
  task. The salesman must take X orders, the craftsman
  make so many articles. How they do it is not specified,
  but what they must achieve is;
* standardization of skills is what has produced
  professions. Doctors, lawyers, teachers and engineers
  are replaceable parts. In theory anyone with the correct
  training can be substituted for any other without
  creating major difficulties of co-ordination. This
  substitutability is captured in the colloquialism, 'He's
  a real pro!'

Mintzberg proposes that organizations divide activities into five broad categories. At the top of the organization there are people whose main role is to determine the goals and policies of the company. These occupy the 'strategic apex'. Below them are the managers and supervisors who have the responsibility of ensuring that policies and procedures are followed: 'the middle line'. They manage the people who work most directly on the outputs or services of the organization and these Mintzberg describes as the 'operating core'. To the right and left of the middle line, and subordinate to the strategic apex, there are people supporting the main workflow of the organization. There are those in the 'technostructure' whose job is to assist the middle line and the operating core by analysing problems and providing solutions and systems for monitoring and implementing them. They include professional workers such as work study analysts, planning and systems analysts, accountants and personnel analysts. The latter assists this analysing and control process by standardizing skills and rewards. The support staff are not directly connected to the main workflow of the organization but they provide services enabling the rest of the organization to function. They include payroll staff, mailroom, cafeteria, reception, legal advice and research and development. In large organizations any one of these departments may be large enough to have the same five-fold structure so that one gets organizations within organizations.

This very general model is most easily recognized in production organizations but it can also describe the structure of schools, universities or hospitals. In a hospital, however, professionals are the operating core: the doctors, nurses, physiotherapists, occupational therapists and radiologists who provide the treatment and care. Other professionals such as planners and trainers are in the technostructure and basic research scientists or laboratory staff are in the support staff. Thus professionals serve different functions within the same organization. Figure 1 presents a conventional tree diagram of a secondary school structure with Mintzberg's concepts overlaid. Note the small technostructure which is provided mainly by the local authority and the inspectorate. They are, strictly speaking, outside the school and this is indicated by a dotted line.

Building on these two sets of concepts and reviewing a large body of literature, Mintzberg concludes there are five basic types of organizations. They are theoretical abstractions but some of them approximate to the pure types and many larger organizations are hybrids of the types or contain examples of more than one pure type within them. Mintzberg continues his fascination with the number five by offering a pentagon model of the pure types. A simplified version appears in figure 2.

The different forms of co-ordination pull the organization towards different structures. The strategic apex pulls the organization structure upwards to centralized decision making and direct supervision. The name for this

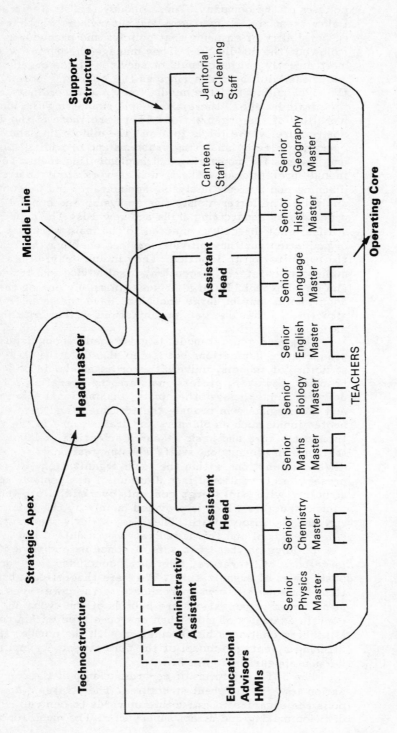

Strategic Apex

Headmaster

Middle Line

Support
Structure

Technostructure

Administrative
Assistant

Educational
Advisors
HMIs

Assistant
Head

Assistant
Head

Senior
Physics
Master

Senior
Chemistry
Master

Senior
Maths
Master

Senior
Biology
Master

Senior
English
Master

Senior
Language
Master

Senior
History
Master

Senior
Geography
Master

Canteen
Staff

Janitorial
& Cleaning
Staff

TEACHERS

Operating Core

HMIs = Her Majesty's Inspectorates

Figure 1

**A tree diagram of a school with Mintzberg's elements of
structure superimposed**

type is 'simple structure' and some of the organizations
that frequently take this form are newer, smaller, autocratic organizations. The technostructure's function is to
standardize and control the work processes so it pulls in
that direction. Mintzberg mixes two metaphors to describe
the resulting structure as a 'machine bureaucracy'. The
bureaucratic element in the metaphor conveys the written
procedures and documents designed to prescribe and control
the system, and the machine element conveys the rationality,
predictability and reliability of the design that has gone
into it. A car or television assembly line plant are good
examples.

The third pull is that exercised by professionals. They
wish to exercise the skills their training has provided and
argue the case for the quality of what they do within the
discretion of their professionalism. This striving for
autonomy is reflected in the small technostructure that
these 'professional bureaucracies' have (see figure 1 for
the school example). Note they are still bureaucratic.
Despite their professionalism, organizational size leads to
greater complexity which requires records to be kept,
minutes taken, standard procedures followed, and professional standards maintained. Hospitals, universities and
craft organizations tend towards this form because the
services they supply need people with complex skills and
professional training. Since they employ so many professionals it is not surprising that their needs and values
influence the way the organization functions.

The fourth group to bid for influence in the design of
the organization is the middle management. They too wish to
be regarded as professionals and have the responsibility for
their production or workflow units. They achieve this only
by agreeing to conform to set standards in the production of
the output or service: that is, standardization of outputs.
The strategic apex co-ordinates the different units and
supplies financial and technical resources but each unit
acquires reasonable autonomy to create the 'divisional
structure'. This is common in conglomerates such as Imperial
Chemical Industries which has separate divisions dealing
with organic chemicals, agriculture, fibres and plastics.
Within each autonomous division, of course, one may find a
different structure: the machine bureaucracy is prevalent,
but if a separate research division exists it may be a
professional bureaucracy or adhocracy.

The support staff represent the final force. Their
preference is to co-ordinate by mutual adjustment and they
are frequently supported in this by the 'operating core'.
This would be the case in the Research Division just mentioned since the operating core would be scientists who are
imbued with values of freedom and innovation. This produces
a structure Mintzberg calls 'adhocracy'. The title attempts
to convey the fact that there are limited formal structures
and that action and responsibility are defined by the
current problem rather than past precedents or personal

Figure 2

Mintzberg's pentagon

From H. Mintzberg (1979), 'The Structuring of Organizations: A synthesis of the research'. Reprinted by permission of Prentice-Hall Inc., Englewood Cliffs, New Jersey.

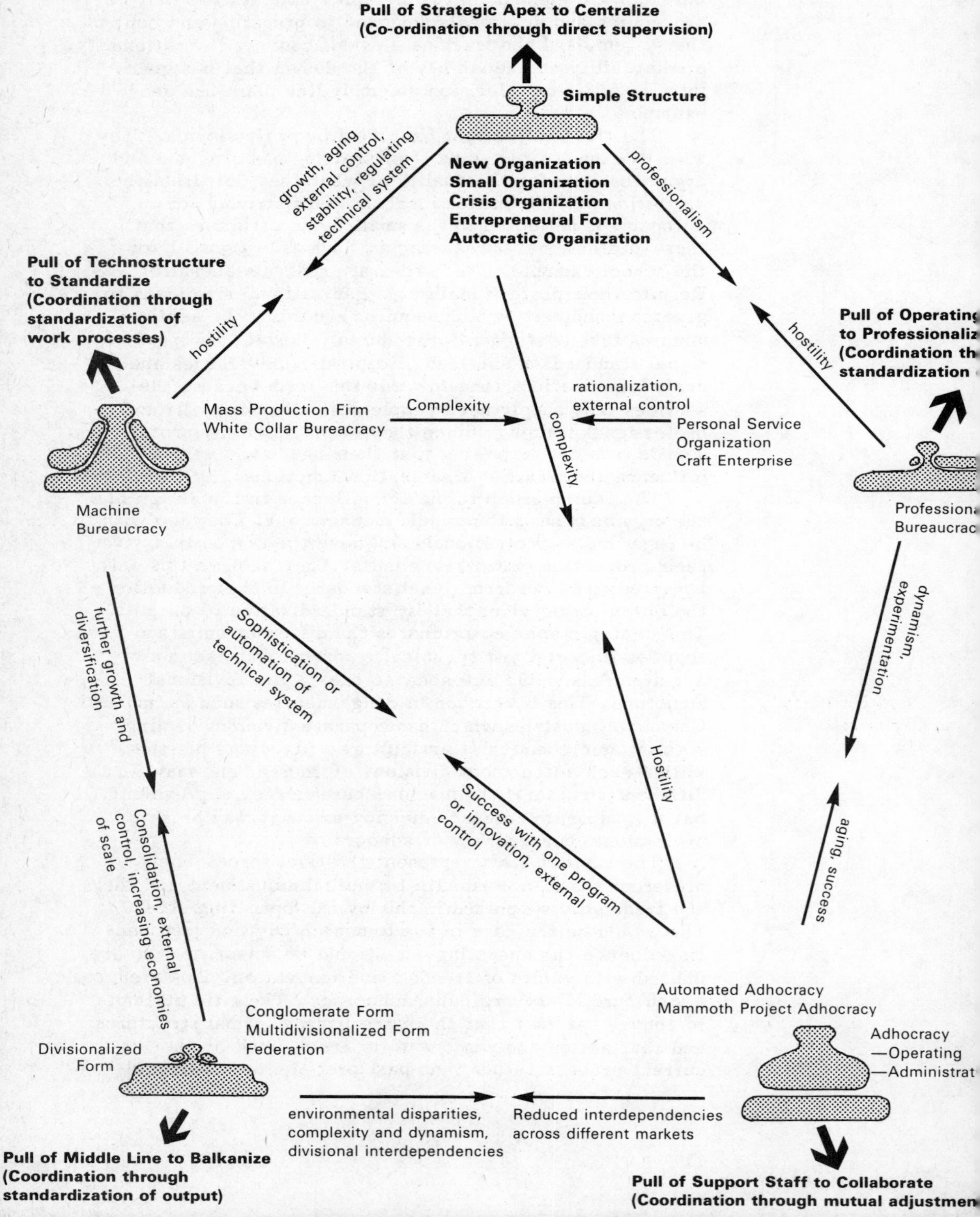

Pull of Strategic Apex to Centralize (Co-ordination through direct supervision)

Simple Structure

**New Organization
Small Organization
Crisis Organization
Entrepreneural Form
Autocratic Organization**

growth, aging, external control, stability, regulating technical system

professionalism

Pull of Technostructure to Standardize (Coordination through standardization of work processes)

hostility

hostility

Pull of Operating to Professionaliz (Coordination th standardization

Mass Production Firm
White Collar Bureacracy

Complexity

complexity

rationalization, external control

Personal Service Organization
Craft Enterprise

Machine Bureaucracy

Profession Bureaucrac

Sophistication or automation of technical system

dynamism, experimentation

further growth and diversification

Consolidation, external control, increasing economies of scale

Success with one program or innovation, external control

Hostility

aging success

Conglomerate Form
Multidivisionalized Form
Federation

Automated Adhocracy
Mammoth Project Adhocracy

Divisionalized Form

Adhocracy
—Operating
—Administrat

environmental disparities, complexity and dynamism, divisional interdependencies

Reduced interdependencies across different markets

Pull of Middle Line to Balkanize (Coordination through standardization of output)

Pull of Support Staff to Collaborate (Coordination through mutual adjustmen

prestige. Large research and development projects sometimes take this form, as do smaller groups of professionals such as advertising organizations. It can also serve the needs of the automated factory. Since automation itself controls and monitors the workflow process, the executives and their technical staff can concentrate on designing new products and the processes to market, produce and distribute them.

Mintzberg's thesis is that all organizations experience these five forces and that in a search for harmony one of the forces becomes dominant at any particular point in the organization's history. The dominant force pulls towards one of the five configurations. As circumstances change, however, the dominant forces change.

The arrows in figure 2 indicate the main forces acting on each type trying to move it towards another type. The results of these forces are the myriad of organizational forms we actually find in the world.

In summary, the very essence of organization is the co-ordination of activities. There appears to be a limited number of ways in which co-ordination is achievable. They are co-ordination by mutual adjustment, direct supervision, standardization of work procedures, standardization of work outputs and standardization of inputs or skills. If any of these forms of co-ordination dominates in an organization they tend to lead to a structure of a particular type. Thus co-ordination by mutual adjustment tends to produce an 'adhocracy'. Direct supervision leads to 'simple structure', whilst standardization of work processes tends to produce the pure 'machine bureaucracy'. The 'divisionalized structure' arises from the desire to co-ordinate by standardizing the quantity and quality of work outputs, whilst standardizing inputs (skills) results in a 'professional bureaucracy'. These are 'pure' types and most organizations contain elements of more than one. We now consider some of the factors that produce these hybrids.

are organizations way they are?

Because people choose, with more or less awareness, to make them that way. It is only too easy to start talking as if organizations make choices, but it is the men and women in them who determine their nature. This is not to say they are totally unconstrained. The fundamental purpose of the organization sets constraints, though organizations doing the same things may organize very differently to do them. A basic distinction is whether the organization manufactures things or provides a service. The latter could include providing treatment, providing education, selling goods or doing research. One reason that this is such a basic choice is that the decision to manufacture almost certainly involves the use of energy, tools and technology to a much greater degree than is likely in providing a service. This area of organizational theory has become known as the 'technological imperative', implying that certain forms of technology force certain kinds of organizational structures.

Quite a lot of empirical research has been done on this subject. Joan Woodward's work (1965) has had a lasting impact. She developed a way of classifying different kinds of production or workflow technology. Note this concept applies to the way products are manufactured, not the nature of the product itself. Woodward constructed a scale of production technology which can be described as ranging along a dimension from simple to complex or, more accurately, as smoothness of production. The least smooth form she called 'unit production'. This is where things are produced one at a time. A craftsman producing hand-made furniture would come into this category, but so would an organization producing ships, railway engines or large, complex computers. Each item is assembled as an individual product. Further along this production technology dimension one moves into mass production, which can be sub-divided into small-batch production such as might characterize a toy manufacturer, and large-batch production which occurs in the motor industry. The most complex and integral form of production technology is in continuous-flow or 'process production', where the product never, or rarely, ceases to be produced. Oil refineries and certain parts of the chemicals industry are good examples.

Table 1 contains an example of the relationship between production technology and an aspect of organizational structure. The table contains information about three different size bands of companies and the average number of people per supervisor in each size band for each of the three product technologies.

Table 1

Number of operators per supervisor classified according to production technology and organizational size
From Woodward (1965); reprinted with permission of Oxford University Press.

Production technology	Size of organization		
	400–500	850–1000	1000–4000
Unit	1:22	1:35	1:26
Mass	1:14	1:14	1:18
Process	1:8	1:8	1:8

In organizations employing unit production technology, the medium-sized organizations (850–1,000 employees) tend to have more employees per supervisor. Regardless of size, unit production employs fewer supervisors than the other two

forms of production technology. This is largely because the
operating core consists of skilled workers whose training
and skill controls the quality of the output: the building
of ships or railway engines is a relevant example. Mass
production technologies are designed to use relatively
unskilled labour and therefore they have to be more closely
supervised. Process production employs the most supervisors
because the technology is complex and mistakes can be very
costly, so the whole process is very closely monitored.
Toxic chemicals and float glass manufacturing illustrate
such processes. In mass production and process production
technologies size appears not to affect the number of
supervisors employed. This latter conclusion from Woodward's data is perhaps the most tenuous (see Hickson et al,
1969).

There is some controversy in the literature as to
whether organizational size or production technology is the
more important determinant of organizational structure. A
large body of work carried out by researchers from the
University of Aston in Birmingham (Pugh and Hickson, 1976;
Pugh and Hinings, 1976) showed organizational size to be a
much stronger predictor of degree of bureaucratization. By
bureaucratization they meant that the organization had
divided its work into specialist roles (high division of
labour) and that co-ordination was achieved by a hierarchical system supported by standardization of procedures which
were formalized into written documents and records. In
Mintzberg's terms it was a machine bureaucracy. Organizational size was correlated with bureaucratization 0.69,
whilst production technology correlated only about 0.30. The
Aston workers did qualify their findings by showing that
technology had a greater impact on the structure at the
bottom of the organization (the operating core). In medium-
sized mass production organizations the operating core would
have more precisely defined jobs and duties than would
operators in a medium sized unit production technology.
However, the roles and role definitions relating to managers
in the two organizations would be very similar.

Summarizing briefly, both the decision to employ a
particular mode of production and the decision to grow
bigger begins to put important constraints on how the
organization should structure and/or organize itself if it
is to succeed. One of Woodward's findings was that organizations which had deviant structures for the technology they
used tended to be the least successful. Other factors
influence the design of the organization, however. Some are
external to the system and some are internal.

External influences on structure
The external ones include the market/clients the organization is trying to serve; the knowledge/technical change that
is occurring in the world; the economic situation resulting
from changes in the availability of resources such as raw
materials and finance; and the political changes resulting

from government legislation. Space prevents a separate
discussion of these, but together they may be construed as
factors which create environmental uncertainty or turbulence
(Metcalfe and McQuillan, 1977). To cope successfully with
such turbulence requires different structures from those
required to survive and develop in a stable and benign
environment. One strategy large corporations adopt is to buy
the suppliers or competitors who may be causing uncertainty.
This diversification also increases the complexity of the
organization so that the divisionalized structure tends to
emerge. One of the general principles for dealing with
environmental complexity is the 'Law of Requisite Variety'
(Ashby, 1956). This states that the variety/complexity
inside a system must be sufficient to match the variety/
complexity of the environment outside the system. Thus the
diversification strategy not only reduces uncertainty but
increases intra-organizational variety which also aids in
coping with turbulence. Less rich organizations cope by
relying much more on their own flexibility and ability to
respond to the uncertainty with new strategies and behaviour. One way they achieve this flexibility and responsiveness is by employing a variety of professional, technical and scientific people, each of whom participates
intimately in the decisions taken within the company. Such
organizations have few rules and regulations. This internal
diversity, however, creates problems of communication and
integration. To achieve co-ordination and integration
special groups are sometimes formed to ensure that the
necessary communication takes place. These 'liaison roles'
(Lawrence and Lorsch, 1967; Chandler and Sayles, 1971) com
to demand special skills and qualities of their own.

A structure specially designed to facilitate co-
ordination in such situations is the 'matrix structure'.
This structure was developed and extensively used by NASA
to complete the US lunar programme. Problems of this scale
do not come neatly packaged by function or department, so
'project groups' were formed which combined specialists from
different functions (e.g. engineering, human factors,
physics, finance). The structure is described as a matrix
because the groups were formed by project and held responsible to the project leader (see table 2) but each member
was also responsible to the head of a functional department.
It is this dual membership which provides the expert back-up
of the function combined with the good communication and
involvement of belonging to a project team. These two responses, the liaison group and the matrix structure, are
variations of the Mintzberg adhocracy. The existence of
these two structures implies that co-ordination by mutual
adjustment sometimes needs some structural support if it is
to succeed in complex environments.

Internal influences on structure
If we turn to Mintzberg's pentagon in figure 2 we can see
some of the forces within the organization which may
influence its structure. These consist of the tensions

le 2

matrix structure

		Functional departments			
		Engineering Head + 7 subs*	Physics Head + 5 subs	Finance Head + 2 subs	Maths Head + 4 subs
	A. leader + 4 members	2		1	1
ject ups	B. leader + 8 members	2	3	1	2
	C. leader + 8 members	1	3	1	3
	D. leader + 6 members	4	1	1	

member of a functional department may be a member of more than one project group.

between the major groups in the organization: the top managers/owners, the professionals in the technostructure and the support structure, and the middle and lower parts of the workflow, the middle line and the operating core. Those in the strategic apex want to maintain as much control as they can, but the technocrats, the middle manager and the professionals in the support structure, fight to increase their autonomy and influence. The technocrats wish to consolidate and automate the successes of the creative research staff, but the latter prefer to continue creating new products and processes. The operating core strive to professionalize their skills and provide better products and/or services to their clients, but the technocrats wish to rationalize and improve what already exists. As Mintzberg says, at any one time there may be harmony amongst these forces, but if the external environment changes the internal environment must respond to it or the organization as a whole will fail. The internal tensions arise again and a new stability emerges through death, amputation, amalgamation or reconciliation.

The professional can now see how he may be caught in any of these cross-fires. The accountant can find himself attached to the apex, the technostructure, the operating core or the middle line. In a hospital the nurse could be in the technostructure, the middle line, the operating core or the support staff. Doctors are trained to diagnose and treat illnesses, teachers to instruct and educate and each progresses in his profession on the basis of his ability in these specific skills. Eventually, however, they become managers, administrators and policy makers with little formal training in these skills. No wonder hierarchical organizations have been accused of promoting people to the point where they reach their level of incompetence (Peter, 1969). This only goes to emphasize the flexibility required of professionals in complex organizations, for the roles they create extend far beyond those for which the professional was originally trained. Indeed, roles provide the link between the broad abstractions so far discussed and the actual behaviour of people at work.

Roles in organizations

The term 'structure' refers to the pattern of offices or positions existing in an organization, and to the nature of the behaviour required of the people filling each of the offices. It is this dramaturgical aspect of structure, the definition of the parts to be played, that leads to the use of 'role' as the central concept. In their work on organizational structure, the Aston group (Pugh and Hickson, 1976) relied heavily on the concept in constructing their major measures, 'role specialization' and 'role formalization', and it is important in other concepts such as 'standardization of procedures' (for roles) and 'configuration' (distribution of roles). A major research project which utilized the concept contains some useful definitions and distinctions (Kahn et al, 1964).

ROLE: the activities and patterns of behaviour that should be performed by the occupant of an office: for example, the nurse must administer drugs and follow the correct procedures in so doing.

ROLE-SET: all other office holders who interact with another office holder, the latter being designated the focal role. Figure 4 illustrates the role-set of a senior occupational therapist in a psychiatric day hospital.

ROLE EXPECTATIONS: the attitudes and beliefs that members of a social system have about what the occupant of any office ought to do; for example, as well as doing their job, teachers are expected to be honest, moral and dedicated to children.

SENT ROLE: the expectations sent to an office holder by other members of his role-set; for example, the head of a department presses a scientist for more research, whilst his colleagues expect him to be a creative theoretician.

RECEIVED ROLE: the role as understood by the occupant based on the expectations sent to him by his role-set; for example, the above-mentioned scientist interprets the message to mean, 'publish as much as you can'.

There may well be a difference between the sent role and the received role. This may be partly due to inadequate information/communication, but can also occur because the receiver, consciously or unconsciously, wishes to see the world in a way which is comfortable or acceptable to him. Cognitive dissonance and perceptual defence are terms used elsewhere in this volume to describe these distorting processes). The disparity may also occur because the role is not clearly specified: small, expanding organizations have often not stopped to clarify who does what and have never written role specifications. Larger organizations are called bureaucracies because they do write rules and they are kept in the 'bureau'. The written word is being used here to delineate the role. We can see from the role-set in figure 3, however, that the senior occupational therapist is at the focus of a disparate set of expectations. Even if all expectations are transmitted accurately (low role ambiguity) they are likely to be in conflict. The psychiatrist may want more group work but the nurses and trainees more individual treatment. Kahn et al defined a number of types of role conflict.

INTER-SENDER CONFLICT: the expectations of two or more role senders are incompatible.

INTER-ROLE CONFLICT: two or more of the roles we occupy are in conflict; for example, manager and trade union representative, worker and father.

INTRA-SENDER CONFLICT: the same role sender has conflicting expectations, for example, increase output and improve quality.

ROLE OVERLOAD: this simply means being unable to meet the legitimate expectations of role-senders.

The fact is, of course, that role-senders also develop illegitimate expectations. This is partly because individuals in organizations are not only concerned with meeting the organization's needs: many are more concerned at meeting their own needs. The ambitious manager may develop all sorts of illegitimate ways round the rules to improve the performance of his department so that he gets promotion and leaves the clearing up to somebody else! On the other hand, we, as the general public, know from bitter personal experience that 'working to rule', the organization's carefully thought out, written down, legalized prescriptions, means inefficiency and frustrations for all. That is, some bending of the rules is actually highly functional for the organization. The universality of this slip between what is and what is supposed to be has been recognized by the concept of 'the informal organization'. The concept of role enables us to see how and why the slippage occurs. More generally the concepts relating to role enable the occupant of an office to analyse why his role is the way it is, and why it is not the way he expected it to be!

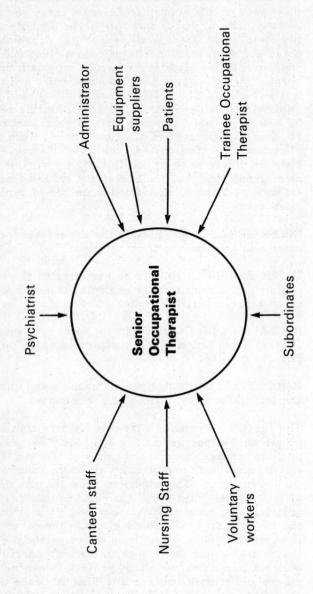

Figure 3

The role-set of a senior occupational therapist in a psychiatric day hospital

In work organizations role-sets do not occur randomly. They
arise from the tasks to be done. In figure 3 we depict one
based on the senior occupational therapist. If we were to
search for others in the hospital setting we would find them
centred on the surgeon's 'firm', on the portering staff, on
the accident department, on the administrative office, on
the junior doctors, and so on. Within each of these role-
sets there would be frequent face-to-face interaction and
high levels of communication. Relationships between them,
however, would be much less clear-cut. In the current jargon
they would be 'loosely-coupled' systems (Weick, 1976)
whereas within a role-set it would be a 'tightly-coupled'
system. It is also obvious that members of one role-set are
often members of another. The surgeon's 'firm' will contain
some of the junior doctors. The surgeon will be on committees guiding policy-making which will also contain members
of the administration. These formally required interactions
open up informal communication channels. It is much quicker,
and perhaps more revealing, to make a direct, informal
approach to another department than to work through the
formal channels where the information has to go up, along,
back, along and then down. It is faster, and perhaps more
satisfying to take the organizational hypotenuse than the
organizational right angle. The fact that many people in
organizations do prefer them is confirmed by studies of how
managers spend their time. About 45 per cent of their time
in communication is spent communicating outside the formal
chain of authority.

These informal 'grapevines' appear everywhere and are
very vigorous. Caplow (1966) studied rumours in war-time
conditions and found they travelled surprisingly quickly and
were often surprisingly accurate. Davis (1953) studied an
organization of 600 people and traced the pattern of various
decisions. For one letter from a customer he found that 68
per cent of the executives received the information but only
three out of the 14 communications passed through the formal
chain of command. Getting things done at all, and certainly
getting them done quickly, depends heavily on knowing and
understanding the nature of the informal organization. It
seems impossible to regulate the behaviour of human beings
by fiat and authority alone. Professional, ideological and
social interests cross the formally defined boundaries and
these reciprocal relationships very quickly begin to twine
themselves around the organization's neatly designed trunk
and branches. As with vines they provide extra support and
bear rich fruits but they sometimes need pruning, or re-
planting. And if they are accidentally uprooted they can
leave the ground exposed, as it may be if a consultant
recommends and installs a different, perhaps more clearly
prescribed structure, but one which breaks up established
relationships. An organization risks relying too heavily on
the informal system which is why formalization and bureaucratization are utilized in the first place, but there is
danger in trying to eliminate it all together. Farris (1979)
contrasts the formal with the informal as in table 3 and it

shows clearly how the informal relies heavily on expectations rather than rules. He quotes several examples of how
the formal organization, or at least the managers representing it, can make use of the informal organization better to
achieve its purposes; for example, by placing newcomers with
people at crucial cross-over points in the informal network
in order to teach them quickly how the system really works.
Effective organizations then allow the formal and informal
to work symbiotically: to sustain and support each other.
Less effective ones fight a battle for the dominance of one
over the other. We can see from Farris' table that the
informal is, in fact, very similar to the co-ordination
principle of mutual adjustment. As Mintzberg's model indicated, all organizations face the problem of resolving the
tensions between the five co-ordinating mechanisms. From th
universality of the informal organization it seems that
adhocracy is never completely defeated. This incipient
victory of adhocracy has an influence on managerial
behaviour as we see in the next section.

The nature of managerial work

The difference between what is specified in a job (role)
description and what actually happens can also be illustrated by the study of how managers actually spend their
time. The classical description of management is that it
involves planning, organizing, co-ordinating and finally
controlling systems and people in order to achieve the goals
outlined in the plans. A relatively small number of researchers have actually studied what managers do and one of the
most influential of these pieces of research has again been
done by Henry Mintzberg (1973). In 1975 Mintzberg compared
folk-lore to fact. The first element of folk-lore he discussed was that the manager is a reflective, systematic
planner.

His own intensive study of five chief executives showed
that only one out of 368 verbal contacts was unrelated to a
specific issue and could be called general planning. A diary
study of 160 British top and middle managers found they
worked for a half hour or more without interruption only
once every two days (Stewart, 1967). Mintzberg concludes
that not only is a manager's work characterized by brevity,
variety and discontinuity but that they actually prefer
action to reflection. Plans, if they exist, are formulated
and re-formulated in the executive's head: they are not
written down and rationally elaborated.

On the other hand, our folk-lore of the modern super-
hero is that the effective executive has no regular duties
to perform. He sits on the Olympian heights waiting the
calls of us lesser mortals. The facts show that he is down
in the valley dealing with the unexpected directly,
encouraging the peasants, negotiating with neighbours, and
even mending the fences.

Executives spend much time meeting important customers
carrying out regular tours round their organizations, and
officiating at rituals and ceremonies. Much of their time is

Table 3

Some contrasts between formal and informal organizations
From Farris (1979): reprinted with permission.

Element	Organization	
	Formal	Informal
Salient goals	Organization's	Individual's
Structural units	Offices/positions	Individual roles
Basis for communication	Offices formally related	Proximity: physical, professional, task social, formal
Basis for power	Legitimate authority	Capacity to satisfy individuals' needs (often through expert or referent power)
Control mechanisms	Rules	Norms (expectations)
Type of hierarchy	Vertical	Lateral

spent scanning the environment for information which can then be passed to their subordinates. This is not 'hard', easily-available information but 'soft', given in confidence or as a favour, but which becomes available only as a result of maintaining regular contacts: informal contacts!

A third piece of conventional wisdom is that senior managers need aggregated information which a formal management information system best provides. Computers have fostered this view as they seemed to be able to make such information up-to-date and easily available. The evidence suggests that managers do not use the information even if it is there. They strongly prefer to rely on meetings and telephone calls. Burns (1954) found managers spent 80 per cent of their time in verbal communication, and Mintzberg 78 per cent. The latter's five managers produced only 25 pieces of mail during the 25 days he investigated them. Only 13 per cent of the mail they received was of specific and immediate use. Managers appear to operate this way because they are future-orientated and their active scanning for hints and gossip is felt to be more useful than detailed understanding of the past. Such behaviour puts a heavy premium on their personal ability to store and sort information. It also makes it difficult for them to transfer their personal images and maps to others in the company.

A related piece of folk-lore is that management is a science and a profession. It is true that the technostructure in large organizations uses mathematical modelling and sophisticated planning and control techniques, but these have little influence on senior managers or even on the managers of the specialists running such facilities. All are still reliant on their intuition and judgement. This is because they manage (i) people and (ii) very complex situations: imagine the problems facing the head of a department of management services in a regional hospital authority who manages 70 professional staff ranging from computer specialists, through work study to behavioural science change agents. That it is correct to give people problems priority over situational problems is reflected in Mintzberg's conclusions about the different roles a manager must perform. These appear diagrammatically in figure 4.

The titles of the ten roles are useful enough not to require further elaboration. The arrows indicate that the organization gives the manager the authority and status to perform the 'interpersonal roles', that this requirement leads him to perform the 'informational roles', and that this forces his involvement in the 'decisional roles'.

Figure 4

The ten roles of the manager
Reprinted by permission of the Harvard Business Review. Exhibit from H. Mintzberg, 'The Manager's Job: Folklore and fact' (July-August, 1975). Copyright ⓒ 1975 by the President and Fellows of Harvard College; all rights reserved.

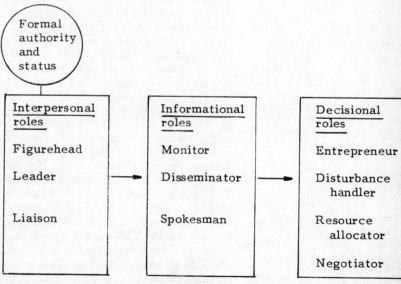

The effective manager is the one who carries out all ten roles but who does so by finding ways to:

* gain control over his time: he tends to be bombarded by others so he must find ways of using these obligations to others to suit his own ends. His only other hope is that people do things for him because of their personal commitment to him. In hierarchical and competitive situations this highly desirable state is often lacking. He may have to be political and devious to achieve his goals;
* some of the time thus gained must be used to determine which issues are really important in the overall picture. This ability has been called the 'helicopter capacity';
* to use the rest of his saved time to ensure that he regularly and systematically shares with colleagues and subordinates his privileged information and how it fits into the images and plans that are guiding his actions.

With this amount of preparation the manager has a good chance of sneaking through the interpersonal barrage that makes up his weekly war. This applies to managers and supervisors at all points in the organization: low, middle or high, in the technostructure or the support structure. For these different positions the task changes in quantity rather than quality, and in the severity of the consequences which result from failure.

Earlier, we reviewed the major forms of organizational structure, the forces which helped to produce them, and the sorts of work they produce for managers and other professional workers. We now wish to examine some of the psychological concepts relevant to understanding the behaviour of people in organizations.

Motivation in organizations

Steers and Porter (1975) distinguish three aspects of motivation:

* what energizes or initiates behaviour?
* what directs or channels the behaviour towards a particular goal or in a particular direction?
* what maintains or sustains the behaviour once it is activated?

The various theories of motivation can be classified under each of these three headings (Hamner and Organ, 1978).

Energizer theories
The most widely known of these is Maslow's (1954) theory of human needs. Simply, men and women are motivated to act in order to satisfy their needs. According to Maslow these needs are arranged in hierarchy of pre-potency. The hierarchical order implies that needs higher up the hierarchy (lower pre-potency) do not motivate behaviour unless there is some degree of satisfaction of the lower-order needs.

Maslow's hierarchy of human needs in order of pre-potency is shown below:

```
                    /\
                   /  \
        Self-actualization
                 /      \
             Autonomy
               /          \
              Ego
             /              \
          Social
           /                  \
        Security
         /                      \
       Physical
      /_____\
```

It is helpful to think of them as following the course of development from infancy to full human maturity. Physical needs refer to food, water, shelter and reproductive needs. Safety needs motivate or direct behaviour when the physiological needs are more or less satisfied or satiated. They force us to seek protection against threat, danger and deprivation. Once we feel this measure of security we are emboldened to seek contact with others in search of friendship, affection and a sense of belonging to an identifiable group. That is to satisfy our social needs. The next set of forces to energize us arises from our need to be valued, liked or esteemed by the groups around us. These are the esteem needs, sometimes called ego needs. Once we have discovered that we compare well with other people we may begin to find that we are not totally happy, either with the standards they set, or with what they actually esteem. We begin to develop our own standards and values which signals the motivating force of our autonomy needs. Provided we achieve sufficient autonomy, and Maslow's view is that many organizations prevent us from achieving it (1965), we may begin to find ourselves driven strongly to develop our talents and potential even to the detriment of the satisfaction of our lower-order needs. The drive to fulfil oneself in this way arises from our self-actualization needs, sometimes called growth needs (Alderfer, 1969). It must be understood that the amount it takes to satisfy any particular need varies enormously across individuals. Gluttons need more food than hermits, risk-takers less security than bankers, extraverts more friends than introverts, the Smiths more cars than the Jones, adventurers more freedom than nuns, artists more fulfilment than executives.

A second energizing theory is proposed by Scott (1966) and is called activation theory. It is a very general theory about how people are energized. High activation occurs as a result of (i) physiological/biochemical differences between people and (ii) the liveliness or demandingness of the environment. The theory states that moderate levels of arousal are the most preferred. Too little and we experience

boredom, too much and we experience anxiety or fear. The
right amount is pleasant and motivating. We are likely to
seek out these conditions again. This takes us to the
question of how behaviour is channelled.

Channeller/director theories

As suggested in the previous paragraph we strive to achieve
situations that have satisfied our needs. Two theories are
relevant. The first is goal-setting theory. Locke (1976) is
its chief proponent. His major point is that individuals
strive to attain that which satisfies them. But the goal,
and not the pleasure from achieving it, is what actually
directs their efforts. Logically and temporarily it comes
prior to the satisfaction. What we value and desire determines the goals we strive for but what directs us are the
goals (intentions) themselves. Locke has done several
experiments showing that setting specific, even difficult
goals leads to more effective performance than setting
general goals such as 'I'll try my best'.

A major management tool incorporating goal-setting is
'management by objectives' (Humble, 1970) or MBO. This is
a systematic technique whereby boss and subordinate agree
on the objectives for the job, agree what would indicate the
successful achievement of the objectives and meet periodically to review if the objectives have been achieved.

A more complex and popular theory with researchers has
been expectancy-instrumentality theory (Vroom, 1964).
Efforts to demonstrate its empirical value have not been
impressive (Campbell and Pritchard, 1976), but it has
intellectual appeal. The theory assumes objects and states
of affairs have differing value, attractiveness or valence.
Valence can be positive (we want it), neutral (we do not
care), negative (we want to avoid it). Our acts lead to
outcomes and in expectancy-instrumentality theory outcomes
are either first-order or second-order. A first-order
outcome enables us to achieve a second-order outcome. For
example, a manager may wish to be promoted (second-order
outcome) and in order to achieve this he works hard,
increases his team's output and is given a merit increase
(first-order outcome). One can see straight away that this
person's strategy depends upon the assumption that increased
performance will lead to promotion. Instrumentality refers
to the strength of this belief: how confident the manager is
that increased performance will lead to promotion. Instrumentality is measured by asking people how certain they are
of this relationship. They can be certain it will, uncertain, or certain it will not. The final concept is expectancy. This refers to the person's subjective beliefs about
the probability of his behaviour leading to the first level
outcome. The person can be 100 per cent certain to totally
unsure. The strength of the person's motivation to proceed
in a particular direction will be a function of these various factors. We are strongly motivated to do something if
we are confident (high expectancy) that the act will lead to

a given outcome (first order) and that this outcome is highly likely (instrumental) to lead to our attaining something we value (second-order valence). Students are likely to work hard for exams if they are confident they can achieve a good result, and are reasonably certain that a good result will lead to the kind of career they have long wanted. Managers will not be motivated if they see no hope of achieving a goal, no matter how certain they are that it will lead to something they dearly want.

Put like this it sounds like a tautology or truism, but it has proved difficult to demonstrate empirically because (i) our success is determined by other factors such as our skill or ability, or the intrusion of unexpected factors; (ii) because it is very difficult for people actually to know what the probabilities connecting instrumentality and expectancy are; and (iii) because real-life behaviour entails several sets of both first- and second-level outcomes making it easy for errors in estimating the probabilities to become compounded.

Nevertheless, the theory highlights some practical aspects of motivation: (i) the organization must provide rewards its employees value: money, fringe benefits, interesting work, security, etc.; (ii) there must be a relation between variations in performance and variations in reward: in many professional/salaried jobs promotion is the only variation in reward; (iii) the organization must make clear what the relationships between effort, performance and rewards are; (iv) the organization must be free to vary the size of rewards sufficiently to encourage people to work harder: some companies employ merit reward systems where extra payment is given solely for higher performance. But sometimes the maximum reward as a percentage of salary may be only three or four per cent which can be so low as to seem demotivating to the dedicated worker.

Maintenance theories of motivation

The most influential maintenance theory has been Herzberg's (1966) two-factor theory. Herzberg set out to understand what it was that gave people satisfaction at work, with the assumption that this would reveal what motivated them to work harder. He proceeded by asking accountants and engineers to describe times when they were dissatisfied and times when they were highly satisfied. Analysis of these interviews showed that these two emotional states were caused by two different sets of conditions.

The things that caused dissatisfaction if they were absent or inadequate were:

* salary or pay;
* relationship with peers;
* job security;
* status;
* company policy;
* working conditions;
* relationship with boss.

176

Herzberg called these hygiene factors. Following the analogy of public health measures, he argued that if they were adequate they would prevent one from becoming dissatisfied, but they would not make one satisfied, just as good sanitation alone will not make one healthy. He argued further that no matter how good the hygiene factors were people would always want more. Most people could always use more money, have better relationships with others, have better working conditions, etc.

The things which people said made themselves satisfied with their work Herzberg called motivators. These were psychological factors such as the interesting nature of the work, feelings of significant achievement, feelings of personal growth and being responsible for worth-while activities. The promotion and recognition that went with these were also motivators. These same findings have been replicated with shop-floor groups, though there is some controversy about whether things are quite as neat as Herzberg's early work showed (cf. House and Wigdor, 1967).

This work has been influential, however, since it played an important part in encouraging organizations to enrich jobs, to make them more complex, more demanding in skill and to increase the degree of control the worker has over his work activities. For example, instead of having each person assemble one part of an electric fire, one could design the job so that each person assembled a complete fire. The principles can extend to allowing workers to set targets and quality standards.

The relevance of the two-factor theory in the present context is that it is interesting work and achievement that sustains high commitment and performance. Pay may get us to work but excitement turns us on once we are there. There is evidence that people low on self-actualization needs do not conform to this pattern. There is also evidence that some people are strongly motivated by money and a good deal of agreement that it has importance for most of us.

Another theory about what maintains our behaviour is social comparison theory. The theory proposes that we compare ourselves with others doing similar work in similar conditions, with similar qualifications and experience, and if the comparison is equitable we continue to sustain our efforts. If the comparison is unfavourable we reduce our input to maintain equity. The skilled coal miner who, when asked why he only attended work four days a week, replied 'because I can't earn enough money in three', may well have been comparing himself with better paid, unskilled car workers. This is quite a good example of why the hygiene factors remain insatiable and why parity arguments are such a powerful force in trade union bargaining. The challenge to the organization is to maintain equity at minimum costs. This means remaining alert to pay rates and working conditions and being flexible in adjusting to changes in them. It also means treating people fairly and equitably.

When we talk about motivating individuals we are usually talking about a change in their behaviour: we want people to work harder, or give a better service, or follow the organization's rules. Learning is defined as a change in behaviour and not surprisingly learning theory has some relevance to understanding behaviour in organizations.

Learning theory and work behaviour

If learning is defined as 'a change in behaviour' we have to ask, 'What causes the behaviour to change?' A common-sense answer might be, 'I decided to do things differently'. 'Why?' would be our next question. The person might reply, 'Because I felt it would be more rewarding to me', or 'Because I would be punished if I didn't'. If we analyse this we can see that learning involves dealing with situations and that depending upon how we behave or respond we may get rewarded or punished: that is, there is an outcome.

Situation ⟶ Behaviour ⟶ Outcome (reward/punishment)

Given we wish people to deal with particular situations and the behaviour is what we want to change, the only things we can manipulate are the outcomes associated with the behaviour. Much research on learning has concentrated on what happens when the outcomes are manipulated in different ways. Two major factors are, first, the nature of the outcome and, second, the frequency with which the behaviour is rewarded/ punished: this is known as the study of schedules of reinforcement.

The nature of outcomes
Four types of outcome are distinguished. Two encourage the behaviour to be repeated and two discourage repetition of the behaviour. Either way behaviour is changed.

1. REINFORCING OR ENCOURAGING OUTCOMES: (i) positive reinforcement: this occurs when the behaviour is followed by a reward which the person likes and wants. The reward encourages the person to repeat the behaviour in the same circumstances or even to generalize the learning by repeating the behaviour in similar circumstances: for example, a worker solves a problem and his superior congratulates him. The solution will be tried again. (ii) Escape learning: by behaving correctly a person escapes being hurt or punished. This is rewarding too and the person is likely to repeat the behaviour: for instance, a worker escapes injury because he was wearing proper safety equipment. This may generalize to his always wearing a seat belt in his car.

2. DISCOURAGING OUTCOMES: (i) expected rewards do not materialize: this is known technically as extinction. A person has got used to being rewarded for a particular behaviour and the rewards cease to be given. Under these conditions the behaviour will eventually cease; for example, under one boss a subordinate is encouraged to read the

technical journals. A new boss never comments on the behaviour so he stops reading. (ii) Punishment occurs when behaviour is followed either by something painful or disliked, such as being publicly told off by one's boss or something one wants is withheld: for example, an expected promotion is not given.

How well the behaviour is learned depends on two things: first, how valued the reward is, or how severe the punishment might be: most people do not deliberately touch a hot iron twice; and second, how frequently the behaviour has been rewarded/punished in the past; that is to say, there are different schedules of reinforcement.

3.   SCHEDULES OF REINFORCEMENT: there are two basic schedules: continuous reinforcement and partial reinforcement. Continuous reinforcement refers to the situation where the behaviour is followed by the same outcome every time the behaviour occurs. In real life this situation very rarely applies. When the conditions are approximated, however, it results in very rapid learning but also in rapid extinction once the reward is withdrawn. This is true unless the behaviour has been rewarded enough for it to become automatic or habitual.

For example, a supervisor can rapidly stop a person making an error if he stands over him, but the error will quickly return unless the behaviour has been overlearned and become a habit. Nurses are carefully watched when preparing drug doses and always punished for mistakes until it does become a habit; and like riding a bike it is probably never extinguished.

Partial reinforcement schedules mean the behaviour is only followed by the outcome some of the time. There are four types, based on whether the rate of reinforcement is fixed or variable, and whether the rate is based on intervals of time or the ratio of reinforced to unreinforced behaviours. Thus fixed interval schedules mean that reinforcement occurs at a fixed time interval: weekly or monthly as does a pay cheque. Fixed-ratio schedules mean that reinforcement is given after every nth response: for example, after every fifth sale is made a saleswoman receives a bonus. The variable schedules mean that the time period or the ratio of responses varies around an average. Research on animals has shown that behaviour which is learned under the variable schedules is more resistant to extinction. One continues the behaviour because one is less sure whether the outcome has really stopped occurring. Gambling behaviour is an obvious example. The reinforcement occurs randomly. The size of the reward varies randomly and the reward immediately follows the behaviour.

An ideal payment schedule based on these ideas might look something like this:

*   a reasonable fixed amount to attract you to the workplace;

* bonus payments based on higher output and paid daily/weekly;
* extra 'lucky draw' tickets, with extra ones being given for exceptional performance, and the lottery being drawn irregularly but including small chances of winning really valuable prizes.

Examples of such systems do exist and these principles for 'shaping' behaviour have been applied to problems such as lateness, absence, under-utilization of public transport, reducing scrap rates, training, and improving the quality of supervisory behaviour. Examples can be found in 'Organizational Behavior Modification' (Luthans and Kreitner, 1975).

Research in this area has been heavily dominated by B. F. Skinner and a statement of his work and the philosophy of behaviourism which has guided it can be found in 'About Behaviorism' (Skinner, 1976). Much of Skinner's research has shown the superiority of positive reinforcement over punishment as a means of controlling and shaping behaviour. The natural world, however, seems to have been uninfluenced by Skinner. It still punishes us viciously, but we learn from the punishments. Many men and women have not heeded Skinner either, the cynics say because giving punishments is rewarding to the punisher. There is doubtless some truth in this. More practically, if we only rely on positively rewarding desired behaviour we have to wait until the behaviour occurs to be able to reward it: it may never do so. So punishment is here to stay, but research indicates that if it has to be used, it is more effective if it is administered immediately following the undesired behaviour, that the person is given an explanation as to why the behaviour is undesirable, that it is administered because of the behaviour and not the person themselves, that it is administered in private to avoid public shaming, that the punishment fits the crime, and that we do not immediately do something nice to the person to make up for the punishment! Such 'model' behaviour leads us to consider a third form of learning: imitation.

Imitation learning
We often change our behaviour by copying someone else. No doubt we learn to model by copying our parents who reward us through the processes of positive and negative reinforcement, but imitative behaviour seems to develop a life of its own. Often we copy behaviour that is not apparently reinforced by outside contingencies. It may be that we just like it, but regardless of its origins it is certainly a major way in which we learn. We can exploit this capacity for ourselves by looking for good models to copy or we can use the process to encourage learning in others. It is a technique frequently used in training (see Goldstein and Sorcher, 1974). Factors which affect the degree of learning through modelling are:

* CHARACTERISTICS OF THE MODEL: they are good at what they do; they are of high status; they control resources desired by the learner; they are similar in age, race and same sex; they are helpful and friendly; the model is rewarded for helping the learner.
* THE PROCESS OF MODELLING: the behaviour is vivid, but detailed; is organized from least to most difficult; is repeated enough for overlearning to occur; avoids irrelevant behaviours; uses several similar models rather than a single model.
* CHARACTERISTICS OF THE LEARNER: is instructed or wants to model; has similar attitudes and background to the model; likes and admires the model; is positively reinforced for modelling.

Our treatment of learning so far has been of a rather mechanical nature: know which carrot to wave when, or how and when to apply a suitable stick and behaviour becomes controllable. Implicit in this sort of learning is the assumption of a standard of desirable behaviour. Otherwise the learner, and the teacher/influencer, would not know when to stop their respective activities. We used the analogy of a machine because machines are designed to behave to specified standards. Recent thinking about human learning and changing human behaviour has raised the important question, how do we learn to change the standards? Argyris and Schon (1974, 1978) call this Model II learning.

Model II learning
One thing that distinguishes man from the animal or physical world is that he can represent, interpret and value it for himself, so that he constructs reality. Man decides whether democracy is good, whether better performances should be better rewarded and whether red is a colour or a communist. In the psychosocial world there are not just facts, but facts and appreciations (Vickers, 1968) of them. Much of the time we are not aware of the nature of our appreciations or value systems and even less aware of how they are influencing our perceptions and the actions we base on them. An everyday example is our injunction to children, 'Don't do as I do; do as I say'. Clearly the message received by the child is not the one we wish to convey; but which message reflects what we really value? Argyris and Schon (1974) refer to the 'do as I say' part of the above statement as the espoused theory. The 'don't do as I do' element they call the theory-in-use; that is, the theory, standards, values which are actually guiding our behaviour.

Based on their research and consultancy Argyris and Schon have concluded that people find it very difficult to understand and to change the principles which are guiding much of their social behaviour. Furthermore, the very principles guiding that behaviour are the ones which prevent the learning of new values or standards. Table 4 contrasts some of the properties of the two models.

Table 4

A comparison of Model I and Model II learning
From Argyris and Schon (1978); 'Organizational Learning: A theory of action perspective'. Addison-Wesley, chapter 6, p. 137, figure 6.1: 'Model II Theory-in-Use'. Reprinted with permission.

Model I		Model II	
Governing variables	Behavioural consequences	Governing variables	Behavioural consequences
1. Define goals and strive to achieve them	Actor is: defensive, competitive, concerned about self, controlling.	1. Striving for valid informatiom	Minimal defensiveness collaborator, facilitator, choice creator
2. To win, not lose	Define, and control what's done	2. Free and informed choice	Trust, risk-taking with support, shared responsibility
3. Minimize generating or expressing negative feeling	Defensive norms (mistrust, conformity, emphasis on diplomacy, power-centred competition)	3. Freely chosen commitment to choices and monitoring of implementation	Norms orientated to learning (open confrontation on difficult issues)
4. Be rational	Low freedom of choice, calculated commitment and calculated risks		

OUTCOME - THINGS STAY AS THEY ARE
EVEN IF THEY APPEAR TO HAVE CHANGED

OUTCOME - NEW, PERHAPS
ORIGINAL PATTERNS EMERGE

One can see that if we start with the goals of being rational and avoiding hurt, of remaining in control and of avoiding defeat, that it becomes painful, irrational and an admission of self-defeat to ask if these guiding principles are wrong! Since we have strived to avoid hurt we have, of course, avoided being punished for using the principles. In other words, our world has reinforced us positively for following them, frequently and over many years. They are habits of thought.

Argyris and Schon (1978) have found them deeply ingrained ones, but ones which many individuals and organizations need to discard if they are to break out of the closed loop such principles create. Sometimes this breaking out occurs naturally as a result of disaster such as bankruptcy, divorce or severe illness. These events force us to recognize the real nature of our theories-in-use and the costs of following them. Since creating crises is hardly a marketable commodity, the main strategy used to develop Model II learning is for the consultant to model the behaviour and force public testing of the effectiveness of current theories in use, and the design and public testing of alternative theories in use. This requires the establishment of open and trusting interpersonal relationships, great skill and integrity on the part of the consultant, and an initial willingness to experiment on the part of the learners. Argyris' (1974) descriptions of his efforts in a major newspaper corporation illustrate the difficulties even when these factors are present. But the evidence that we are victims of our values is incontrovertible: and poignantly emphasized by Vickers (1968). 'The sanest, like the maddest of us, cling like spiders to a self-spun web, obscurely moored in vacancy and fiercely shaken by the winds of change' (Vickers, 1968).

Leadership in Organizations

Whilst there is a large and distinctive body of research on leadership, it overlaps with the study of managerial behaviour and decision making. Its importance lies in its evaluation of the effectiveness of particular styles of managing and in determining which styles are most appropriate in different situations.

The word manager is derived from the French word 'la main' which conveys handling and manipulating. In contrast, 'lead' means heading in a direction with the assumption that others will follow. The essence of leadership then is influencing people to follow your lead. French and Raven (1959) propose people can be influenced in several ways: they call them the bases of social power. They are described below.

*   Coercion or the power to punish.
*   Reward or ability to allocate resources.
*   Authority or legitimate power.
*   Referent power: one is liked or admired.
*   Expert power: the authority of knowledge.

In the numerous studies of leadership behaviour there has been a striking consensus about the major and most frequently used styles. The two most frequently discovered are (i) a concern for people and (ii) a concern for ensuring the task is done and done properly. Some of the labels used to describe these two basic styles are listed below:

People		Tasks
Employee-centred	versus	Production-centred
Consideration structure	versus	Initiation structure
Democratic	versus	Autocratic
Concern for people	versus	Concern for production
Consults, joins	versus	Tells, sells

A less frequently identified aspect of behaviour is one which Cooper (1966) called 'leader's task relevance' and which Bass (1967) called 'task-orientation'. It refers to the leader's personal commitment to and competence in the skills and knowledge inherent in the task. If the leader was a surgeon the commitment would be to surgery, if an academic to scholarship, if a manager to management, if a trade unionist to labour history and union organization. We prefer to call it the technical-professional style because task-centred has been used to describe the production-centred autocratic style too. The parallels between these empirically discovered styles of leadership and the bases of social influence is, we hope, apparent.

All three styles have been shown, and have not been shown, to be related to the effectiveness of the group. It is differences in the situation which cause these variations. Fiedler (1967) was the first to collect a body of empirical research from which he developed his 'contingency model of leadership effectiveness'.

Fiedler measured three aspects of the situation:

* leader-member relations: were they good or poor?
* task structure: highly structured tasks have (i) clearly stated goals, (ii) low variety of tasks, (iii) low requirements for members to co-operate with each other, and (iv) involve decisions where it is easy to verify the success of failure of the decision. Assembly lines are highly structured; governing boards are low.
* leader's position power: the degree of power the leader has by virtue of his formal authority and his informal influence.

These three measures were combined to produce an eight-fold classification of situations. Underlying this classification, however, is the important theoretical proposition that the relationship between leadership style and group effectiveness is moderated by the degree to which the situation allows the leader to influence his team members. Figure 5 shows these eight situations ordered from most to

least favourable in allowing the leader to influence subordinate behaviour. If leader-member relations are good, the
task is highly structured and the leader has strong position
power (situation 1) so he can more easily influence his
group. Beneath each of the eight situations we have indicated by the letters P, N and T the most effective leadership style. This summarizes many studies on many different
kinds of groups. Fiedler only measured person (P) and task-
centred (T) styles of leadership. 'N' refers to situations
where there is no relationship between these leadership
styles and group performance. Task-centred styles are more
effective if the situation is either very favourable or very
unfavourable, and obviously for very different reasons.
People-centred styles are most effective in situations where
it is only moderately easy for the leader to influence team
members. Three practical suggestions arise from this work:

* change the leader's style to match the situational
  demands;
* change the situation to match the leader's style;
* select people to match situations.

There is some debate as to whether leaders can change
their behaviour so easily. One study of UK managers showed
that subordinates were most dissatisfied with managers who
had no consistent style. Fiedler believes behaviour is
difficult to change and favours changing situations, but
others have shown that leaders treat sub-groups of their
teams differently anyway. The inner 'cadre' of a team are
given freedom and respect and the rest, the 'hired-hands',
are treated more formally and autocratically. Freedom to
change both situations and behaviours are also frequently
constrained by organizational rules, practices and the
physical plant. Once again the findings are best used as
general guidelines for understanding particular situations.
A short, up-to-date summary of leadership can be found in
Evans (1979).
The difficulties encountered by lone individuals
(leaders) attempting to create change in large organizations
are universal and are partly responsible for the growth of a
new breed of behavioural science consultants who practise
organization development (OD).

Organizational development

OD has two major strands to its short history. One is the
evidence that management development alone does not improve
an organization. A second is the increasing recognition
that emotional and interpersonal factors play a major role
in determining behaviour. Even well-educated men are not
totally rational, or even reasonable beings. It was also
recognized that understanding feelings, emotions and
attitudes requires different learning and teaching methods
from passing on cognitively based knowledge. In the late

Leader member relations	Good				Poor			
Task structure	structured		unstructured		structured		unstructured	
Leader position	high	low	high	low	high	low	high	low
	1	2	3	4	5	6	7	8
Type of leader most effective in the situation	T	T	N	P	P	N	T	T

Favourable for leader →→→ Unfavourable for leader

Key: P = Person-centered leadership style

T = Task-centered leadership style

N = No relationship

Figure 5

Leadership effectiveness in situations
Adapted from F. E. Fiedler, 'A Theory of Leadership

1940s psychologists, psychiatrists and their students began
to work together in groups to understand what was happening
within the group itself. The distinction between teacher and
student was suspended, people were encouraged to say how
they felt about things and why they felt the way they did.
Group members were pressed to be honest about what other
people's looks, actions or mannerisms did to them. Openness,
honesty, sharing and trust were encouraged in order for
people to understand themselves and the processes going on
within groups. This grew into a world-wide movement with
a vast array of techniques for helping people understand
themselves and others. They range from groups where everybody is nude and which last continuously for 48 hours to
conventional counselling. I do not know of any organizations
which have used the nude marathon but many have used less
risky techniques to develop their social skills and actually
to work with each other to solve personal and interpersonal
problems. The OD consultant's job is to help them to do this
without them damaging each other.

For many years this 'sensitivity-training' or 'process
consultation' was the OD consultant's main role. Experience
taught them, however, that it is not enough merely to get
people talking and listening to each other effectively. The
communication needed to be used to get the organization's
work done more efficiently and effectively. This required an
understanding of the technology and tasks of the organization and the role structures associated with them. Organization development requires creating harmony amongst people,
tasks, technology and structures. It is about helping the
organization to develop its capacities to learn for itself,
to do its own Model II learning. The consultant's job is to
facilitate the processes that lead to this. The truly
successful consultants make themselves redundant forever.

Table 5 outlines an OD programme to illustrate how all
levels and parts of the organization are involved in the
change programme. If it is a success people feel a greater
sense of integration with each other, with the goals of the
company, and have a greater willingness to risk new ven-
tures. It becomes a genuine learning system as opposed to a
set of individual learners.

This is an idealized view. In practice few organizations
have experienced such total OD programmes. It is more typical to find consultants working with parts of the organization or using OD techniques and principles to assist the
implementation of a technological or structural change, such
as job enrichment or decentralization. The author and three
colleagues (Warr et al, 1978) carried out an intervention in
a steel works where we did work with groups from the top
to the bottom of the organization. But the focus was on
problems facing each particular group and ways the group
might go about solving them for themselves. This actually
raised problems which could only be resolved by the Steel
Corporation more generally and there was little success with
these issues, but many local problems were successfully
tackled.

Table 5

A six phase OD programme
From: Blake and Mouton (1978): reprinted with permission of
Gulf Publishing Company.

0.   The top management give the go-ahead.

1.   Learning the language and principles: small groups of
managers from different parts and levels of the company meet
for one week to learn about the programme, its language and
their own leadership styles. An open climate is encouraged.

2.   Team development: actual work teams meet for a week
to work on how they work. Starts with the top group and
works down. Openness, trust encouraged.

3.   Inter-group development: groups and departments that
have important working relationships spend several days
exchanging views of each other and working out plans to
improve relationships. Plans implemented.

4.   Top management team's relationships should now be good
enough to develop an ideal model for the organization. They
spend a week developing the basic ideas and months refining
them.

5.   The ideal strategic model is implemented. Special teams
are set up to achieve this. The consultant may still be
involved.

6.   The strategic model is systematically evaluated and
adjustments planned, made, and evaluated ...

In his fascinating book 'Behind the Front Page', Argyris
(1974) describes how he acted as a consultant to the top
management team of a major American newspaper. He concentrated on developing good interpersonal relationships
amongst the team and worked with them over many months.

Concepts in organizational behaviour: some common threads
This chapter is replete with concepts and labels. Figure 6
attempts to show that there are some common threads amongst
most of those used. There is a progression from left to
right implying that organizations develop certain dominant
forms and patterns of behaviour if the individuals who lead
them make particular assumptions about what motivates men
and women at work. The philosophies of man are taken from
Schein (1965) and follow Maslow's need hierarchy up until
complex man where Schein proposes that men learn and adapt
circumstances force them to change and that motivation is a
complex, ever-altering force. Historically, however, and in
different organizations now, these different philosophies
have been more or less popular. It is proposed in figure 6

that these motivational assumptions lead to different
learning/shaping processes, that they depend on different
bases of social power which lead to different leadership
styles and decision-making procedures. These processes are
most easily supported by structures of particular types.
Once again, they are pure types, but figure 6 is intended to
convey the nature of their purity, the possible combinations
of impure types and to act as a summary of essential facts.

Before finishing, however, let us deal briefly with the
role of professionals in organizations.

Professional roles in organizations

We saw at the beginning of this chapter that professionals
can be located in all parts of the organization's structure
and that this would demand different responses from them. A
general model for examining the nature of these tensions has
been proposed by Gowler and Legge (1980). They use it to
derive a table showing the methods that different professional groups use to deal with the varying demands made upon
them. This table is shown with the addition of trade union
official (table 6). Apart from revealing the variety of professional relationships it shows how professionals need to
change roles within their organization. The scientist who
manages research becomes a professional manager. The trade
union official also becomes a manager of his staff. The
values and methods of these different professions are rarely
in sympathy.

Table 6

The variety of professional roles
From Gowler and Legge (1980): reprinted by permission of
J. Wiley & Sons.

Provider	Values/Beliefs	Core method	Outcomes	User
Scientist	Cognitive/ technical	Experimental	Prediction	Other scien- tists
Doctor	Therapeutic	Diagnostic	Prescrip- tion	Patient
Lawyer	Judicial	Negotiated adjudication	Proscrip- tion	Client
Adminis- trator	Bureaucratic	Organization	Regulation	Employ- ees
Manager	Entrepreneurial	Pragmatic	Transac- tion	Custo- mers
Trade union official	Welfare and protection	Negotiation	Agreements	Member- ship

The stresses in professional roles are further elaborated by Gowler and Legge with the model in figure 7. This

Figure 6

Concepts in organizational behaviour – some common threads

Dominant philosophy of man	Dominant learning process	Dominant basis of social power	Dominant style of leadership	Dominant organiz-ational form
Economic man	→ Punishment and extinction	→ Coercion/ authority	→ Initiation structure (tells/sells)	→ Simple structure/ machine bureaucrac
Social man	→ Reward and avoidance learning	→ Reward	→ Consideration structure (consults)	→ Professional bureaucrac
Self-actualizing man	→ Imitation/ learning	→ Referent/ expert (about facts)	→ Task-orientated (joins)	→ Adhocracy
Complex man	→ Model II Learning/ appreciative behaviour	→ Referent/ expert (about process)	→ Facilitator (unites)	→ ? (Flexitocracy

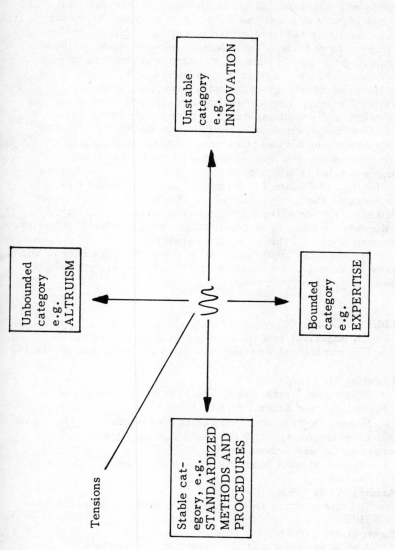

Figure 7

The cruciform effect in professional roles

model describes 'the cruciform effect' to emphasize the competing tensions inherent in professional roles. The tensions can only be resolved by the choices of the professional himself. As figure 7 shows, the professional is expected to provide a service to his clients based on the expertise derived from his training. Professionals as 'worthy' people, however, are expected to demonstrate goodness, kindness and other altruistic behaviour. But this is not clearly defined and takes them outside their expertise. Similarly they are pulled in opposing directions by demands to provide a reliable and comprehensive service requiring the application of standard methods and procedures, and yet as good professionals to be either using or actually creating the latest innovation. In these authors' words, 'The professional is trapped between morality and expediency as he attempts to match the absolutism which vindicates professional authority with the relativism which vindicates professional practice'. How these tensions will appear in specific roles in specific organizations it is not possible to predict. You will have to fill out the boxes for yourself, but the models will help to identify the general nature of the issues you are likely to face. The cruciform effect has a visual similarity to a role-set, of course, and that model would be helpful too in putting bones on this ubiquitous skeleton.

Indeed, the whole chapter is a series of skeletons, but they do constitute an introduction to the anatomy and physiology of organizations.

References

Alderfer, C.P. (1969)
An empirical test of a theory of human needs.
Organizational Behavior and Human Performance, 4, 142-175.

Argyris, C. (1974)
Behind the Front Page. San Francisco: Jossey-Bass.

Argyris, C. and Schon, D.A. (1974)
Theory in Practice: Increasing professional effectiveness. San Francisco: Jossey-Bass.

Argyris, C. and Schon, D.A. (1978)
Organizational Learning. Reading, Mass.: Addison-Wesley.

Ashby, W.R. (1956)
An Introduction to Cybernetics. London: Chapman & Hall.

Bass, B.M. (1967)
Social behavior and the orientation inventory.
Psychological Bulletin, 68, 260-292.

Blake, R.R. and Mouton, J.S. (1978)
The New Managerial Grid. Houston: Gulf Publishing Co.

Burns, T. (1954)
The directions of activity and communication in a departmental and executive group. Human Relations, 7, 73-97.

Campbell, J.P. and Pritchard, R.D. (1976)
Motivation theory in industrial and organizational psychology. In M.D. Dunnette (ed.), Handbook of Industrial and Organizational Psychology. Chicago: Rand McNally.

Caplow, T. (1966)
Rumours in War. In A.H. Rubenstein and C.H. Haberstroth (eds), Some Theories of Organization. Homewood, Ill.: Irwin-Dorsey.

Chandler, M.K. and Sayles, L.R. (1971)
Managing Large Systems. New York: Harper & Row.

Cooper, R.C. (1966)
Leader's task relevance and subordinate behaviour in industrial work groups. Human Relations, 19, 57-84.

Davis, K. (1953)
Management communication and the grapevine. Harvard Business Review, Sept.-Oct., 43-49.

Evans, M.G. (1979)
Leadership. In S. Kerr (ed.), Organizational Behavior. Columbus, Ohio: Grid Publishing.

Farris, G.F. (1979)
The informal organization in strategic decision-making. International Studies of Management and Organization, 9, 131-152.

Fiedler, F.E. (1967)
A Theory of Leadership Effectiveness. New York: McGraw-Hill.

French, J.R.P. Jr and Raven, B. (1959)
The bases of social power. In D. Cartwright (ed.), Studies in Social Power. Ann Arbor, Mich.: Institute for Social Research.

Goldstein, A.P. and Sorcher, M. (1974)
Changing Supervisor Behavior. New York: Pergamon Press.

Gowler, D. and Legge, K. (1980)
Evaluative practices as stressors in occupational settings. In C.L. Cooper and R. Payne (eds), Current Concerns in Occupational Stress. Chichester: Wiley.

Hamner, W.C. and Organ, D.W. (1978)
Organizational Behavior: An applied psychological approach. Dallas: Business Publications Inc.

Herzberg, F. (1966)
Work and the Nature of Man. Cleveland: World Publishing.

Hickson, D.J., Pugh, D.S. and Pheysey, D.C. (1969)
Operations technology and organizational structure: an empirical reappraisal. Administrative Science Quarterly, 378-397.

House, R.J. and Wigdor, L.A. (1967)
Herzberg's dual-factor theory of job satisfaction and motivation: a review of the evidence and a criticism. Personnel Psychology, 10, 368-389.

Humble, J. (1970)
Management by Objectives in Action. London: McGraw-Hill.

Kahn, R.L., Wolfe, D.M., Quinn, R.P., Snoek, J.D. and Rosenthal, R.A. (1964)
Organizational Stress. New York: Wiley.

Lawrence, P.R. and Lorsch, J.W. (1967)
Organization and Environment. Boston: Harvard Business School.

Locke, E.A. (1976)
The nature and causes of job satisfaction. In M.D. Dunnette (ed.) (1976), Handbook of Industrial and Organizational Psychology. Chicago: Rand McNally.

Luthans, F. and Kreitner, R. (1975)
Organizational Behavior Modification. Glenview, Ill.: Scott, Foresman & Co.

Maslow, A.H. (1954)
Motivation and Personality. New York: Harper & Row.

Maslow, A.H. (1965)
Eupsychian Management. Homewood, Ill.: Irwin-Dorsey.

Metcalfe, L. and McQuillan, W. (1977)
Managing turbulence. In P.C. Nystrom and W.H. Starbuck (eds), Prescriptive Models of Organization. Amsterdam: North-Holland Publishing Co.

Mintzberg, H. (1973)
The Nature of Managerial Work. New York: Harper & Row.

Mintzberg, H. (1975)
The manager's job: folklore and fact. Harvard Business Review, July-August, 49-61.

Mintzberg, H. (1979)
The Structuring of Organizations. Englewood Cliffs, NJ: Prentice-Hall.

Peter, L.F. (1969)
The Peter Principle. New York: William Morrow.

Pugh, D.S. and Hickson, D.J. (eds) (1976)
Organizational Structure in its Context. Farnborough: Saxon House/Teakfield Press.

Pugh, D.S. and Hinings, C.R. (1976)
Organization Structure Extensions and Replications. Farnborough: Saxon House.

Schein, E.H. (1965)
Organizational Psychology. Englewood Cliffs, NJ: Prentice-Hall.

Scott, W.E. Jr (1966)
Activation theory and task design. Organizational Behavior and Human Performance, 1, 3-30.

Skinner, B.F. (1976)
About Behaviorism. New York: Vintage Books.

Steers, R. and Porter, L.W. (1975)
Motivation and Work Behavior. New York: McGraw-Hill.

Stewart, R. (1967)
Managers and their Jobs. London: Macmillan.

Vickers, G. (1968)
Value Systems and Social Process. London: Tavistock.

Vroom, V.H. (1964)
Work and Motivation. New York: Wiley.

Warr, P.B., Finemen, S., Nicholson, N. and Payne, R.L.
(1978)
Developing Employee Relations. Farnborough: Saxon
House/Teakfield.

Weick, K.E. (1976)
Educational organizations as loosely coupled systems.
Administrative Science Quarterly, 1-19.

Woodward, J. (1965)
Industrial Organization: Theory and practice. Oxford:
Oxford University Press.

estions

1. Describe the different ways by which organizations
   attempt to achieve co-ordination. Give examples of
   each.
2. What is a matrix organization? When is it likely to be
   used? What are its strengths and weaknesses?
3. What type of organizational structure(s) would you
   expect to find in (i) a medium-sized general hospital;
   (ii) a department store?
4. Illustrate your understanding of the concepts related to
   role-set by analysing the role of student (or any
   suitable variation of that).
5. Compare and contrast the formal versus the informal
   organization. Provide examples from an organization of
   which you are a member.
6. Why do informal organizations develop?
7. What is the cruciform effect? How might it apply to the
   job of social worker (or any suitable variant)?
8. Why is it not possible for organizational psychology to
   make the kind of predictions that the physical sciences
   can make?
9. Imagine you are a newly appointed manager and find your
   workers are not putting in much effort. What would the
   motivational theories of how to energize behaviour
   suggest about changing this situation?
10. What theories of motivation deal with the channelling
    of behaviour? Use one of them to explain/illustrate the
    behaviour of you and your fellow students.
11. Illustrate your understanding of Herzberg's two-factor
    theory by comparing the following jobs: coal miner,
    general medical practitioner and a travelling salesman
    paid partly by commission.
12. What factors enable one person to influence another?
    Which ones would be dominant in (i) a military
    organization; (ii) a college or university?
13. Describe the different ways in which people learn. Do
    some seem to be superior to others? If so, why?
14. What advice would you give to a young manager who asked
    you about how to discipline people?
15. What would be an optimally reinforcing payment system
    according to reinforcement theory? What sorts of jobs
    would it be applicable to? What sorts of jobs would it
    not be applicable to?

16. Why is there no one best leadership style?
17. Describe Fiedler's contingency model of leadership effectiveness.
18. A leader is in octant 8 of Fiedler's contingency model. He is doing badly. What kind of situation is he in and what kind of leadership style is he likely to have? What should be done to make things better?
19. What is organization development and why did it develop as an activity?
20. Compare and contrast stereotypes about managerial roles with what managers actually do.
21. Why might the training of a professional worker fail to prepare him properly for a career in a large organization?
22. Which of the main types of organizational structure most appeals to you personally? Why?
23. What is model II learning? Why is it difficult to get people to do this sort of learning?
24. Can motivational theory help explain why it is difficult to get people to do model II learning?
25. What factors influence the structural characteristics of organizations? Give examples.

Annotated reading

Mintzberg's ideas are only available in his recent book (1979) The Structuring of Organizations. Englewood Cliffs, NJ: Prentice-Hall.

    This is a detailed review and synthesis of a mass of literature on organizations. The first chapter describes the five co-ordinating mechanisms and the last describes the five types of structures and the pentagon model.

Child, J. (1977) Organization: A guide to problems and practice (paperback). New York: Harper & Row.

    A readable and informed account of the meaning of organizational structure. It discusses the choices managers have when faced with designing an organization around the issues of shaping the jobs/roles people do, having tall or flat chains of command, grouping activities by function, product or some mixture, mechanisms for integrating the divisions so created, and how to control the humans working in the system. Child also discusses how to change organizations and the future forms they may need/choose to adopt.

Handy, C. (1976) Understanding Organizations. Harmondswor Penguin.

    This is an extremely well-written and lively book, rich with pertinent examples. The first part introduces basic concepts for understanding organizations: motivation, roles, leadership, power and influence, group processes, structure and politics. The second part applies the concepts to problems such as how to design organizations, how to develop and change them and the working

of the various aspects of organizations as systems
(budgets, communications, computers, bargaining). The
last chapter describes what it is like to be a manager
and the dilemmas they face. The book has a very useful
third section which is a guide to further study for each
of the 12 chapters.

Warr, P.B. (ed.) (1978) Psychology at Work (2nd edn).
Harmondsworth: Penguin.
This book contains 16 chapters, each written by
different authors. It is moderately technical in places,
but much of it is quite understandable to the non-
psychologist. The chapters cover the following topics:
hours of work and the 24-hour cycle, workload and
skilled performance, training, the design of machines
and systems that optimize human performance, accidents,
computers and decision making, selection, interviewing,
negotiation and collective bargaining, leadership,
attitudes and motives, job redesign and employee
participation, work stress, counselling in work
settings, how to change organizations and organizational
systems as psychological environments.

Some journals which cover these subjects but which aim
their content at practitioners and which are widely
available in UK are: Harvard Business Review, Personnel
Review, Personnel Management, Management Today.

Part four

Stress in the Workplace

9

Sources of Stress on Managers at Work
Cary L. Cooper

The complexity of industrial organizational life is increasingly a source of stress for managers. Brummet, Pyle and Flamholtz (1968) suggest that managers are suffering extreme physiological symptoms from stress at work, such as disabling ulcers or coronary heart disease (CHD), which force them to retire prematurely from active work before they have had an opportunity to complete their potential organizational life. These and other stress-related effects (e.g. tension, poor adjustment, etc.) also feed into the family, becoming potential sources of disturbance and thus pervading the whole quality of managerial life. The mental and physical health effects of job stress are not only disruptive influences on the individual managers, but also a 'real' cost to the organization, on whom many individuals depend: a cost which is rarely, if ever, seriously considered either in human or financial terms by organizations, but one which they incur in their day-to-day operations. In order to do something positive about sources of stress on managers at work, it is important to be able to identify them. The success of any effort to minimize stress and maximize job satisfaction will depend on accurate diagnosis, for different stresses will require different action. Any approach to the management of stress in an organization which relied on one particular technique (e.g. OD or job enrichment or TM), without taking into account the differences within work groups or divisions, would be doomed to failure. A recognition of the possible sources of management stress, therefore, may help us to arrive at suggestions of ways to minimize its negative consequences. It was with this in mind that I decided to bring together the research literature in the field of management and organizational stress in a framework that would help to identify sources of managerial satisfaction and stress more clearly.

A survey of the management literature reveals a formidable list of over 40 interacting factors which might be sources of managerial stress and satisfaction: those to be dealt with here were drawn mainly from a wider body of theory and research in a variety of fields; medicine, psychology, management sciences, etc. Additional material has been drawn from exploratory studies carried out by Cooper and Marshall (1978, 1979). Seven major categories of

Figure 1
_____

Seven major categories of stress

SOURCES OF MANAGERIAL   MANIFESTATIONS OF
STRESS (AND SATISFACTION)   MANAGERIAL STRESS

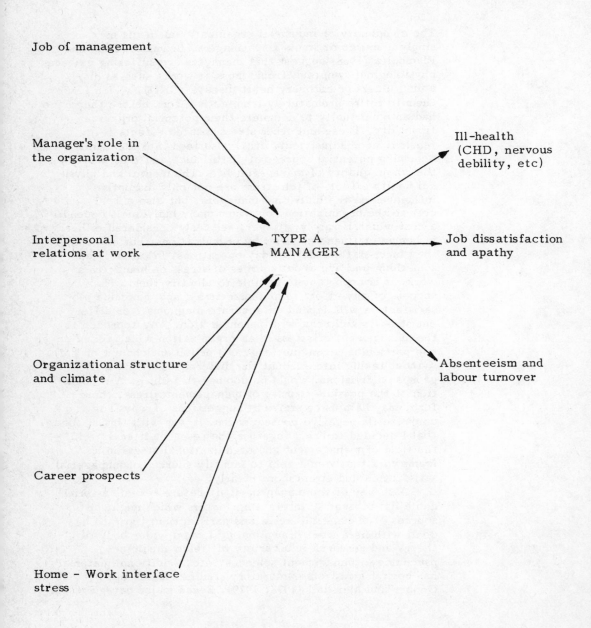

Job of management

Manager's role in
the organization

Interpersonal
relations at work

Organizational structure
and climate

Career prospects

Home – Work interface
stress

TYPE A
MANAGER

Ill–health
(CHD, nervous
debility, etc)

Job dissatisfaction
and apathy

Absenteeism and
labour turnover

stress can be identified. Figure 1 is an attempt to represent these diagramatically: they are dealt with in a natural progression from those related to the job, organization and individual.

Factors intrinsic to the 'job of management' were a first and vital focus of study for early researchers in the field (Stewart, 1976) and 'shop-floor' (as opposed to management) studies are still the main preoccupation. Stress can be caused by too much or too little work, time pressures and deadlines, having too many decisions to make (Sofer, 1970), working conditions, excessive travel, long hours, having to cope with changes at work and the expenses (monetary and career) of making mistakes (Kearns, 1973). It can be seen that every job description includes factors which for some individuals at some time will be a source of pressure.

One of the most important sources of stress for managers is their tendency to work long hours and to take on too much work. Research into work overload has been given substantial empirical attention. French and Caplan (1973) have differentiated overload in terms of quantitative and qualitative overload. Quantitative refers to having 'too much to do', whilst qualitative means work that is 'too difficult'. Miller (1960) has theorized that 'overload' in most systems leads to breakdown, whether we are dealing with single biological cells or managers in organizations. In an early study, French and Caplan (1970) found that objective quantitative overload was strongly linked to cigarette smoking (an important risk factor or symptom of CHD). Persons with more phone calls, office visits, and meetings per given unit of work time were found to smoke significantly more cigarettes than persons with fewer such engagements. In a study of 100 young coronary patients, Russek and Zohman (1958) found that 25 per cent had been working at two jobs and an additional 45 per cent had worked at jobs which required (due to work overload) 60 or more hours per week. They add that, although prolonged emotional strain preceded the attack in 91 per cent of the cases, similar stress was only observed in 20 per cent of the controls. Breslow and Buell (1960) have also reported findings which support a relationship between hours of work and death from coronary disease. In an investigation of mortality rates of men in California, they observed that workers in light industry under the age of 45, who are on the job more than 48 hours a week, have twice the risk of death from CHD compared with similar workers working 40 or under hours a week. Another substantial investigation on quantitative work load was carried out by Margolis et al (1974) on a representative national US sample of 1,496 employed persons of 16 years of age or older. They found that overload was significantly related to a number of symptoms or indicators of stress: escapist drinking, absenteeism from work, low motivation to work, lowered self-esteem, and an absence of

suggestions to employers. The results from these and other
studies (Cooper and Marshall, 1978, 1979) are relatively
consistent and indicate that this factor is indeed a potential source of managerial stress that adversely affects both
health and job satisfaction.

There is also some evidence that 'qualitative' overload
is a source of stress for managers. French et al (1965)
looked at qualitative work overload in a large university.
They used questionnaires, interviews and medical examinations to obtain data on risk factors associated with CHD for
122 university administrators and professors. The greater
the 'quality' of work expected of the professor, the lower
the self-esteem. Several other studies have reported an
association of qualitative work overload with cholesterol
level, including one concerning a tax deadline for accountants (Friedman et al, 1958), and another on medical students
performing a medical examination under observation (Dreyfus
and Czackes, 1959). French and Caplan (1973) summarize
this research by suggesting that both qualitative and
quantitative overload produce at least nine different
symptoms of psychological and physical strain: job satisfaction, job tension, lower self-esteem, threat, embarrass-
ment, high cholesterol levels, increased heart rate, skin
resistance, and more smoking. In analysing these data,
however, one cannot ignore the vital interactive relationship of the job and manager: objective work overload, for
example, should not be viewed in isolation but relative to
the manager's capacities and personality.

Such caution is sanctioned by much of the American and
some UK literature which shows that overload is not always
externally imposed. Many managers (perhaps certain personality types more than others) react to overload by working
longer hours. For example, in reports on an American study
(Uris, 1972), it was found that 45 per cent of the executives investigated worked all day, in the evenings, and at
weekends, and that a further 37 per cent kept weekends free
but worked extra hours in the evenings. In many companies
this type of behaviour has become a norm to which everyone
feels they must adhere.

Manager's role in the organization
Another major source of managerial stress is associated with
a person's role at work. A great deal of research in this
area has concentrated on role ambiguity and role conflict,
following the seminal investigations of the Survey Research
Center of the University of Michigan (Kahn et al, 1964).

Role ambiguity exists when a manager has inadequate
information about his work role: that is, where there is
lack of clarity about the work objectives associated with
the role, about work colleagues' expectations of the work
role and about the scope and responsibility of the job.
Kahn et al (1964) found in their study that men who suffered
from role ambiguity experienced lower job satisfaction,
higher job-related tension, greater futility, and lower

self-confidence. French and Caplan (1970) found, in a sample of 205 volunteer engineers, scientists, and administrators at one of NASA's bases, that role ambiguity was significantly related to low job satisfaction and to feelings of job-related threat to one's mental and physical well-being. This also related to indicators of physiological strain such as increased blood pressure and pulse rates. Margolis et al (1974) also found a number of significant relationships between symptoms or indicators of physical and mental ill health with role ambiguity in their representative national sample (n = 1,496). The stress indicators related to role ambiguity were depressed mood, lowered self-esteem, life dissatisfaction, low motivation to work, and intention to leave job.

Role conflict exists when an individual in a particular work role is torn by conflicting job demands or doing things he really does not want to do or does not think are part of the job specification. The most frequent manifestation of this is when a manager is caught between two groups of people who demand different kinds of behaviour or expect that the job should entail different functions. Kahn et al (1964) found that men who suffered more role conflict had lower job satisfaction and higher job-related tension. It is interesting to note that they also found that the greater the power or authority of the people 'sending' the conflicting role messages, the more role conflict produced job dissatisfaction. This was related to physiological strain as well, as the NASA study (French and Caplan, 1970) illustrates. They telemetered and recorded the heart rate of 22 men for a two-hour period while they were at work in their offices. They found that the mean heart rate for an individual was strongly related to his report of role conflict. A larger and medically more sophisticated study by Shirom et al (1973) found similar results. Their research is of particular interest as it tries to look simultaneously at a wide variety of potential work stresses. They collected data on 762 male kibbutz members aged 30 and above, drawn from 13 kibbutzim throughout Israel. They examined the relationships between CHD, abnormal electro-cardiographic readings, CHD risk factors (systolic blood pressure, pulse rate, serum cholesterol levels, etc.), and potential sources of job stress (work overload, role ambiguity, role conflict, and lack of physical activity). Their data was broken down by occupational groups: agricultural workers, factory groups, craftsmen, and managers. It was found that there was a significant relationship between role conflict and CHD (specifically, abnormal electro-cardiographic readings), but for the managers only. In fact, as we move down the ladder from occupations requiring great physical exertions (e.g. agriculture) to those requiring least (e.g. managerial), the greater was the relationship between role ambiguity/conflict and abnormal electro-cardiographic findings. It was also found that as we go from occupations involving excessive physical activities to those with less such activity, CHD increased significantly. Drawing together these data, it might be hypothesized that managerial and professional occupations are more likely to suffer occupational stress from role-related stress and other interpersonal dynamics and less from the physical conditions of work.

Another aspect of role conflict was examined by Mettlin and Woelfel (1974). They measured three aspects of inter-personal influence - discrepancy between influences, level of influence, and number of influences - in a study of the educational and occupational aspirations of high school students. Using the Langer Stress Symptom questionnaire as their index of stress, they found that the more extensive and diverse an individual's interpersonal communications network, the more stress symptoms he showed. A manager's role which is at a boundary - that is, between departments or between the company and the outside world - is, by definition, one of extensive communication nets and of high role conflict. Kahn et al (1964) suggest that such a posi-tion is potentially highly stressful. Margolis and Kroes (1974) found, for instance, that foremen (high role conflict-prone job) are seven times as likely to develop ulcers as shopfloor workers.

Another important potential source of stress associated with a manager's role is 'responsibility for people'. One can differentiate here between 'responsibility for people' and 'responsibility for things' (equipment, budgets, etc.). Wardwell et al (1964) found that responsibility for people was significantly more likely to lead to CHD than responsi-bility for things. Increased responsibility for people frequently means that one has to spend more time interacting with others, attending meetings, working alone and, in consequence, as in the NASA study (French and Caplan, 1970) more time in trying to meet deadline pressures and sched-ules. Pincherle (1972) also found this in the UK study of 2,000 executives attending a medical centre for a check-up. Of the 1,200 managers sent by their companies for their annual examination, there was evidence of physical stress being linked to age and level of responsibility; the older and more responsible the executive, the greater the pro-bability of the presence of CHD risk factors or symptoms. French and Caplan support this: in their NASA study of managerial and professional workers, they found that res-ponsibility for people was significantly related to heavy smoking, raised diastolic blood pressure, and increased serum cholesterol levels; the more the individual had responsibility for 'things' as opposed to 'people', the lower were each of these CHD risk factors.

Having too little responsibility (Brook, 1973), lack of participation in decision making, lack of managerial sup-port, having to keep up with increasing standards of per-formance and coping with rapid technological change are other potential role stressors mentioned repeatedly in the literature but with little supportive research evidence. Variations between organizational structures determine the differential distribution of these factors across differing occupational groups. Kay (1974) does suggest, however, that (independent of employing organizations) some pressures are to be found more at middle than at other management levels. He depicts today's middle manager as being particularly hard pressed:

*   by pay compression, as the salaries of new recruits increase;
*   by job insecurity: they are particularly vulnerable to redundancy or involuntary early retirement;
*   by having little real authority at their high levels of responsibility;
*   by feeling 'boxed' in.

erpersonal
ations

A third major potential source of managerial stress has to do with the nature of relationships with one's boss, sub-ordinates, and colleagues. Behavioural scientists have long suggested that good relationships between members of a work group are a central factor in individual and organizational health (Cooper, 1980). Nevertheless, very little research work has been done in this area either to support or negate this hypothesis. French and Caplan (1973) define poor relations as 'those which include low trust, low supportiveness, and low interest in listening to and trying to deal with problems that confront the organizational member'. The most notable studies in this area are by Kahn et al (1964), French and Caplan (1970) and Buck (1972). Both the Kahn et al (1964) and the French and Caplan studies came to roughly the same conclusions, namely that mistrust of persons one works with is positively related to high role ambiguity, which leads to inadequate communications between people and to 'psychological strain in the form of low job satisfaction and to feelings of job-related threat to one's well-being'.

Relationships with boss
Buck (1972) focussed on the attitude and relationship of workers and managers to their immediate boss using Fleishman's leadership questionnaire on consideration and initiating structure. The consideration factor was associated with behaviour indicative of friendship, mutual trust, respect and a certain warmth between boss and subordinate. He found that those managers who felt that their boss was low on 'consideration' reported feeling more job pressure. Managers who were under pressure reported that their boss did not give them criticism in a helpful way, played favourites with subordinates, 'pulled rank' and took advantage of them whenever they got a chance. Buck concludes that the 'considerate behaviour of superiors appears to have contributed significantly inversely to feelings of job pressure'.

Relationships with subordinates

Officially, one of the most critical functions of a manager is his supervision of other people's work. It has long been accepted that an 'inability to delegate' might be a problem, but now a new potential source of stress is being introduced in the manager's interpersonal skills: he must learn to 'manage by participation'. Donaldson and Gowler (1975) point to the factors which may make today's zealous emphasis on participation a cause of resentment, anxiety and stress for the manager concerned:

* mismatch of formal and actual power;
* the manager may well resent the erosion of his formal role and authority (and the loss of status and rewards);
* he may be subject to irreconcilable pressures: for example, to be both participative and to achieve high production;
* his subordinates may refuse to participate.

Particularly for those with technological and scientific backgrounds (a 'things orientation'), relationships with subordinates can be a low priority (seen as 'trivial', 'petty', time consuming and an impediment to doing a job well) and one would expect their interactions to be more a source of stress than those of 'people-orientated' managers.

Relationships with colleagues

Besides the obvious factors of office politics and colleagues' rivalry we find another element here: stress can be caused not only by the pressure of poor relationships but also by its opposite: a lack of adequate social support in difficult situations (Lazarus, 1966). At highly competitive managerial levels, it is likely that problem sharing is inhibited for fear of appearing weak; and much of the (American) literature particularly mentions the isolated life of the top executive as an added source of strain (see Cooper and Marshall, 1978, for an extensive bibliography on this).

Morris (1975) encompasses this whole area of relationships in one model: what he calls the 'cross of relationships'. While he acknowledges the differences between relationships on two continua - one axis extends from colleagues to users and the other intersecting axis from senior to junior managers - he feels that the focal manager must bring all four into 'dynamic balance' in order to be able to deal with the stress of his position. Morris' suggestion seems 'only sensible' when we see how much of his work time the manager spends with other people. In a research programme to find out exactly what managers do, Mintzberg (1973) showed just how much of their time is spent in interaction. In an intensive study of a small sample of chief executives he found that in a large organization a mere 22 per cent of time was spent in desk work sessions, the rest being taken up by telephone calls (6 per cent), scheduled meetings (59 per cent), unscheduled meetings (10 per cent) and other activities (3 per cent). In small organizations basic desk work played a larger part (52 per cent), but nearly 40 per cent was still devoted to face-to-face contacts of one kind or another.

reer prospects

Two major clusters of potential managerial stressors can be identified in this area:

* lack of job security: fear of redundancy, obsolescence or early retirement, etc;
* status incongruity: under- or over-promotion, frustration at having reached one's career ceiling, etc.

For many managers their career progression is of overriding importance: by promotion they earn not only money but also status and the new job challenge for which they strive. Typically, in the early years at work, this striving and the aptitude to come to terms quickly with a rapidly changing environment is fostered and suitably rewarded by the company. Career progression is, perhaps, a problem by its very nature. For example, Sofer (1970) found that many of his sample believed that 'luck' and 'being in the right place at the right time' play a major role.

At middle age, and usually middle management levels, one's career becomes more problematic and most executives find their progress slowed, if not actually stopped. Job opportunities become fewer, those jobs that are available take longer to master, past (mistaken?) decisions cannot be revoked, old knowledge and methods become obsolete, energies may be flagging or demanded by the family, and there is the 'press' of fresh young recruits to face in competition. Both Levinson (1973) and Constandse (1972) - the second of these refers to this phase as the 'male menopause' - depict the manager as suffering these fears and disappointments in 'silent isolation' from his family and work colleagues.

The fear of demotion or obsolescence can be strong for those who know they have reached their 'career ceiling': and most will inevitably suffer some erosion of status before they finally retire. Goffman (1952), extrapolating from a technique employed in the con-game, 'cooling the mark out', suggests that the company should bear some of the responsibility for taking the sting out of this (felt) failure experience.

From the company perspective, on the other hand, McMurray (1973) puts the case for not promoting a manager to a higher position if there is doubt that he can fill it. In a syndrome he labels 'the executive neurosis', he describes the over-promoted manager as grossly overworking to keep down a top job and at the same time hiding his insecurity: he points to the consequences of this for his work performance and the company. Age is no longer revered as it was; it is becoming a 'young man's world'. The rapidity with which society is developing (technologically, economically, and socially) is likely to mean that individuals will now need to change career during their working life (as companies and products are having to do). Such trends breed uncertainty and research suggests that older workers look for stability (Sleeper, 1975). Unless managers adapt their expectations to suit new circumstances 'career development' stress, especially in later life, is likely to become an increasingly common experience.

Organizational structure and climate

A fifth potential source of managerial stress is simply 'being in the organization' and the threat to an individual's freedom, autonomy, and identity this poses. Problem areas, such as little or no participation in the decision-making process, no sense of belonging, lack of effective consultation, poor communications, restrictions on behaviour, and office politics, are some of those with the most impact here. An increasing number of research investigations are being conducted in this area, particularly into the effect of employee participation in the work place. This research development is contemporaneous with a growing movement in North America and in the EEC countries of work participation programmes, involving autonomous work groups, worker directors, and a greater sharing of the decision-making process throughout the organization. The early work on participation was in terms of its effect on production and attitudes of workers. For example, Coch and French (1948) examined the degrees of participation in a sewing factory. They found that the greater the participation, the higher was the productivity, the greater the job satisfaction, the lower the turnover and the better the relationship between boss and subordinate. These findings were later supported by a field experiment in a footwear factory in Southern Norway where greater participation led to significantly more favourable attitudes by workers towards management and more involvement in their jobs (French et al, 1960).

The research more relevant to our interests here, however, is the recent work on lack of participation and stress-related disease. In the NASA study (French and Caplan, 1970), for example, they found that managers and other professional workers who reported greater opportunities for participation in decision making reported significantly greater job satisfaction, low job-related feelings of threat, and higher feelings of self-esteem. Buck (1972) found that both managers and workers who felt 'under pressure' most, reported that their bosses 'always ruled with an iron hand and rarely tried out new ideas or allowed participation in decision making'. Managers who were under stress also reported that their bosses never let the persons under them do their work in the way they thought best. Margolis et al (1974) found that non-participation at work, among a national representative sample of over 1,400 workers, was the most consistent and significant predictor or indicator of strain and job-related stress. They found that non-participation was significantly related to the following health risk factors: overall poor physical health, escapist drinking, depressed mood, low self-esteem, low life satisfaction, low job satisfaction, low motivation to work, intention to leave job, and absenteeism from work. Kasl (1973) also found that low job satisfaction was related to non-participation in decision making, inability to provide feedback to supervisors, and lack of recognition for good performance; and that poor mental health was linked to close supervision and no autonomy at work (Quinn et al, 1971). Neff (1968) has highlighted the importance of lack of participation and involvement by suggesting that 'mental health at work is to a large extent a function of the degree to which output is under the control of the individual worker'. To summarize, research seems to indicate that greater participation leads to lower staff turnover and higher productivity; and that when participation is absent lower job satisfaction and higher levels of physical and mental health risks may result.

me-work interface esses

The sixth 'source' of managerial stress is more of a 'catch-all' for all those interfaces between life outside and life inside the organization that might put pressure on the manager: family problems (Pahl and Pahl, 1971), life crises (Dohrenwend and Dohrenwend, 1974), financial difficulties, conflict of personal beliefs with those of the company, and the conflict of company with family demands (Cooper, 1981).

The area which has received most research interest here is that of the manager's relationship with his wife and family. (It is widely agreed that managers have little time for 'outside activities' apart from their families. Writers who have examined their effects on the local community (cf. Packard, 1975) have pointed to the disruptive effects of the executive's lack of involvement.) The manager has two main problems vis-à-vis his family:

*   the first is that of 'time-management' and 'commitment-management'. Not only does his busy life leave him few resources with which to cope with other people's needs, but in order to do his job well the manager usually also needs support from others to cope with the 'background' details of house management, etc., to relieve stress when possible, and to maintain contact with the outside world;
*   the second, often a result of the first, is the spill-over of crises or stresses in one system which affect the other.

As these two are inseparable we now go on to discuss them together.

P

Marriage patterns

The 'arrangement' the manager comes to with his wife is of
vital importance to both problem areas. Pahl and Pahl (1971)
found that the majority of wives in their middle-class sample saw their role in relation to their husband's job as a
supportive, domestic one; all said that they derived their
sense of security from their husbands. Barber (1976),
interviewing five directors' wives, finds similar attitudes.
Gowler and Legge (1975) have dubbed this bond 'the hidden
contract', in which the wife agrees to act as a 'support
team' so that her husband can fill the demanding job to
which he aspires. Handy (1978) supports the idea that this
is 'typical' and that it is the path to career success for
the manager concerned. Based on individual psychometric
data, he describes a number of possible marriage-role
combinations. In his sample of top British executives (in
mid-career) and their wives, he found that the most frequent
pattern (about half the 22 couples interviewed) was the
'thrusting male-caring female'. This he depicts as highly
role segregated with the emphasis on 'separation', 'sil-
ence', and complementary activities. Historically, both the
company and the manager have reaped benefits from maintaining the segregation of work and home implicit in this
pattern. The company thus legitimates its demand for a
constant work performance from its employee, no matter wha
his home situation, and the manager is free to pursue his
career but keeps a 'safe haven' to which he can return to
relax and recuperate. The second and most frequent combination was 'involved-involved': a dual career pattern, with
the emphasis on complete sharing. This, while potentially
extremely fulfilling for both parties, requires energy
inputs which might well prove so excessive that none of the
roles involved is fulfilled successfully.

It is unlikely that the patterns described above are
negotiated explicitly or that in the long term they are
'in balance'. Major factors in their continuing evolution
are the work and family demands of particular life stages.
A recent report (Beattie et al, 1974), for example, highlights the difficult situation of the young executive who,
in order to build up his career, must devote a great deal of
time and energy to his job just when his young housebound
wife, with small children, is also making pressing demands.
The report suggests that the executive fights to maintain
the distance between his wife and the organization, so that
she is not in a position to evaluate the choices he has to
make; paradoxically, he does so at a time when he is most
in need of sympathy and understanding. Guest and Williams
(1973) examined the complete career cycle in similar terms,
pointing out how the demands of the different systems change
over time. The addition of role-disposition and personality-
disposition variations to their 'equations' would, however,
make them even more valuable.

Mobility

Home conflicts become particularly critical in relation to managerial relocation and mobility. Much of the literature on this topic comes from the United States where mobility is much more a part of the national character than in the UK (Pierson, 1972), but there is reason to believe that here, too, it is an increasingly common phenomenon.

At an individual level the effects of mobility on the manager's wife and family have been studied (Cooper and Marshall, 1978). Researchers agree that whether she is willing to move or not, the wife bears the brunt of relocations, and they conclude that most husbands do not appreciate what this involves. American writers point to signs that wives are suffering and becoming less co-operative. Immundo (1974) hypothesizes that increasing divorce rates are seen as the upwardly aspiring manager races ahead of his socially unskilled, 'stay-at-home' wife. Seidenberg (1973) comments on the rise in the ratio of female to male alcoholics in the United States from 1:5 in 1962 to 1:2 in 1973 and asks the question, 'Do corporate wives have souls?' Descriptive accounts of the frustrations and loneliness of being a 'corporate wife' in the US and UK proliferate. Increasing teenage delinquency and violence is also laid at the door of the mobile manager and the society which he has created.

Constant moving can have profound effects on the life style of the people concerned: particularly on their relationships with others. Staying only two years or so in one place, mobile families do not have time to develop close ties with the local community. Immundo (1974) talks of the 'mobility syndrome', a way of behaving geared to developing only temporary relationships. Packard (1975) describes ways in which individuals react to the type of fragmenting society this creates: for example, treating everything as if it is temporary, being indifferent to local community amenities and organizations, living for the 'present' and becoming adept at 'instant gregariousness'. He goes on to point out the likely consequences for local communities, the nation, and the rootless people involved.

Pahl and Pahl (1971) suggest that the British reaction is, characteristically, more reserved and that many mobiles retreat into their nuclear family. Managers, particularly, do not become involved in local affairs due both to lack of time and to an appreciation that they are only 'short-stay' inhabitants. Their wives find participation easier (especially in a mobile rather than a static area) and a recent survey (Middle Class Housing Estate Study, 1975) suggested that, for some, involvement is a necessity to compensate for their husband's ambitions and career involvement which keep him away from home. From the company's point of view, the way in which a wife does adjust to her new environment can affect her husband's work performance. Guest and Williams (1973) illustrate this by an example of a major

international company who, on surveying 1,800 of their
executives in 70 countries, concluded that the two most
important influences on overall satisfaction with the
overseas assignment were the job itself and, more
importantly, the executive's wife's adjustment to the
foreign environment.

The Type A manager
Sources of pressure at work evoke different reactions from
different managers. Some are better able to cope with these
stressors than others; they adapt their behaviour in a way
that meets the environmental challenge. On the other hand,
some managers are psychologically predisposed to stress:
that is, they are unable to cope or adapt to the stress-
provoking situations. Many factors may contribute to these
differences: personality, motivation, being able or ill-
equipped to deal with problems in a particular area of
expertise, fluctuations in abilities (particularly with
age), insight into one's own motivations and weaknesses,
etc. It would be useful to examine, therefore, those
characteristics of the individual that research evidence
indicates are predisposers to stress. Most of the research
in this area has focussed on personality and behavioural
differences between high and low stressed individuals.

The major research approach to individual stress
differences began with the work of Friedman and Rosenman
(Rosenman et al, 1964, 1966; Friedman, 1969) in the early
1960s and developed later showing a relationship between
behavioural patterns and the prevalence of CHD. They found
that individuals manifesting certain behavioural traits were
significantly more at risk to CHD. These individuals were
later referred to as the 'coronary-prone behaviour pattern
Type A' as distinct from Type B (low risk of CHD). Type
A was found to be the overt behavioural syndrome of style
of living characterized by 'extreme of competitiveness,
striving for achievement, aggressiveness, haste, impatience,
restlessness, hyperalertness, explosiveness of speech,
tenseness of facial musculature and feelings of being under
pressure of time and under the challenge of responsibility'.
It was suggested that 'people having this particular behavioural pattern were often so deeply involved and committed to their work that other aspects of their lives were
relatively neglected' (Jenkins, 1971). In the early studies,
persons were designated as Type A or Type B on the basis
of clinical judgements of doctors and psychologists or peer
ratings. These studies found higher incidence of CHD among
Type A than Type B. Many of the inherent methodological
weaknesses of this approach were overcome by the classic
Western Collaborative Group Study (Rosenman et al, 1964,
1966). It was a prospective (as opposed to the earlier
retrospective studies) national sample of over 3,400 men
free of CHD. All these men were rated Type A or B by
psychiatrists after intensive interviews, without knowledge
of any biological data about them and without the

individuals being seen by a heart specialist. Diagnosis was made by an electro-cardiographer and an independent medical practitioner, who were not informed about the subjects' behavioural patterns. They found the following result: after $2\frac{1}{2}$ years from the start of the study, Type A men between the ages of 39 and 49, and 50 and 59, had 6.5 and 1.9 times respectively the incidence of CHD than Type B men. They also had a large number of stress risk factors (e.g. high serum cholesterol levels, elevated beta-lipoproteins, etc.). After $4\frac{1}{2}$ years of the follow-up observation in the study, the same relationship of behavioural pattern and incidence of CHD was found. In terms of the clinical manifestations of CHD, individuals exhibiting Type A behavioural patterns had significantly more incidence of acute myocardial infarction and angina pectoris. Rosenman et al (1967) also found that the risk of recurrent and fatal myocardial infarction was significantly related to Type A characteristics. Quinlan and his colleagues (Quinlan et al, 1969) found the same results among Trappist and Benedictine monks. Monks judged to be Type A coronary-prone cases (by a double-blind procedure) had 2.3 times the prevalence of angina and 4.3 times the prevalence of infarction as compared to monks judged Type B.

An increasingly large number of studies have been carried out which support the relationship between Type A behaviour and ill-health (Caplan, Cobb and French, 1975). From a management perspective the most significant work was carried out by Howard et al (1976). Two hundred and thirty-six managers from 12 different companies were examined for Type A behaviour and for a number of the known risk factors in CHD (blood pressure, cholesterol, triglycerides, uric acid, smoking and fitness). Those managers exhibiting extreme Type A behaviour showed significantly higher blood pressure (systolic and diastolic) and higher cholesterol and triglyceride levels. A higher percentage of these managers were cigarette smokers and in each age group studied, Type A managers were less interested in exercise (although differences in cardio-respiratory fitness were found only in the oldest age group). The authors conclude that Type A managers were found to be higher on a number of risk factors known to be associated with CHD than Type B managers.

**e management of
ess**

Cooper and Marshall (1978) have argued that understanding the sources of managerial pressure, as we have tried to do here, is only the first step in stress reduction. Next, we must begin to explore 'when' and 'how' to intervene. There are a number of changes that can be introduced in organizational life to begin to manage stress at work. For example:

* to re-create the social, psychological, and organizational environment in the work place to encourage greater autonomy and participation by managers in their jobs;

    *   to begin to build the bridges between the work place and
the home; providing opportunities for the manager's wife
to understand better her husband's job, to express her
views about the consequences of his work on family life,
and to be involved in the decision making process of
work that affects all members of the family unit;

    *   to utilize the well-developed catalogue of social and
interactive skill training programmes in order to help
clarify role and interpersonal relationship difficulties
within organizations;

    *   and, more fundamentally, to create an organizational
climate to encourage rather than discourage
communication, openness and trust, so that individual
managers are able to express their inability to cope,
their work-related fears, and are able to ask for help
if needed.

There are many other methods and approaches of coping
and managing stress, depending on the sources activated and
the interface between these sources and the individual make-
up of the manager concerned, but the important point that
we are trying to raise here is that the cure (intervention
or training technique) depends on the diagnosis. It is
important to try and encourage organizations to be sensitive
to the needs of its managers and begin to audit managerial
(di)stress. As Wright (1975) so aptly suggests, 'the
responsibility for maintaining health should be a reflection
of the basic relationship between the individual and the
organization for which he works; it is in the best interests
of both parties that reasonable steps are taken to live and
work sensibly and not too demandingly'.

References

Barber, R. (1976)
Who would marry a director? Director, March, 60-62.
Beattie, R.T., Darlington, T.G. and Cripps, O.M. (1974)
The management threshold. BIM Paper OPN 11.
Breslow, L. and Buell, P. (1960)
Mortality from coronary heart disease and physical
activity of work in California. Journal of Chronic
Diseases, 11, 615-626.
Brook, A. (1973)
Mental stress at work. The Practitioner, 210, 500-506.
Brummet, R.L., Pyle, W.C. and Flamholtz, E.G. (1968)
Accounting for human resources. Michigan Business
Review, 20, 20-25.
Buck, V. (1972)
Working Under Pressure. London: Staples Press.
Caplan, R.D, Cobb, S. and French, J.R.P. (1975)
Relationships of cessation of smoking with job stress,
personality and social support. Journal of Applied
Psychology, 60, 211-219.
Coch, L. and French, J.R.P. (1948)
Overcoming resistance to change. Human Relations, 11,
512-532.

Constandse, W.J. (1972)
A neglected personnel problem. Personnel Journal, 51, 129-133.

Cooper, C.L. (1980)
The Stress Check. London: Prentice Hall.

Cooper, C.L. (1981)
Stressing Exe utive Families. London: Prentice Hall.

Cooper, C.L. and Marshall, J. (1978)
Understanding Executive Stress. London: Macmillan.

Dohrenwend, B.S. and Dohrenwend, B.P. (1974)
Stressful Life Events. New York: Wiley.

Donaldson, J. and Gowler, D. (1975)
Prerogatives, participation and managerial stress. In Gowler, D. and Legge, K. (eds), Managerial Stress. Epping: Gower Press.

Dreyfuss, F. and Czackes, J.W. (1959)
Blood cholesterol and uric acid of healthy medical students under stress of examination. Archives of Internal Medicine, 103, 708-711.

French, J.R.P. and Caplan, R.D. (1970)
Psychosocial factors in coronary heart disease. Industrial Medicine, 39, 383-397.

French, J.R.P. and Caplan, R.D. (1973)
Organizational stress and individual strain. In A.J. Marrow, (ed.), The Failure of Success. New York: AMACOM.

French, J.R.P., Israel, J. and As,D. (1960)
An experiment in participation in a Norwegian factory. Human Relations, 13, 3-20.

French, J.R.P., Tupper, C.J. and Mueller, E.I. (1965)
Workload of university professors. Unpublished research report. Ann Arbor, Mich.: University of Michigan.

Friedman, M. (1969)
Pathogenesis of Coronary Artery Disease. New York: McGraw-Hill.

Friedman, M., Rosenman, R.H. and Carroll, V. (1968)
Changes in serum cholesterol and blood clotting time in man subjected to cyclic variations of occupational stress. Circulation, 17, 852-861.

Goffman, E. (1952)
On cooling the mark out. Psychiatry, 15, 451-463.

Gowler, D. and Legge, K. (1975)
Stress and external relationships - the 'Hidden Contract'. In D. Gowler and K. Legge (eds), Managerial Stress. Epping: Gower Press.

Guest, D. and Williams, R. (1973)
How home affects work. New Society, 23, 114-117.

Handy, C. (1978)
The family: help or hindrance. In C.L. Cooper and R. Payne (eds), Stress at Work. Chichester: Wiley.

Howard, J.H., Cunningham, D.A. and Rechnitzer, P.A. (1976)
Health patterns associated with Type A behaviour: a managerial population. Journal of Human Stress, 2, 24-31.

Immundo, L.V. (1974)
Problems associated with managerial mobility. Personnel
Journal, 53, 910.
Jenkins, C.D. (1971)
Psychological and social precursors of coronary disease.
New England Journal of Medicine, 284, 307-317.
**Kahn, R.L., Wolfe, D.M., Quinn, R.P., Snoek, J.D. and
Rosenthal, R.A.** (1964)
Organizational Stress. New York: Wiley.
Kasl, S.V. (1973)
Mental health and the work environment. Journal of
Occupational Medicine, 15, 509-518.
Kay, E. (1974)
Middle management. In J. O'Toole (ed.), Work and the
Quality of Life. Cambridge, Mass.: MIT Press.
Kearns, J.L. (1973)
Stress in Industry. London: Priory Press.
Lazarus, R.S. (1966)
Psychological Stress and the Coping Process. New York:
McGraw-Hill.
Levinson, H. (1973)
Problems that worry our executives. In A.J. Marrow
(ed.), The Failure of Success. New York: AMACOM.
McMurray, R.N. (1973)
The executive neurosis. In R.L. Noland (ed.), Industrial
Mental Health and Employee Counselling. New York:
Behavioral Publications.
Margolis, B.L. and Kroes, W.H. (1974)
Work and the health of man. In J. O'Toole (ed.), Work
and the Quality of Life. Cambridge, Mass.: MIT Press.
Margolis, B.L., Kroes, W.H. and Quinn, R.P. (1974)
Job stress: an unlisted occupational hazard. Journal of
Occupational Medicine, 16, 654-661.
Marshall, J. and Cooper, C.L. (1978)
Executives Under Pressure. London: Macmillan.
Marshall, J. and Cooper, C.L. (1979)
Work experience of middle and senior managers: the
pressures and satisfactions. Management International
Review, 19, 81-96.
Mettlin, C. and Woelfel, J. (1974)
Interpersonal influence and symptoms of stress. Journal
of Health and Social Behavior, 15, 311-319.
Middle Class Housing Estate Study (1975)
Unpublished paper. Civil Service College, UK.
Miller, J.G. (1960)
Information input overload and psychopathology. American
Journal of Psychiatry, 116, 695-704.
Mintzberg, H. (1973)
The Nature of Managerial Work. New York: Harper & Row
Morris, J. (1975)
Managerial stress and 'The Cross of Relationships'. In
D. Gowler and K. Legge (eds), Managerial Stress. Eppin
Gower Press.

Neff, W.S. (1968)
Work and Human Behavior. New York: Atherton Press.
Packard, V. (1975)
A Nation of Strangers. New York: McKay.
Pahl, J.M. and Pahl, R.E. (1971)
Managers and Their Wives. London: Allen Lane.
Pierson, G.W. (1972)
The Moving Americans. New York: Knopf.
Pincherle, G. (1972)
Fitness for work. Proceedings of the Royal Society of Medicine, 65, 321-324.
Quinlan, C.B., Burrow, J.G. and Hayes, C.G. (1969)
The association of risk factors and CHD in Trappist and Benedictine monks. Paper presented to the American Heart Association, Louisiana, New Orleans.
Quinn, R.P., Seashore, S. and Mangione, I. (1971)
Survey of Working Conditions. US Government Printing Office.
Rosenman, R.H., Friedman, M. and Jenkins, C.D. (1967)
Clinically unrecognised myocardial infarction in the Western collaborative group study. American Journal of Cardiology, 19, 776-782.
Rosenman, R.H., Friedman, M. and Strauss, R. (1964)
A predictive study of CHD. Journal of American Medical Association, 189, 15-22.
Rosenman, R.H., Friedman, M. and Strauss, R. (1966)
CHD in Western collaborative group study. Journal of American Medical Association, 195, 86-92.
Russek, H.I. and Zohman, B.L. (1958)
Relative significance of heredity, diet and occupational stress in CHD of young adults. American Journal of Medical Science, 235, 266-275.
Seidenberg, R. (1973)
Corporate Wives - Corporate Casualties. New York: American Management Association.
Shirom, A., Eden, D., Silberwasser, S. and Kellerman, J.J. (1973)
Job stress and risk factors in coronary heart disease among occupational categories in kibbutzim. Social Science and Medicine, 7, 875-892.
Sleeper, R.D. (1975)
Labour mobility over the life cycle. British Journal of Industrial Relations, 13, 194-214.
Sofer, C. (1970)
Men in Mid-Career. Cambridge: Cambridge University Press.
Stewart, R. (1976)
Contrasts in Management. New York: McGraw-Hill.
Uris, A. (1972)
How managers ease job pressures. International Management, June, 45-46.
Wardwell, W.I., Hyman, M. and Bahnson, C.B. (1964)
Stress and coronary disease in three field studies. Journal of Chronic Diseases, 17, 73-84.

Wright, H.B. (1975)
Executive ease and dis-ease. Epping: Gower Press.

N.B. Some of the research literature reviewed here was draw
from Cary L. Cooper's book, written with Judi Marshall,
'Understanding Executive Stress', London: Macmillan, 1978.

Questions

1. What are the sources of occupational stress that are common to most jobs?
2. What is Type A behaviour and why is it important to be aware of it?
3. Studs Terkel in his book 'Working' suggests 'work is, by its very nature about violence ... to the spirit as well as to the body. It is about ulcers as well as accidents, about shouting matches as well as fist fights, about nervous breakdowns as well as kicking the dog around. It is, above all, about daily humiliations.' Discuss.
4. Is there any evidence that 'worker participation' can work?
5. William Faulkner once said, 'You can't eat for eight hours a day nor drink for eight hours a day nor make love for eight hours a day ... all you can do for eight hours a day is work. Which is the reason why man makes himself and everybody else so miserable and unhappy.' Discuss.
6. Differentiate between 'qualitative' and 'quantitative' overload and between 'role ambiguity' and 'role conflict'.
7. Is stress a result of the mismatch between the person and the work environment?

Annotated reading

Buck, V.E. (1972) Working Under Pressure. London: Staples.
This is an early book in the stress field, which highlights a seminal study in the area. It explores the nature of boss-subordinate relationships, but is limited by the method of data analysis and the theoretical frame work it adopts.

Caplan, R.D. et al (1975) Job Demands and Worker Health. Washington, DC: US Department of Health, Education and Welfare.
This is a much more comprehensive study of a variety of occupations in terms of job stressors and their manifestations. It examines both blue and white collar occupations.

Cooper, C.L. and Marshall, J. (1978) Understanding Executive Stress. London: Macmillan.
This book reviews the field of managerial stress, highlighting the potential stressors at work in the home It draws on work published in medical, social science and management journals and books.

Marshall, J. and Cooper, C.L. (1979) Executives Under Pressure. London: Macmillan.
    This book examines the quality of managerial life. It focusses on the problems of managerial redundancy, early retirement, job mobility, training and the home-work interface.

Cooper C.L. and Payne, R. (1980) Current Concerns in Occupational Stress. Chichester: Wiley.
    This is an edited volume of distinguished contributors who explore a range of issues that affect people at work. It looks at the impact of job transfers, dual career marriages, shift work, hazardous occupations, boundary roles (e.g. shop stewards) and also explores the potential methods of coping with the exigencies of industrial life.

Part five

Approaches to Change

10

Transition: Understanding and Managing Personal Change
Barrie Hopson

> In the ongoing flux of life, (the person) undergoes many
> changes. Arriving, departing, growing, declining,
> achieving, failing - every change involves a loss and a
> gain. The old environment must be given up, the new
> accepted. People come and go; one job is lost, another
> begun; territory and possessions are acquired or sold;
> new skills are learned, old abandoned; expectations are
> fulfilled or hopes dashed - in all these situations the
> individual is faced with the need to give up one mode of
> life and accept another (Parkes, 1972).

Today, more than at any other time in our history, people
have to cope with an often bewildering variety of transitions: from home to school; from school to work; from being
single to being married and - increasingly - divorced; from
job to job; from job to loss of employment; retraining and
re-education; from place to place and friend to friend; to
parenthood and then to children leaving home; and finally to
bereavements and death. Alongside these and other major life
events people are having to learn to cope with the passage
from one stage of personal development to another: adolescence, early adulthood, stabilization, mid-life transition
and restabilization.

What is a transition?
We define a transition as a discontinuity in a person's life
space (Adams, Hayes and Hopson, 1976). Sometimes the discontinuity is defined by social consensus as to what constitutes a discontinuity within the culture. Holmes and Rahe
(1967) provide evidence to show the extent of cultural
similarity in perceptions of what are important discon-
tinuities, in the research they conducted to produce their
social readjustment rating scale. The life changes represented here (see table 1), along with their weighted
scores, were found to be remarkably consistent from culture
to culture: Japan, Hawaii, Central America, Peru, Spain,
France, Belgium, Switzerland and Scandinavia. For example,
death of a spouse requires about twice as much change in
adjustment worldwide as marriage, and ten times as much as
a traffic violation. The correlation between the items
ranged from 0.65 to 0.98 across all the cultures.

Another way of defining a discontinuity is not by general consensus but by the person's own perception. These two may not always coincide: for example, adolescence is considered to be an important time of transition in most western cultures, whereas in other cultures like Samoa it was not considered to be a time of stressful identity crisis. Also, in a common culture some children experience adolescence as a transition while others do not. Consequently it cannot be assumed that everyone experiences a transitional event (e.g. a change of job) in the same way.

Table 1

The Holmes and Rahe social readjustment rating scale

LIFE EVENT	Mean value
1. Death of a spouse	100
2. Divorce	73
3. Marital separation from mate	65
4. Detention in jail or other institution	63
5. Death of a close family member	63
6. Major personal injury or illness	53
7. Marriage	50
8. Being fired at work	47
9. Marital reconciliation with mate	45
10. Retirement from work	45
11. Major change in the health or behaviour of a family member	44
12. Pregnancy	40
13. Sexual difficulties	39
14. Gaining a new family member (e.g. through birth, adoption, oldster moving in, etc.)	39
15. Major business readjustment (e.g. merger, reorganization, bankruptcy, etc.)	39

16. Major change in financial state
    (e.g. a lot worse off or
    a lot better off than usual)   38

17. Death of a close friend   37

18. Changing to a different line of work   36

19. Major changes in the number of arguments
    with spouse (e.g. either a lot more
    or a lot less than usual regarding
    childbearing, personal habits, etc.)   35

20. Taking on a mortgage greater than
    $10,000 (e.g. purchasing a home,
    business, etc.)   31

21. Foreclosure on a mortgage or loan   30

22. Major change in responsibilities
    at work (e.g. promotion,
    demotion, lateral transfer)   29

23. Son or daughter leaving home (e.g.
    marriage, attending college, etc.)   29

24. In-law troubles   29

25. Outstanding personal achievement   28

26. Wife beginning or ceasing work
    outside the home   26

27. Beginning or ceasing formal schooling   26

28. Major change in living conditions
    (e.g. building a new home, remodelling,
    deterioration of home or neighborhood)   25

29. Revision of personal habits (dress,
    manners, associations, etc.)   24

30. Trouble with the boss   23

31. Major change in working hours or
    conditions   20

32. Change in residence   20

33. Changing to a new school   20

34. Major change in usual type and/or
    amount of recreation   19

35. Major change in church activities (e.g. a lot more or a lot less than usual)   19

36. Major change in social activities (e.g. clubs, dancing, movies, visiting, etc.)   18

37. Taking on a mortgage or loan less than $10,000 (e.g. purchasing a car, TV, freezer, etc.)   17

38. Major change in sleeping habits (a lot more or a lot less sleep, or change in part of day when asleep)   16

39. Major change in number of family get-togethers (e.g. a lot more or a lot less than usual)   15

40. Major change in eating habits (a lot more or a lot less food intake, or very different meal hours or surroundings)   15

41. Vacation   13

42. Christmas   12

43. Minor violations of the law (e.g. traffic tickets, jaywalking, disturbing the peace, etc.)   11

For an experience to be classed as transitional there should be:

* PERSONAL AWARENESS of a discontinuity in one's life space; and
* NEW BEHAVIOURAL RESPONSES required because the situation is new, or the required behaviours are novel, or both.

A person can sometimes undergo a transitional experience without being aware of the extent of the discontinuity or that new behavioural responses are required. This at some point will probably cause the person or others adaptation problems. For example, following the death of her husband, the widow may not be experiencing strain - she might even be pleased that he is dead - but suddenly she becomes aware that no house repairs have been done, and a new dimension or loss becomes evident along with the awareness of new behavioural responses required.

Why is an understanding of transitional experience important?
Life in post-industrial society is likely to bring more and

more transitions for people in all arenas of living. Any transition will result in people being subjected to some degree of stress and strain. They will be more or less aware of this depending upon the novelty of the event and the demands it makes upon their behavioural repertoires. Thus, there is likely to be a rise in the number of people experiencing an increased amount of stress and strain in the course of their daily lives.

Many practitioners in the helping professions are dealing directly with clients who are in transition. It is vital for them to understand how people are likely to react during transition, and to recognize the symptoms of transitional stress. Professionals also need helping techniques to ensure that individuals cope more effectively with their transitions, and to make organizations and social groups more aware of what they can do to help people in transition.

there a general ►del of transitions?

As we began to discover other work on different transitions, increasingly a general picture began to emerge. It appeared that irrespective of the nature of the transition, an overall pattern seemed to exist. There were differences, of course, especially between those transitions that were usually experienced as being positive: for example, marriage and desired promotion, and those usually experienced negatively, like bereavement and divorce. But these differences appeared to reflect differences of emphasis rather than require a totally different model.

The major point to be made in understanding transitions is that whether a change in one's daily routine is an intentional change, a sudden surprise that gets thrust upon one, or a growing awareness that one is moving into a life stage characterized by increasing or decreasing stability, it will trigger a CYCLE of reactions and feelings that is predictable. The cycle has seven phases, and the identification of these seven phases has come about through content analysis of reports from over 100 people who have attended transition workshops for the purpose of understanding and learning to cope more effectively with transitions they were experiencing and through extending the findings reported above.

Immobilization

The first phase is a kind of immobilization or a sense of being overwhelmed; of being unable to make plans, unable to reason, and unable to understand. In other words, the initial phase of a transition is experienced by many people as a feeling of being frozen up. It appears that the intensity with which people experience this first phase is a function of the unfamiliarity of the transition state and of the negative expectations one holds. If the transition is not high in novelty and if the person holds positive expectations, the immobilization is felt less intensely or perhaps not at all. Marriage can be a good example of the latter.

Minimization

The way of getting out of this immobilization, essentially, is by movement to the second phase of the cycle, which is characterized by minimization of the change or disruption, even to trivialize it. Very often, the person will deny that the change even exists. Sometimes, too, the person projects a euphoric feeling. Those readers who recall seeing Alfred Hitchcock's film 'Psycho' will remember that Tony Perkins spent considerable time shrieking at his mother in the house on the hill. It is not until the end of the film that one learns the mother has been dead for some time, and it is her semi-mummified body with which he has been carrying on his 'dialogue'. That is an extreme example of denying or minimizing the reality of a major change in one's life. Denial can have a positive function. It is more often a necessary phase in the process of adjustment. 'Denial is a normal and necessary human reaction to a crisis which is too immediately overwhelming to face head-on. Denial provides time for a temporary retreat from reality while our internal forces regroup and regain the strength to comprehend the new life our loss has forced upon us' (Krantzler, 1973).

Depression

Eventually, for most people - though not for Tony Perkins in 'Psycho' - the realities of the change and of the resulting stresses begin to become apparent. As people become aware that they must make some changes in the way they are living, as they become aware of the realities involved, they sometimes begin to get depressed: the third phase of the transition cycle. Depression is usually the consequence of feelings of powerlessness, of aspects of life out of one's control. This is often made worse by the fear of loss of control over one's own emotions. The depression stage has occasional high energy periods often characterized by anger, before sliding back into a feeling of hopelessness. They become depressed because they are just beginning to face up to the fact that there has been a change. Even if they have voluntarily created this change themselves, there is likely to be this dip in feelings. They become frustrated because it becomes difficult to know how best to cope with the new life requirements, the ways of being, the new relationships that have been established or whatever other changes may be necessary.

Letting go

As people move further into becoming aware of reality, they can move into the fourth phase, which is accepting reality for what it is. Through the first three phases, there has been a kind of attachment, whether it has been conscious or not, to the past (pre-transition) situation. To move from phase three to phase four involves a process of unhooking from the past and of saying 'Well, here I am now; here is what I have; I know I can survive; I may not be sure of what I want yet but I will be OK; there is life out there waiting for me.' As this is accepted as the new reality, the person's feelings begin to rise once more, and optimism becomes possible. A clear 'letting go' is necessary.

Testing
This provides a bridge to phase five, where the person becomes much more active and starts testing himself vis-à-vis the new situation, trying out new behaviours, new life styles, and new ways of coping with the transition. There is a tendency also at this point for people to stereotype, to have categories and classifications of the ways things and people should or should not be relative to the new situation. There is much personal energy available during this phase and, as they begin to deal with the new reality, it is not unlikely that those in transition will easily become angry and irritable.

Search for meaning
Following this burst of activity and self-testing, there is a more gradual shifting towards becoming concerned with understanding and for seeking meanings for how things are different and why they are different. This sixth phase is a cognitive process in which people try to understand what all of the activity, anger, stereotyping and so on have meant. It is not until people can get out of the activity and withdraw somewhat from it that they can begin to understand deeply the meaning of the change in their lives.

Internalization
This conceptualizing, in turn, allows people to move into the final phase of internalizing these meanings and incorporating them into their behaviour. Overall, the seven transition phases represent a cycle of experiencing a disruption, gradually acknowledging its reality, testing oneself, understanding oneself, and incorporating changes in one's behaviour. The level of one's morale varies across these phases and appears to follow a predictable path. Identifying the seven phases along such a morale curve often gives one a better understanding of the nature of the transition cycle.

Interestingly, the Menninger Foundation's research on Peace Corps volunteers' reactions to entering and experiencing training (a transition for each person) produced a very similar curve. More recently, Elisabeth Kubler-Ross and those who joined her death and dying seminars have also charted a very similar curve of the reaction cycle people go through upon learning they are terminally ill, which is the ultimate transition.

Before proceeding, it is necessary to make it clear that seldom, if ever, does a person move neatly from phase to phase as has been described above. It can help someone in distress, however, to be made aware that what they are experiencing is not uncommon, that it will pass, and that they have a great deal they can do in determining how quickly it will pass.

It is also important to point out that each person's experience is unique and that any given individual's progressions and regressions are unique to their unique circumstances. For example, one person may never get beyond denial or minimization. Another may end it all during depression. Yet another might experience a major failure just as things begin to look up, and slip back to a less active, more withdrawn posture.

What is important is the potential for growth arising from any major disruption or calamity. One realizes this potential and moves toward it when one lets go and fully accepts the situation for what it is; one dies a 'little death' to become larger.

What effects do transitions have on people?

It is important to note here that all transitions involve some stress, including those considered by society to be positive changes, such as being left large sums of money, parenthood or marriage (Holmes and Rahe, 1967). Our own studies investigating this relationship show the following results:

* transitions are most stressful if they are unpredictable, involuntary, unfamiliar, of high magnitude (degree of change), and high intensity (rate of change);
* the incidence of illness is positively correlated with the amount of life change one undergoes;
* lack of feedback on the success of attempts to cope with strain-inducing events causes more severe stress-related diseases than when relevant feedback is present;
* interpersonal warmth and support during stressful periods seems to reduce the impact of the stress;
* viruses alone do not cause illnesses. The incidence of bad emotional experiences seems to upset the body and allow the viruses to take over;
* hypertension occurs more often in environments characterized by high stressors and few ways of responding to those stressors;
* the more major the life changes the higher the risk of coronary heart disease.

Every transition contains 'opportunity value' for the mover

However undesirable a particular transition may be for the mover, there is always opportunity for personal growth and development contained within it. If one takes a severe example such as death of a spouse, for the majority of those bereaved nothing will compensate for that loss. On the other hand, given that the loss is out of their control, what is under their control is what they decide to do with their lives from there on. There are opportunities for new relationships, travel, career change, new interests, etc. Obviously, during the grief process - which is essential - the opportunities are difficult and often obnoxious to contemplate but part of the 'letting go' stage involves doing exactly that. The Chinese have two symbols for the concept of 'crisis': one means 'danger' while the other signifies 'opportunity'.

What are the coping tasks relevant to all transitional events?

We believe that there are common elements in any transition, which enable us to talk generally about transitional behaviour. We also assert that in dealing with any transitional event a person has two tasks to perform as he moves through the phases of the model:

* MANAGEMENT OF STRAIN: to manage the degree of strain generated by the stress in such a way that the individual can engage with the external problems caused by the transition.
* COGNITIVE COPING TASKS: a transition will always necessitate adjustment. Any adjustment requires decisions to be made about the appropriateness of new and old behaviour patterns. The individual will be asking himself questions such as: (i) How can I accept this situation?; (ii) What behaviour is expected of me?; (iii) What do I want from this situation?

How successfully he manages these two tasks determines the speed with which he completes the transition.

What are the coping tools relevant to transitions?

At the Counselling and Career Development Unit at Leeds University we have been working for a number of years on developing training programmes to help adults in transition and to teach transition coping skills to young people in schools and colleges.

We have developed a questionnaire to be used to help people identify the transition coping skills they already possess and which simultaneously highlights the deficits in their coping repertory. Figure 1 reproduces the questionnaire designed for use with adults. People are asked to answer 'yes' or 'no' to all the questions. Each time they reply 'no', it suggests an area where they are lacking in some theoretical understanding of the nature of transitions, or deficient in cognitive or behavioural skills. Each of the items is dealt with briefly below, along with some teaching points we make to participants. In a workshop, this learning would take place experientially and participants would have an opportunity to develop and practise their skills. The language used is written to convey the flavour of the workshop approach. The following text should be read in conjunction with the questionnaire.

Figure 1

Coping skills questionnaire

1. KNOW YOURSELF

a. Would I have chosen for this to have happened?
b. Am I proactive in new situations: do I take initiatives, have a purpose as opposed to sitting back and waiting on events?
c. Do I know what I want from this new situation?
d. Do I know what I don't want from this new situation?
e. If I feel under stress do I know what I can do to help myself?
f. Do I know how to use my feelings as indicators of where I am?

2. KNOW YOUR NEW SITUATION

a. Can I describe the transition?
b. Do I know how I'm expected to behave?
c. Can I try out the new situation in advance?

3. KNOW OTHER PEOPLE WHO CAN HELP: do I have other people:

a. To depend on in a crisis?
b. To discuss concerns?
c. To feel close to - a friend?
d. Who can make me feel competent and valued?
e. Who can give me important information?
f. Who will challenge me to sit up and take a good look at myself?
g. With whom I can share good news and good feelings?
h. Who will give me constructive feedback?

4. LEARN FROM THE PAST

a. Is there anything similar that has happened to me?
b. Can I identify what I did which helped me get through that experience?
c. Can I identify what I would have done differently?

5. LOOK AFTER YOURSELF

a. Do I know how to use supportive self-talk?
b. Do I get regular exercise or have a personal fitness programme?
c. Am I eating regularly and wisely?
d. Do I know how to relax?
e. Am I keeping to a regular schedule?
f. Do I know my 'personal anchor points'?
g. Do I give myself 'treats' when under stress?
h. Do I have other people who will take care of me?
i. Can I survive?

j. Do I know when my low points are likely to be?

6. LET GO OF THE PAST

a. Do I easily let go of old situations?
b. Do I continuously feel that this should not happen to me?
c. Do I know how to vent my anger constructively?

7. SET GOALS AND MAKE ACTION PLANS

a. Do I know how to set goals?
b. Do I know what my goals are for this transition and for my life generally?
c. Do I know how to make and implement action plans?
d. Do I know how to set priorities?
e. Do I know how to make effective decisions?
f. Do I know how to generate alternatives, because there is always an alternative?

8. LOOK FOR THE GAINS YOU HAVE MADE

a. Can I find one thing which is positive about this experience?
b. Can I list a variety of new opportunities that did not exist before or that I would not have thought of previously?
c. Have I learned something new about myself?

Know yourself

1. WOULD I HAVE CHOSEN FOR THIS TO HAVE HAPPENED? You may not have chosen this situation. This could make it more difficult for you to accept the transition. But it has happened. You now have three alternatives:

(A) accept it and put up with it
(B) refuse to accept
(C) accept it and try to benefit from it

(A) will help you to survive. (B) will bring you nothing but bad feelings and worse; you will be less able to cope with the tasks facing you in the new situation. (C) will help you to grow in addition to merely surviving.

Given the inevitable, ask yourself the key question: 'What is the worst thing that could happen?' Having identified that, ask yourself if you can cope with that. Is it really so terrible?

It is essential to remember that problematic situations constitute a normal aspect of living. It is also useful to recall the variety of transitions that you have encountered and survived up until now. Through having survived you will probably have developed some skills. If, on looking back, you feel dissatisfied with how you managed a transition, it is important to ask yourself whether you had all the skills needed to deal effectively with that situation. More than likely you did not. Do not berate yourself for not having these skills. Instead be glad that you have identified the need for additional skills, for that in itself is the first stage of skill development.

2. AM I PROACTIVE IN NEW SITUATIONS: DO I TAKE INITIATIVES, HAVE A PURPOSE, AS OPPOSED TO SITTING BACK AND WAITING ON EVENTS? To be proactive involves a certain sequence of behaviour:

*   knowing what you want;
*   knowing alternative ways of achieving this;
*   choosing one alternative;
*   evaluating the results against your original objective.

The essence of proactive behaviour is that there is a REASON for it, even if the end result involves no action. The reason, however, must stem from what Maslow (1968) calls a 'growth' need as opposed to a 'deficiency' need. Deciding not to give a public talk (objective), and knowing various ways of avoiding this (knowing alternatives), choosing one, and thereby achieving the objective at first glance seems to fit the description of 'proactive behaviour'. However, if the reason is based on fear of making a fool of oneself, this would not be classed as proactive. If it were due to over-commitment, or the feeling that you are not the best equipped person to do it, that would be proactive.

3. DO I KNOW WHAT I WANT FROM THIS NEW SITUATION

4. DO I KNOW WHAT I DO NOT WANT FROM THIS NEW SITUATION? If you are unclear as to what you want or do not want from a new situation this usually signifies a lack of knowledge about your own values or about what the new situation has to offer. There is an entire educational tech-nology designed to help young people and adults to crystal-lize their needs and values. It has been developed in the USA and is known generically as values clarification (Simon, Howe and Kirschenbaum, 1972; Simon, 1974; Howe and Howe, 1975; Kirschenbaum, 1977). Obtaining more information about the new situation is dealt with in the next section.

5. IF I FEEL UNDER STRESS DO I KNOW WHAT I CAN DO TO HELP MYSELF? Avoid situations where you might over react. If you have recently separated from your spouse and it is still painful, do not accept an invitation to an event where you know you will encounter your spouse again. Make as few decisions as possible as you will not be thinking clearly enough. Do not make more than one transition at a time. It is amazing how often people choose one transition to be the stimulus for a host of others. If you have changed your job, do not change your spouse, residence and/or life style all at the same time. A new broom can sometimes sweep you over!

Look after yourself (see section on this below).
Do not waste time blaming yourself (see below).
Remember that time itself will not eliminate the stress
or heal you, it is what you do with that time. There are a
variety of cognitive shielding techniques that you can use
to minimize the strain. These all involve controlling the
amount of stimulation in the environment. Some examples are:

* time management: making priorities;
* making lists;
* queuing: delaying decisions during a difficult period
  by queuing them up, dealing with them one at a time,
  and not thinking about future decisions until the time
  to make them arrives. Writing down a decision in a diary
  to be made at a future date is a good way of queuing.
* temporary drop-out: refusing to resolve decisions until
  after a recuperation period. This can appear initially
  as reactive; however, it is correctly termed proactive
  as the mover is deliberately opting out of the situation
  temporarily as part of a strategy to move in later and
  thereby more effectively.

There are now some excellent resources available for
techniques of preventing and managing stress; for example,
Sharpe and Lewis' 'Thrive on Stress' (1977), Lamott's
'Escape from Stress' (1975), and Forbes' 'Life Stress'
(1979).

6.   DO I KNOW HOW TO USE MY FEELINGS AS INDICATORS
OF WHERE I AM? Many people, especially men, as a result
of their upbringing are emotionally illiterate: that is,
they have not developed the skills of 'reading' their own
emotions. One's 'gut' feelings are the surest indicator of
how one is coping at any particular time. The skill is in
learning to recognize the changes in feelings when they
occur and then having an emotional vocabulary to be able
to label them correctly. Often when people are asked what
they are feeling they will answer you in terms of only
what they are thinking (see Hopson and Scally, 'Lifeskills
Teaching Programmes no. 1 - How to manage negative
emotions', 1980a; Johnson's 'Reaching Out', 1972).

Know your new situation
1.   CAN I DESCRIBE THE TRANSITION? An essential
prerequisite to successful transition coping is to know that
you are in one. It is essential to be aware of when the
transition began, where you are in relation to it and what
are all the variables involved. For example, considering
changing your job might involve geographical change,
relationship changes, financial implications, holiday plans
for this year, etc.

2.   DO I KNOW HOW I AM EXPECTED TO BEHAVE? Transitions are naturally accompanied by stress even if they are
desired. Anxiety certainly increases the less information

you have about your new situation. Collect as much data as you can about what others expect of you, what society expects and how you are to behave. You may decide not to live up to or down to those expectations, but again you need the initial data before you can make that decision. You also need to know the consequences of any decision before you make it.

You can ask people who have made a similar transition or indeed are presently going through the same transition. A variety of self-help and special interest groups have developed in recent years to provide mutual support and information to people undergoing similar transitions: ante-natal classes, induction courses, orientation programmes, women's and men's 'rap' groups for people redefining their sex roles, widows' clubs, singles' clubs, one-parent family groups, etc.

It is important to remember that other people often forget, or in some cases are not even aware, that this is a new situation for you. They may need reminding. For example one new day at the end of your first week at a new job constitutes 20 per cent of the time you have worked there. For someone who has been here for five years, one new day represents less than 0.4 per cent of the time he has been there. Consequently, his feelings about that day are likely to be quite different from your feelings about the same day.

3. CAN I TRY OUT THE NEW SITUATION IN ADVANCE?
Some transitions can be 'sampled' in advance, for example, starting a new job, moving to another country; even a divorce or death can sometimes be anticipated. Reading books about anticipated transitions can be valuable, as can talking to others who have experienced it, while remembering that no one will experience it just like you. Where appropriate you can visit places, meet people, watch films, etc., prior to your transition.

Knowing other people who can help
There is now considerable evidence to show the beneficial effects on stress reduction of talking problems through with people: friends, colleagues, even strangers.

We often make the mistake of expecting too few people, typically a spouse and children, to satisfy too great a proportion of our needs. Check the list in the questionnaire. How many categories of person do you have available to you in your life? Are there any gaps? How many different people make up your 'support' group? How dependent are you on one or two?

We are also better at developing some forms of support at the expense of others. For example, people are often better at developing friendships than relationships with people who challenge us. The challengers in most people's support systems are about as abrasive as a marshmallow. Yet sometimes challengers are exactly what we require to shift us out of stereotyped thinking. Who are the challengers in your support systems? Remember, you may not even like them

Learn from the past

Our past is an important part of our present. Our past is
the history of our successes and our failures and is thereby
a record of our learning. As such, we can continue to learn
from our past experiences. 'Mistakes' are another way of
labelling 'opportunities for learning'. If we can identify
times in the past when we have had similar feelings or
experienced similar transitions, we have an opportunity to
monitor those chapters of our history and evaluate our
performances against the criteria of our own choosing. What
did we do that really did not help the situation? What would
we avoid if we were to have that experience again? Can we
learn from that experience and generalize it to the new
transition? A sense of one's own history is a prerequisite
to a fully functioning present and a portent for one's range
of possible futures.

Look after yourself

1.   DO I KNOW HOW TO USE SUPPORTIVE SELF-TALK?
Many of the problems we create for ourselves and much of
the support that we give ourselves derives from the same
source: our internal dialogue with ourselves. This dialogue
continues throughout most of our waking hours. These
'cognitions' are vital to our survival and growth. They
enable us to adapt to new situations, to learn, to feel and
to enact cognitively a variety of scenarios without having
to perform any of them. Ellis (1975), with his RATIONAL
EMOTIVE THERAPY, for years has claimed that the way we
think determines what we feel, with the corollary that if we
can change how we think we can also change how we feel.
His therapeutic method involves retraining people to talk
internally to themselves to minimize the negative emotions
which they otherwise would create. Ellis claims that most
people carry a variety of 'irrational beliefs' in their
heads unfounded in reality, but which result in their creating bad feelings for themselves as a result of 'shoulds' and
'oughts' which they believe are infallible. These beliefs
usually belong to one of three categories, which Ellis calls
the 'Irrational Trinity' on the road to 'mustabation':

*   A belief that I should be a certain sort of person, or
    a success, or perfect, or loved by everyone, and if I'm
    not, I'm a failure and worthless;
*   a belief that you, or other people, should do as I want
    them to do: love me, work for me, understand me, etc.,
    and if they do not, it is terrible, and I deserve to be
    miserable or they should be made to suffer;
*   a belief that things should be different; there should
    not be racial hatred, this organization should run
    better, our parents should not have to die, etc., and if
    things are not as I want them to be it is awful and
    either I cannot cope and deserve to be miserable, or I
    have every right to be furious.

Since it takes years to develop our patterns of self-talk,

changing them involves practice. There are a variety of programmes now available for helping people to restructure their self-talk into more supportive statements. Mahoney and Mahoney (1976) call this process 'cognitive ecology': cleaning up what you say to yourself.

2. DO I GET REGULAR EXERCISE OR HAVE A PERSONAL FITNESS PROGRAMME? Physical fitness is related to one's ability to cope with stress. It has also been shown to be related to the ability to create effective interpersonal relationships (Aspy and Roebuck, 1977) which in turn is related to stress reduction.

You need to be fit to cope effectively with transitions. Yet, of course it is often when we are most in need of fitness that we are often least inclined to make time for it. There are a number of well-researched fitness programmes available (Health Education Council, 1976; Carruthers and Murray, 1977; Cooper, 1977; Royal Canadian Air Force, 1978).

3. AM I EATING REGULARLY AND WISELY? Now is not the time for a rash diet. Your body needs all the help it can get. People in transition often have neither the time nor inclination to eat wisely. There is sometimes a reliance on quick junk foods, take-away meals or eating out. Remember to eat something every day from the four major food groups: meat, fish, poultry; dairy products; fruits and vegetables; bread and cereals.

Do not replace food with alcohol or smoking. Obviously there are times when alcohol will help you get through a lonely evening. You need a holiday from self-work as much as from any other kind of work. The danger signs are when alcohol or a cigarette is used as a substitute for meals.

Be wary of developing a dependence on drugs at this time. Sleeping tablets can sometimes be helpful during a crisis, but get off them quickly. They can serve to prevent you from developing healthier coping strategies.

It is a good idea to acquire an easy to read book on diet but one that is critical of food fads. The Health Education Council's booklet, 'Look After Yourself' (1976), contains a simple introduction to good nutrition, and Breckon's 'You Are What You Eat' (1976) is a fascinating survey of dietary facts and fiction, arguing strongly against overdosing oneself with vitamins and dealing in a balanced way with the hysteria over additives.

4. DO I KNOW HOW TO RELAX? There are two ways of reducing stress. One is to organize your life to minimize the number of stressors working on you. The other concerns how to reduce the effect of stress WHEN it hits you. The latter is typically the biggest problem when coping with a transition. Unfortunately, the very people who are most prone to stress illnesses often exacerbate the problem by packing their lives with transitions.

There are numerous relaxation methods, each of which have their advocates. A brief guide follows.

* Learn a relaxation technique. Progressive relaxation is simple and easy to learn. It is described in 'Exercises in Personal and Career Development' by Barrie Hopson and Patricia Hough (1973). It is described there as a classroom exercise. Transcendental meditation is now well researched and strong claims are made for it as a technique which directly affects the body's physiology. Most cities have a TM centre. You could also read 'The Transcendental Meditation Technique' by Peter Russel (1977). For those who do not enjoy the ritual cliquishness that accompanies TM, read Herbert Benson's 'The Relaxation Response' (1977).
* Direct body work to encourage relaxation: massage. The basics can be learned quickly on a course. If there is a Personal Growth centre near you, make contact as they might run courses. Read 'The Massage Book' by G. Downing (1972). You will need to keep an open mind regarding some of the sweeping generalizations made on behalf of some of these techniques.

5. AM I KEEPING TO A REGULAR SCHEDULE? If your internal world is in crisis, keep your external world in order. Keeping irregular hours, eating at strange times, going to lots of new places, meeting new people; all these can be disorientating.

6. DO I KNOW MY 'PERSONAL ANCHOR POINTS'? Toffler (1970) described this concept as one antidote to 'future shock'. When all around us things are changing we need an anchor point to hold on to. For some people it is their home, for others a relationship, children, a job, a daily routine, a favourite place or a hobby. Anchor points are plentiful, and it is vital to have at least one. In the midst of instability a stable base offers confirmation of identity, disengagement from the problem, and maybe even relaxation.

7. DO I GIVE MYSELF 'TREATS' WHEN UNDER STRESS? This list of tips has been packed with work. But play is vital too. If you are feeling low, or under stress, how about simply giving yourself a treat? It might even be a reward for accomplishing a difficult test or situation, but it does not have to be.

Draw up a list of treats. Try to become an expert on self-indulgence: a theatre trip, a massage, a book, see friends, make love, have a disgustingly 'bad for you' meal, take a holiday, or pamper yourself.

The only warning about treats is: do not spend so much time treating yourself that you use these as a diversion from coping directly with the transition.

8. DO I HAVE OTHER PEOPLE WHO WILL TAKE CARE OF ME? It is all right to be taken care of sometimes. Allow a friend, lover or colleague to look after you. If they do not offer, be proactive, ask them. Be brave enough to accept help from others. Recall what you feel when others close to you ask for help. There are pay-offs for helpers as well as those who receive help.

9. CAN I SURVIVE? Of course you can. You may doubt it at the moment. Perhaps it will help to remind yourself that what you are feeling now is normal for someone having experienced what you are experiencing. It is also neces ary before you can move on to the next stage of finding out more about you and what this transition can do FOR you instead of TO you.

Do not worry about feelings of suicide. Sometimes survival does not seem like such a good idea. If these feelings really seem to be getting out of hand see a counsellor, ring a Samaritan, or consult a doctor; you will probably get more librium than counselling, but that can take off the pressure until you have regrouped your resources.

The feeling will pass. Talk to people, keep a regular routine, treat yourself; at the end of each day recall one good experience, then you can match it with a bad one, then another good experience followed by a bad one, etc., or contract with a friend to call you at certain times.

10. DO I KNOW WHEN MY LOW POINTS ARE LIKELY TO BE? These can usually be predicted quite easily; after a phone call to your children (in the case of a divorced parent), seeing your ex-spouse with a new partner, just seeing your ex-spouse, discovering a personal belonging of your dead spouse, seeing an old workmate (redundancy, retirement), etc.

Keep a diary or a journal. This will help you to clarify your thoughts and feelings as well as to identify times, places and people to avoid. If you are experiencing the loss of a love it is usually advisable to fill your Sundays, bank holidays and Saturday nights!

Let go of the past
1. DO I EASILY LET GO OF OLD SITUATIONS? Sometimes people cannot let go because they try too hard to hold on. It is permissible to grieve. Grief shows that you are alive. Think about what you are missing, feel it. Ask people if you can talk to them about it. They will often be too embarrassed to mention it or worry that it will 'upset' you. Cry, rage, scream, recognize the loss, do not deny the pain. Wounds hurt when you dress them, but you know that is the first stage of the wound getting better. It is permissible to feel anger too.

2. DO I CONTINUOUSLY FEEL THAT THIS SHOULD NOT HAPPEN TO ME? Then you are guilty of making yourself

unhappy by hitting yourself over the head with 'shoulds' and 'oughts'. You need to look again at the section on supportive self-talk.

3. DO I KNOW HOW TO VENT MY ANGER CONSTRUCTIVELY? Allow yourself to feel the anger. If it is kept inside it will only hurt you. Feel angry at the person who left you, at the person who took something from you, at the world that let you down or at friends who cannot be trusted. Hit a pillow, scream aloud (in a closed car this is very effective; just like an echo chamber) or play a hectic sport. Do not hurt anyone, including yourself.

Anger is only a feeling. It cannot hurt anyone. Only behaviour hurts. Once the anger is cleared away, you are then freer to begin to evaluate, make plans and decide.

Set goals and make action plans
1. DO I KNOW HOW TO SET GOALS? Some people fail to manage their transitions effectively because they have not identified a desirable outcome. 'If you don't know where you're going, you'll probably end up somewhere else' (David Campbell, 1974).

It is essential to identify what you want to achieve in terms which are as behaviourally specific as possible, such as 'I want a new job worth £8,000 per annum where I have overall responsibility for financial operations of a medium-scale department.' 'In six months I want to be able to go out on my own, to visit friends by myself, and to have developed one new interest' (this was an objective of a recent widow in one of my workshops).

2. DO I KNOW WHAT MY GOALS ARE FOR THIS TRANSITION AND FOR MY LIFE GENERALLY? This requires the specific skill of knowing how to set, define, and refine objectives.

3. DO I KNOW HOW TO MAKE AND IMPLEMENT ACTION PLANS? Once the objectives are clear the action steps follow next. There are a variety of resources available with guidelines on making effective action plans. Carkhuff's two books, 'The Art of Problem Solving' (1974a) and 'How to Help Yourself' (1974b), are useful. An action plan needs to be behaviourally specific: 'I will make an appointment to see the solicitor tomorrow morning'. It needs to be in terms of 'what I will do now', not in terms of 'what I will do sometime', or 'what we will do eventually'. An action plan should read like a computer programme, with each step so clearly defined that someone else would know how to carry it out.

4. DO I KNOW HOW TO SET PRIORITIES? Having a variety of goals is one thing, having the time to achieve them all is another. Skills of time management are required along with a systematic way of measuring the desirability of one goal with another.

5. DO I KNOW HOW TO MAKE EFFECTIVE DECISIONS?
Katz (1968) has talked about the importance, not so much
of making wise decisions but of making decisions wisely.
There are a variety of teaching programmes now available to
help people become more proficient at making choices (Hopson
and Hough, 1973; Watts and Elsom, 1975).

6. DO I KNOW HOW TO GENERATE ALTERNATIVES,
BECAUSE THERE IS ALWAYS AN ALTERNATIVE? Often
people do not make as good a decision as they might have
simply because they have not generated enough alternatives.
The techniques of 'brainstorming', 'morphological forced
connections' and 'synectics' (all described in Adams, 1974)
are all ways of doing this. The key quite often, however,
is the belief that no matter now hopeless the situation, how
constrained one feels, there is always an alternative, no
matter how unpalatable it may initially appear, and that you
can choose. This is the central concept in the model of the
'self empowered person' described by Hopson and Scally
(1980b).

Look for the gains you have made
If gains are not immediately apparent, review the section
again under 'Know yourself'. Have you had to cope with
something with which you have not had to cope before? If so,
this will have shed light on a new facet of your personality. What is it? Do you like it? Can you use it to any
advantage in the future?

**Quick check-list on
client's transition
coping skills**

1. DOES HE KNOW WHAT HE WANTS FROM THE NEW
SITUATION? If not, you must help him to define what he
wants; getting him to be as specific as possible. He may not
be used to thinking in terms of objectives. You will have to
teach him. Write down options on a blackboard, flip chart,
or a note book. Help him to evaluate the costs and benefits
of different alternatives. Give him homework on this to be
discussed at a future session.

2. DOES HE TEND TO BE PROACTIVE IN NEW SITUATIONS
OR TO SIT BACK AND WAIT FOR THINGS TO HAPPEN? If
he appears to be proactive, check out that it really is
proactivity and not just acting to minimize anxiety, for
instance jumping into something to alleviate ambiguity. If
he is reactive you will need to point out that this will
minimize his chances of getting what he wants and you will
need to give him a task which is small enough for him to
complete successfully (e.g. doing some homework) in order
to develop his confidence in the ability to make things
happen. Give him a suitable book to read (see the section
on self-help books) which is simultaneously instructive and
a task to be completed.

3. DOES HE HAVE OTHER PEOPLE HE CAN RELY ON
FOR HELP? Get him to specify who and what they can do

for him. If he is deficient in help, steer him towards an appropriate self-help group.

4. HAS ANYTHING LIKE THIS HAPPENED TO HIM BEFORE? Look for links with previous experiences. Help him to discover what he did then which helped, and what in retrospect he would now choose to do differently.

5. HOW WELL CAN HE LOOK AFTER HIMSELF? Is he physically fit and eating sensibly? If not, advise him of the importance of this. Similarly, help him to discover the 'anchor points' in his life and persuade him to keep to a regular schedule. Encourage him to give himself a treat from time to time. Help him to identify when the low points are likely to be and to plan to minimize the impact of these: for example, always have something planned for Sunday when you are newly divorced.

6. CAN HE LET GO OF THE PAST? If not, encourage him to experience the grief and the anger as a way of discharging it and accepting that these feelings are normal and acceptable. They only become a problem if we can never let go of them.

7. CAN HE SET GOALS AND MAKE ACTION PLANS? Persuade him to begin thinking about specific goals as outlined under point 1. Help him define priorities, generate alternatives, and weigh them up.

8. CAN HE SEE POSSIBLE GAINS FROM HIS NEW SITUATION? Gently pressure him to begin to look for gains. The timing of this is vital. If he has not sufficiently let go of the past your intervention can appear heartless. Empathy is essential, but also you are trying to get him to see that however much he may not have chosen for an event to happen, that there will be something to gain.

it possible to train people to cope more effectively with transitions?

This has had to be empirically tested. Our general hypothesis is that people experiencing transitions will have similar tasks to cope with, namely, managing strain and dealing with cognitive tasks presented by the transition. We are assuming that to a considerable extent people's reactions to being in transition are learned as opposed to being inherited. To the extent that individuals' reactions are learned, we should be able to develop preventive, educative and re-educative strategies to help them manage their affairs and relationships more effectively at lower psychological costs, and derive greater benefits from the opportunity values embedded in every major transition.

This means that training programmes could be generated to help develop more effective coping styles for a number of people either (i) experiencing different transitional events, or who are anticipating transitional events, or

(ii) as general training for any presently unknown future transitions.

We have already conducted a variety of transitions workshops in the UK, the USA and Scandinavia with populations including managers, trade unionists, counsellors, organization development specialists, social workers, case workers, teachers and youth workers. These have been primarily designed for participants who in turn will have to deal with individuals in transition. We believe that it is only possible to do such work when one has a clear understanding not just of a theoretical orientation, a collection of coping skills and teaching techniques, but also of one's own transitional experiences, skills and deficits, joys, confusion and sadness.

The final question is always 'why'? Why spend the energy, use the time, deplete the resources, all of which could be directed to something else?

We can only give our answer. A transition simultaneously carries the seeds of our yesterdays, the hopes and fears of our futures, and the pressing sensations of the present which is our confirmation of being alive. There is danger and opportunity, ecstasy and despair, development and stagnation, but above all there is movement. Nothing and no one stays the same. Nature abhors vacuums and stability. A stable state is merely a stopping point on a journey from one place to another. Stop too long and your journey is ended. Stay and enjoy but with the realization that more is to come. You may not be able to stop the journey, but you can fly the plane.

References

Adams, J.L. (1974)
Conceptual Blockbusting. San Francisco: Freeman.
Adams, J.D., Hayes, J. and Hopson, B. (1976)
Transition: Understanding and managing personal change. London: Martin Robertson.
Aspy, D.N. and Roebuck, F.N. (1977)
Kids Don't Learn From People They Don't Like. Amherst, Mass.: Human Resource Development Press.
Benson, H. (1977)
The Relaxation Response. London: Fountain Well Press.
Breckon, W. (1976)
You Are What You Eat. London: BBC Publications.
Campbell, D. (1974)
If You Don't Know Where You're Going You'll Probably End Up Somewhere Else. Hoddesdon, Herts: Argus Publications.
Carkhuff, R.R. (1974a)
The Art of Problem Solving. Amherst, Mass.: Human Resource Development Press.
Carkhuff, R.R. (1974b)
How To Help Yourself. Amherst, Mass.: Human Resource Development Press.
Carruthers, M. and Murray, A. (1977)
F/40: Fitness on forty minutes a week. London: Futura.

Cooper, K. (1977)
The New Aerobics. New York: Bantam.
Downing, G. (1972)
The Massage Book. New York: Random House.
Ellis, A. and Harper, R. (1975)
A New Guide to Rational Living. Hollywood, Ca:
Wilshire Books.
Forbes, R. (1979)
Life Stress. New York: Doubleday.
Health Education Council (1976)
Look After Yourself. London: Health Education Council.
Holmes, T.H. and Rahe, R.H. (1967)
The social readjustment rating scale. Journal of
Psychosomatic Research, 11, 213-218.
Hopson, B. and Hough, P. (1973)
Exercises in Personal and Career Development. Cambridge:
Hobsons Press.
Hopson, B. and Scally, M. (1980a)
How to cope with and gain from life transitions. In B.
Hopson and M. Scally, Lifeskills Teaching Programmes
No. 1. Leeds: Lifeskills Associates.
Hopson, B. and Scally, M. (1980b)
Lifeskills Teaching: Education for self-empowerment.
London: McGraw-Hill.
Howe, L.W. and Howe, M.M. (1975)
Personalizing Education: Values clarification and
beyond. New York: Hart.
Johnson. D.W. (1972)
Reaching Out. Englewood Cliffs, NJ: Prentice-Hall.
Katz, M.R. (1968)
Can computers make guidance decisions for students?
College Board Review, No. 72.
Kirschenbaum, H. (1977)
Advanced Value Clarification. La Jolla, Ca: University
Associates.
Krantzler, M. (1973)
Creative Divorce. New York: M. Evans.
Lamott, K. (1975)
Escape from Stress. New York: Berkley.
Mahoney, M.J. and Mahoney, J. (1976)
Permanent Weight Control. New York: W.W. Norton.
Maslow, A. (1968)
Towards a Psychology of Being (2nd edn). New York: Van
Nostrand.
Parkes, C. Murray (1972)
Bereavement: Studies of grief in adult life. London:
Tavistock.
Royal Canadian Air Force (1978)
Physical Fitness. Harmondsworth: Penguin.
Russel, P. (1977)
The Transcendental Meditation Technique. London:
Routledge & Kegan Paul.
Sharpe, R. and Lewis, D. (1977)
Thrive on Stress. London: Souvenir Press.

Simon, S. (1974)
Meeting Yourself Halfway. Hoddesdon, Herts: Argus
Publications.

Simon, S., Howe, L.W. and Kirschenbaum, H. (1972)
Value Clarification. New York: Hart.

Toffler, A. (1970)
Future Shock. New York: Random House.

Watts, A.G. and Elsom, D. (1975)
Deciding. Cambridge: Hobsons Press.

Questions

1. Why is an understanding of the psychological processes of level 1 transitions important to your profession?
2. What are the major types of transition and how are they related?
3. How would you set about rating the impact of life events on people?
4. Critically evaluate the Hopson-Adams model of transitions.
5. What effect do transitions have on people?
6. What are the coping tasks relevant to all transitions?
7. Describe the coping skills which are relevant to transitions.
8. Which will be the most important influence in ensuring a successful transition and why? Is it the coping skills of the mover or the structure and practices of the organization, institution or social norms?
9. Describe a life transition in terms of the stages the person might go through and what he could do to maximize the chances of coping with it effectively and gaining from the experience.
10. How effectively can we train people to improve their transition coping skills?

Annotated reading

Adams, J.D., Hayes, J. and Hopson, B. (1976) Transition: Understanding and managing personal change. London: Martin Robertson.

This is the first attempt to provide a conceptual framework to describe the psychological sequence of a transition. It is primarily a theoretical book, although some guidelines for the practitioner are available.

Hopson, B. and Scally, M. (1980) How to cope with and gain from life transitions. In B. Hopson and M. Scally, Lifeskills Teaching Programmes No. 1. Leeds: Lifeskills Associates.

This is for a classroom teacher of young people and consists of a series of carefully described group exercises to teach young people about transitions and how to cope more effectively with them.

Parkes, C. Murray (1975) Bereavement: Studies of grief in adult life. Harmondsworth: Penguin.

This book is about more than bereavement, although it is discussed at great length. Parkes generalizes from bereavement to other aspects of separation and loss in people's lives.

11

Creating Change
H. R. Beech

Politicians and kings have perhaps made the most distinctive
and historically interesting attempts to change the behaviour of those they seek to control. Sometimes this has
involved extreme measures, such as torture and execution,
sometimes more subtle legal approaches to behaviour control,
but these attempts perversely - and to the bafflement of the
controller - have often failed to produce the desired
outcome. Somehow, it seems, human nature appears to be
resistant to change.

Psychologists are disposed to argue that such failures
are mainly attributable to two causes. First, until
recently, there was an obvious lack of the technology to
effect changes with any degree of reliability: the methods
which had been used before were both crude and unsystema-
tically applied. Second, sometimes the attempts to effect
change involved very fundamental aspects of human functioning and it might not be within the capacity of the
species to accomplish them. Indeed, the contention of the
behavioural psychologist these days might be that substantial changes can be wrought in carefully selected
behaviours where the appropriate techniques can be freely
applied. This is not to say, of course, that some psychologists fail to perceive in these strategies a means of
acquiring very substantial or near complete control over
human nature or, indeed, the means by which the very fabric
of society could be altered. Of course, it would be unwise
to allow psychologists (even if their techniques did permit
such achievements) also to determine the types of change to
be brought about. Psychologists are in no better position to
decide what kind of society we should live in than is any
other group.

For the most part, however, the aims and aspirations of
psychologists are generally less ambitious and merely
involve the deployment of strategies for change to areas
where help is needed and requested. But to understand the
origin of these strategies it is first useful to describe
the influence exerted by Freud and Pavlov.

Freud's theories (Munroe, 1955) were important because
they gave an entirely new interpretation to 'bad', 'wrong'
or 'unacceptable' behaviour. Rather than seeing these behaviours as the reflection of something defective in the very

substance of man, Freud argued that such conduct arose out of environmental experiences. Indeed, Freud is often thought of as a thoroughgoing psychic determinist, believing that all behaviour is determined by prior experience and, in a very real sense, is programmed to be just the way it is, free will and choice being merely illusory. In short, enormous importance is attached to the influence of the environment as a determinant of what we are.

Pavlov (1927) was also interested in how behaviour became modified (although primarily concerned with how the physiological systems of animals worked) and devised the method of classical conditioning to assist in this endeavour. The definitive experiment carried out in his laboratory was to show that, after training, the sound of a bell could produce salivation in dogs. Clearly the dog does not start life with this capacity and needs to learn this reaction, and it is the process by which such learning takes place that is called 'classical conditioning'. Briefly, the process involves presenting the new stimulus (bell) before the old stimulus (food) to the response (salivation). Repetitions of this arrangement, with only a brief (say half a second) interval between the sound of the bell and pre- sentation of food leads to the new association being formed. Instead of requiring food before salivating, the dog now has come to salivate at the sound of the bell alone.

Perhaps not of itself a particularly compelling piece of learning, but to many psychologists this type of association appeared as one of the fundamental building blocks of learn- ing; such learning could be seen as underpinning all human behaviour.

An early enthusiast of Pavlov's work, Watson, was said to have been so impressed by such demonstrations of condi- tioning that he declared that any American child might be turned into the President using these methods. Whether or not Watson accorded such power to classical conditioning, he was certainly enthusiastic to use it and has achieved an important place in psychological history through his Little Albert experiment (1920).

In this study Watson's aim was to investigate the acquisition of emotional responses, arguing that they are probably learned by the associative process called condi- tioning. For this demonstration he chose an 11-month-old boy called Albert and set out to create a learned emotional reaction in this child. Watson had observed Albert's fondness for a tame white rat and chose to reverse this feeling by arranging for a loud noise to be made (by crashing two metal plates together behind Albert's head) whenever the child reached out for this pet. After just a few trials of this kind, Albert's fear, occasioned by the sudden loud noise, was transferred to the white rat so that every time this animal appeared Little Albert would whimper and crawl away. Furthermore, it was noted that the new fear reaction had transferred to other objects with some similarity to the rat (e.g. a ball of cotton wool) and it appeared to be enduring over the period of observation.

This latter observation led Watson to speculate upon the fate of a more mature Albert, lying on the psychoanalyst's couch, and vainly trying to understand how he came to worry about white fluffy objects! But the conditioning process might well be the basis for all our irrational (neurotic) fears.

It is important to point out, however, that the environment is not the only contributing factor to learning since, from Pavlov on, it has been observed that not all learning opportunities are realized or, if they are, there are individual differences in the character of the learning which is affected.

The earliest experimental observations of such limitations of a purely environmentalist approach were made by Pavlov. He is said to have first formed this conclusion as a result of flood waters entering his laboratories in Leningrad, finding that this had made some of the animals very disturbed while others appeared to treat the matter with indifference. Later, experiments showed more conclusively that some animals appeared to be susceptible to disturbance and others more phlegmatic, these two types being labelled 'weak' and 'strong' nervous systems respectively. This differentiation has been repeatedly confirmed in the experimental work of other investigators and clearly shows that an opportunity to learn is not all that is involved: a major influence is the basic temperament of the organism which is doing the learning.

Another study which points to this conclusion was conducted by Rachman (1966). The problem posed by the investigator here was that of whether or not fetishistic behaviour (sexual arousal to unusual stimuli) could be acquired by a simple associative process. Briefly, three male volunteers were exposed to conditions in which pictures of boots were linked with pictures of an erotic nature to see if bonding occurred in such a way that the sight of boots alone would produce sexual excitement. Such was in fact found to be the case and establishes that fetishes can come about through associations of this kind. However, the point to be made here is that the subjects took varying numbers of trials to lose such reactions; in short, the disposition of the individual seems to be very much implicated in what we learn and how well such learning is preserved.

Generally these results are thought to reflect some permanent characteristics of the individuals concerned, but it is important to add that even temporary states of the organism can affect learning, a point which has been made by Beech and others (see Vila and Beech, 1978).

Clinical experience would tend to indicate that symptoms of distress (e.g. inability to go out of the house or to meet others socially without feeling anxious) often appear to be preceded by a period of general tension and emotional upset; it is as if such states prepare the ground for certain kinds of learning to take place: as if they put the organism on a defensive footing, ready to react adversely to relatively minor provocation. The kind of disturbance referred to here is quite commonly experienced by women in the few days prior to menstruation and has been given the name of pre-menstrual tension. If this condition is a good parallel to the situation in which abnormal fears can arise, then it should be possible to show a propensity for 'defensive' or adverse learning in pre-menstrual days which is not present at other times in the cycle. This is, in fact, what has been found. The evidence indicates that the state of the organism at the time when some noxious event is present not only determines the speed at which learning takes place but also any tendency for the learning to be preserved over time. One might be tempted to argue that this 'natural' disposition to acquire neurotic symptoms could explain why disproportionately large numbers of women complain of neurotic symptoms.

Another influence to be taken into account as limiting the scope of a purely environmentalist view of human behaviour is that of biological potential for learning. The argument here has been cogently presented by Seligman and Hager (1972), who conclude that all organisms appear to show a great readiness to acquire certain associations while other connections will be made only with difficulty or even not at all. Among the examples cited by Seligman and Hager is that of the dog which can very quickly associate the operation of a latch with its paw to escape from a box, but seems quite unable to learn to effect escape by wagging its tail. It is not that tail-wagging is a difficult action for the dog to perform or even that it is an uncommon reaction; rather it seems that the problem lies in making the connection itself. It is argued that the species has no biological propensity to make such a connection; the evolutionary history of the dog did not prepare the animal for this kind of learning.

It is not yet known to what extent humans are affected by preparedness, although it is obvious that certain connections appear to be 'natural' and made quite easily, while others are not. It has been suggested that a good example of preparedness is to be found in the prevalence of spider and snake phobia found in populations not at all at risk from these creatures. A more purely environmentalist approach might argue that one would need to be bitten by a spider or snake before a phobic reaction could be developed yet, obviously, there seems to be a great readiness in many people to display a wariness about spiders in a country such as England, while no such widespread fear is evoked by horses or hamsters. Somewhere in our evolutionary history, it can be argued, the species has acquired a readiness to respond with fear to potential dangers, including spiders and snakes. Perhaps this is why open spaces present a problem for many people; such 'exposure' was to be avoided in the interests of survival and this potential for acquiring a fear of open spaces is easily tapped.

The thoroughgoing environmentalist would want to argue that man is virtually a blank sheet, a complicated learning machine and, given the appropriate incentives and opportunities, can be moulded to any desired pattern. In the light of the limitations to learning which have been mentioned it is obviously appropriate to take a more moderate view and regard man as a creature highly susceptible to modification through learning, but far from infinitely so. As yet, we do not know quite how far the capacity to learn can take us. Can it, for example, so change human nature that one becomes entirely altruistic, greed, selfishness and other 'human failings' becoming totally alien? There are those, like Dawkins (1978) who would not think this possible but, on the other hand, Skinner (1953) and many others see almost limitless possibilities to behaviour modification with the psycho-technology currently available even now.

For Skinnerians the basic principle of change can be stated quite simply; the consequences of any piece of behaviour affects the future of that behaviour. If the consequence is rewarding then the behaviour is strengthened (i.e. rendered more likely to occur again); if it is punishing, then the same response tends to be weakened. Using this basic proposition, it is argued, far-reaching changes can be made to occur.

Of course, such a view is as profoundly hedonistic as Pavlov's or Freud's, the basic contention being that man is simply a pleasure-maximizing, pain-minimizing organism; this is as much part and parcel of his make-up as any other creature. Changing behaviour, according to this view, depends upon the nature, timing and other attributes of rewards and punishments rather than upon appeals to reason or religious precepts.

There is, understandably, considerable resistance to accepting such a stark view of man's nature; it appears to accord no place at all to free will and choice, nor does it allow man any special place in biological or other terms. Hedonism is the key mechanism in what we are; man can (and does) learn to do and to be anything, providing that the rewards and punishments are there to chart the way.

What we can now do is to examine the achievements to date; to see how far Pavlovian and Skinnerian principles of learning have been effective in producing change. It is anyone's guess how much further it is possible to go.

Aversive learning

Most of us subscribe to the validity of the adages that 'the burnt child dreads the fire' or 'once bitten, twice shy'. These sayings simply embody the importance of pain avoidanc in our biological make-up. Clearly, deprived of such protection the species could hardly be expected to survive; we learn pretty quickly and thoroughly if the consequences of some actions are painful. Yet there appear to be some notable exceptions to such a compelling principle; martyrs and heroes often seem to subject themselves to avoidable pain while hard-bitten criminals may appear unaffected by the punishment society metes out to them. Obviously the problem is more complex than at first sight appears. Perhaps one should not be overly influenced by these exceptions, since the rule does seem to hold in general, but it is just as well to begin by recognizing that the results of punishment are unpredictable. For that matter, the outcome of rewarding behaviours shows much the same variability and such findings make fools of those who argue for simple solutions. For example, on the one hand there are those who want to create a better society by wreaking extreme retribution upon all who infringe rules while, on the other, the 'progressives' appear to think that the solution to crime is to remove all sources of discomfort and irritation. Both views, obviously, are patently absurd; crime has persisted in spite of great harshness in past years and, as is now well documented, the rate has risen dramatically as the number of social workers, leisure centres and social welfare has increased.

There are several arguments advanced to explain why punishment fails to achieve good effects in the context under discussion. In the first place it is said that its application is seldom timely: it works very well if immediate, but poorly or not at all if the crime and later court sentence are separated by lengthy intervals of time. Second, it is said that the rate of successful to unsuccessful crime is unfavourable to learning to resist temptation: numerous crimes may be rewarded before one act leads to punishment. A third argument is that the rate of criminal behaviour is inversely related to the strength of punishment, and that deterrents are not nearly strong enough to be effective. Yet another reason is said to be the temperament of the habitual criminal who, it is alleged, does not generate the kind of anxiety which most of us experience when 'wrong doing'. This last point refers to evidence that the nervous systems of individuals appear to extend over a range from the excessive 'jumpiness' of the chronically anxious at one end of the spectrum to those who appear to be 'psychopathically' resistant to showing disturbance to even strong stimulation.

There is probably something to be said for each of these points and, at least, all serve to indicate the complexities which may underlie the application of punishments.

To some extent it is possible to avoid a number of these problems when aversive consequences are part of a treatment programme; here, more of what takes place is under the control of the therapist or experimenter. Perhaps the best-known example of this is to be found in the treatment of alcoholism. With this, an attempt is made to ensure that drinking (and stimulus situations related to it) leads to aversive consequences; a convenient means of achieving this in practice has been to administer an emetic drug and, when this is beginning to take effect, the individual is permitted to sip the alcohol to which he is addicted. Unpleasant feelings of nausea and vomiting will, in this way, become associated with the particular sight, smell and taste involved (Voegtlin and Lemere, 1942).

Of course, it can be argued that simply punishing the 'wrong' response is hardly likely to lead to the adoption of a socially-acceptable reaction. What, for example, can the homosexual do with the sexual impulses he experiences after the usual way in which these are expended have been denied to him by punishment? Accordingly, more sophisticated attempts to help have included not only punishment but also opportunities to escape from punishment. In the context of treating homosexuals, for instance, the individual concerned has been allowed access to slides depicting homosexual activity only at the cost of receiving strong electric shocks, while the rejection of such slides and their substitution by heterosexual material can lead to the avoidance of punishment altogether.

A perennial problem of aversive training has been that of securing appropriate levels of co-operation and motivation and, no doubt, many failures are attributable to this difficulty. A simple example of this clarifies the point in practical terms. The investigation here was of a young boy whose habit of thumb-sucking was to be dealt with by capitalizing upon his enjoyment of cartoons. The therapist arranged for the boy to sit through protracted showings of cartoon films but these showings ceased abruptly if thumb-sucking occurred, and the film would only be continued when this behaviour stopped. It took a relatively short time for the boy to control his bad habit during the film shows but it was noted that the training had no effect upon what happened outside that situation! Indeed, one might reasonably argue that, in this case, the boy had learned how to control the behaviour of the psychologist, rather than the opposite!

Since aversion therapy is given only to those voluntarily submitting themselves to this form of training, one should be able to assume a reasonable level of motivation to change. However, as we all recognize from personal experience, our commitment to change can be quite ephemeral and today's resolution to give up smoking (or whatever) can disappear completely tomorrow. Perhaps this is only another way of saying that the aversive condition has not been applied sufficiently vigorously or intensively to inhibit the temptation: the associative bond between aversive feelings and the 'unwanted' action is insufficiently strongly made. Nevertheless, it is apparent that this problem is a major obstacle to the success of punishment as a means of control.

Systematic desensitization

Few doubt the power of anxiety to alter and disrupt ordinary behaviour patterns; anxiety can handicap our attempts to cope with a whole range of life's problems, it may prevent anything approaching an adjustment to quite ordinary events and it may totally ruin our enjoyment of relationships and circumstances which should be pleasurable. The capacity to deal with and eliminate anxiety can be regarded as of major importance to the effective control of our

behaviour since, essentially, anxiety is a disruptive
influence which erodes our capacity to control our own
thought and action. In short, changing behaviour often seems
to involve removing anxiety.

The behavioural strategy to resolve this problem appears
to be surprisingly direct and simple. All that is needed is
a gradual, step-by-step approach to the feared object or
situation together with some means of inhibiting anxiety at
each of these stages. The technique for accomplishing this
was developed and refined by Wolpe (1969). More than 30
years earlier Mary Cover Jones (1924) had described essentially the same method in successfully eliminating the
children's fears and, in a sense, there seems to be nothing
particularly remarkable or novel in the method. Nevertheless, Wolpe's standardization of an effective technique for
the analysis of anxiety and the application of a treatment
strategy was enormously important from both practical and
theoretical points of view.

The basic argument is that fear (or anxiety) has inad-
vertently, through a process of association, become a
learned reaction to the presence of certain cues. For
example, fear may be triggered by the presence of several
people because, at some time in the past, the individual has
been made anxious in a social setting; or anxiety is aroused
by the sound of quarrelling voices because, at some time,
the individual was threatened by the belligerence of others.
The task of treatment, therefore, is to sever this connection: to detach anxiety from the innocuous cue.

Some years ago the author was asked for help in removing
an extreme fear of spiders in a lady so incapacitated by
this anxiety that she was unable to perform household
chores. Any article of furniture moved or corner dusted
might dislodge one of these alarming creatures and so occa-
sion acute anxiety. Being outdoors clearly also presented
problems to this lady, although she recognized that her fear
was actually groundless in the sense that none of the
spiders she encountered, indoors or out, could actually harm
her.

Questioning revealed that the fear she experienced could
be broken down into a number of separate components which,
in various combinations, could evoke either more or less
anxiety. Size, for example, was an important variable: the
larger the spider the more fear would be experienced.
Similarly, blackness, hairiness, degree of activity, and
proximity all affected the amount of fear experienced. It
was possible, therefore, to describe 'spider situations'
which would produce little by way of upset, and others which
would create a good deal. A small, light-coloured, apparently hairless spider, quite dead and at some distance
away, would cause only mild apprehension, while an active,
large, black and hairy spider, galloping across her body,
would produce a sense of panic.

One must begin, in desensitization treatment, with the
least anxiety-provoking situation and as each of these

ceases to produce anxiety, so one moves on to the next step
in the hierarchy. In the spider phobic case quoted, one can
obviously begin with exhibiting a small, dead, pale-
coloured, hairless spider in one corner of the room, while
the patient sits in the opposite corner. When this condition
ceases to produce anxiety, then the insect can be moved a
little closer or, alternatively, some characteristic can be
changed (e.g. substitution of a slightly larger specimen) so
that we have moved one notch up the fear hierarchy.

What is notable here is that each step in the hierarchy
appears to produce a smaller reaction than was anticipated
before treatment; it is as if accomplishing each step has
resulted in some small but discernible loss in the total
anxiety now experienced. This kind of psychological arith-
metic applies with every step taken, so that the total
amount of anxiety to be eliminated becomes less and less.

So far so good, but systematic desensitization involves
some means of INHIBITING anxiety at each stage, for only
in this way can the anxiety connection be broken. Each
hierarchical step, therefore, must be capable of producing
some amount of fear, but this must be sufficiently small to
be extinguished by some other feeling state, and the most
convenient means of achieving this is to train the individual in muscle relaxation.

It is argued that muscle relaxation is in fact an ideal
counter to anxiety feelings, since it is both easy to learn
and very effective. In short, there is good evidence that
one cannot be anxious and completely relaxed at the same
time; relaxation effectively inhibits the experience of
fear. Accordingly, such training precedes the hierarchical
presentation of fear stimuli; the individual is instructed
to remain as relaxed as possible each time the fear-stimulus
is presented so that the experience of anxiety is controlled. In this way a new type of association is being
learned: that in the presence of certain cues which
previously occasioned fear, no such feelings are present.

Understandably, while this method may work quite well
it is not one which is easily put into practice in all
cases. The various spider specimens needed to form the
hierarchy may be easily secured, but in the case of, say, a
fear of flying, there are serious practical problems. One
could not, for example, easily arrange that the aeroplane
merely completes the dash down the runway (as one item on
the hierarchy) without actually taking off (which may occupy
a very different hierarchical level). The necessary control
over the situation here, and in numerous other cases, simply
could not be achieved.

This problem is solved by presenting such situations as
imagined scenes instead of as real-life experiences. This
obviously makes it very much easier to arrange for events to
accord precisely with treatment requirements and allows all
the refined control over circumstances that one would wish
to have. The only question to ask about this solution is
that of whether or not dealing with an imagined situation is

as beneficial as dealing with the real one. The evidence indicates that it is, although all therapists like to include experience of the real event (the real spider, lift, aeroplane, etc.) as a way of consolidating and affirming the new found absence of fear. Merely learning not to experience anxiety in imagined examples of fear aspects or situations, using the little-by-little approach and suppressing any worry by preserving muscle relaxation, can produce important changes in behaviour.

This approach is widely used in the treatment of major and incapacitating phobias with considerable success, but it is worth pointing out that less extreme conditions, including those commonly found in young children, respond very well to sympathetic handling along these lines. Fear of school, of being left by mother, of playing with strange children, of insects, of the car, and many others respond well to the graduated approach described and, of course, the benefit to behaviour generally of shedding such fears makes the effort well worth while.

gnitive learning

It will be apparent from the description of the behavioural approaches given so far that they seem to depend upon a rather mechanical conception of learning. Insight, explanation, logic and other ways in which we come to modify or correct our view of things appear to count for nothing: the assumption is that we simply cannot talk anyone out of being alcoholic or experiencing acute anxiety; they must be taught to do so by a painstaking and carefully conceived programme of training which avoids any appeal to the 'mind'. Yet we are aware that cognitive learning does occur since we can behave differently as a result of being told that this or that is the case, or by receiving instructions to do something in a particular way. Indeed, if everything about our behaviour had to be acquired by trial and error or successive approximations, then learning would be tedious, slow and in many cases inefficient.

The charge often levelled at the behavioural approach is that it ignores the conceptual thinking that is so peculiarly and importantly human. But this is to misunderstand the situation since it is apparent that the kind of learning process required to effect change appears to depend upon what it is about our behaviour that we are trying to modify. Furthermore, it has been argued that mental events (cognitions, thoughts) are also behaviours and amenable to the same laws and, to an extent, the same training methods.

A good example is the technique called 'thought stopping'. Essentially this represents the attempt to produce the disruption or inhibition of a mental process in much the same way as some more overt activity might be stopped. It is usual to begin (see Wolpe, 1969) with a demonstration by the therapist that a sudden, unexpected and loud noise (banging the table, for example) can interrupt a particular focus of attention. In the same way, it is pointed out, an unpleasant and persistent idea can be interrupted and, with practice, might become permanently inhibited. By stages, the control of the interruptive signal is transferrred from therapist to patient and then from an external signal (banging on the table) to an internal one (saying 'stop' to oneself).

It is readily apparent that this strategy is direct, simple, and treats ideas or cognitions in much the same way as any reflex or motor action. There is, in the application of this technique, nothing special about mental events: they are simply regarded as internal behaviours.

A rather less rigorous behaviour approach is to be found in Rational Emotive Therapy; indeed, many hard-nosed behaviourists would reject any claim that RET derives from learning or conditioning theories and deny that there is any identifiable trace of the behavioural tradition in RET. Nevertheless, this cognitive approach has features which are 'behavioural' in character; for example, the emphasis upon the here-and-now rather than the influence of early life experiences, the parsimonious theoretical formulations, the implicit and explicit dependence upon reinforcing experiences and the directness of attack upon a clearly-identified source of malfunctioning. The main thrust of the technique (Ellis, 1962) derives from the assumption that faulty thinking is revealed in what people say to themselves; such 'self-talk' influences overt behaviours, so changing the cognitions can influence the way we act and feel.

Part of the immediate appeal of this technique lies in the very obviousness that 'self-talk' is a major preoccupation of us all when we are beset by difficulties. As a simple example, when girl informs boy that their relationship is ended a positive torrent of internal conversations is likely to be triggered: 'I am in a terrible mess ... I can't believe it ... there's no hope ... what can I do, nothing matters any more ...' etc. Such self-talk is likely to be accompanied by observable behaviour such as weeping, not eating or sleeping, refusing to socialize, failing to deal adequately with work assignments, and so on.

RET concentrates attention upon those things which are objectively true (e.g. 'she no longer loves me') and those which are not ('no one cares ... life is over ... there'll never be anyone else for me ...'). It is contended that when one is forced to examine the illogicality of deducing certain conclusions from the premise 'she doesn't love me', then shifts toward more positive emotions and behaviours have to occur. Attention is, of course, directed to all faulty ideas which serve as props for disappointment and disillusion: many of these quite commonplace errors of thinking which we are better rid of. For example, that one must always appear competent and without sign of weakness, that one must always have evidence that one is loved, needed and approved of, or that any adverse comment means that no one is to be trusted.

There is no doubt that this kind of counselling approach can help us to gain a perspective on life's bumps and abrasions and so prevent exaggerated and damaging emotional reactions. Yet there are obviously important limitations to an approach which depends so heavily upon exposing the illogicality of much self-talk; the point about such states of mind, as about prejudices of all kinds, is that they tend to be rather resistant to a logical approach. There is, it often seems, a strong desire to bring ideas into line with the feelings being experienced.

Furthermore, a cognitive strategy tends to pay little attention to the internal alterations of state which can often prompt the appearance of faulty ideas. Anyone with experience of depression will recognize that talking someone out of such a state is not just a tall order but pretty well impossible. No doubt where the pattern of gloomy thoughts and ideas arise out of what may be a purely environmental circumstance - a lost job, a failed exam, a lost love - a logical analysis of thoughts and feelings can be beneficial, but perhaps such circumstances are less common than one might at first suppose. Perhaps in part these environmental traumas are not random events but, to a degree, are visited upon those of us who are already vulnerable to an extent.

A cognitive technique which translates rather better from the traditional areas of behavioural concern to mental events is covert sensitization (Cautela, 1966). Basically, this method represents the application of aversive control to thoughts (as opposed to 'actions' such as drinking alcohol or operating a fruit machine) and involves imagined scenes of the unwanted behaviour followed by imagined noxious consequences. For example, the overweight gluttonous lady may be asked to conjure up images of a table groaning under the weight of delicious food, stuffing herself to bursting with cream cake and other goodies and then to create the mental picture of being sick: vomit spilling out over the table, over her dress, on to the food, and so on. In short, it is hoped to create the cognitive equivalent of real events with the consequences of overeating being highly unpleasant and embarrassing.

Another example comes from Foa (1976), whose male client derived sexual gratification from dressing in woman's clothing. This had brought him to the courts, where he was then referred for treatment. Covert sensitization took the form of requiring the patient to imagine that he is driving along in his car when he sees a clothes line on which desirable articles of clothing are hanging; he stops, gets out and attempts to take these clothes, but as he does so, he is overcome by intense feelings of nausea. He is then required to imagine throwing the clothes away and feeling very much better.

It is worth pointing out that in this case, as in other examples of aversive training, the unwanted habit returned again following an initially successful outcome. Generally, the therapist takes account of the need to deal with this problem by arranging 'booster' courses of treatment as and when the need arises.

Operant training

It is apparent from the accounts given that the behavioural approach to change is strongly hedonistic; organisms learn when rewarded and 'unlearn' when punished. Perhaps more than in any other technique of learning, operant training exemplifies this dependence upon the manipulation of the consequences of behaviour: a consequence which is rewarding (positively reinforcing) will strengthen some reaction or response, while one which is punishing (negatively reinforcing) will weaken and discourage further behaviour of the same kind.

It was not until B. F. Skinner's 1953 publication that there was any systematic account of the circumstances under which rewards and punishments work best. Experimenting with small animals, often rats, Skinner was able to demonstrate convincingly that if some observable piece of behaviour (response) was followed consistently by reward, the chances of the same behaviour occurring in a similar situation on subsequent occasions would increase. Similarly, if a response was punished, it would become less likely to occur. Three very important aspects of the apparently simple relationship between response and consequences arose from these animal studies. First, it is imperative that the reinforcement applied to the subject really is rewarding or punishing for them. A puff at a cigarette is obviously pleasant and rewarding to some humans but would probably prove aversive to most rats, whereas the dry food pellets enjoyed by rats would be of little interest to most humans. The second point was that, at least initially, the reinforcement (reward or punishment) must follow immediately after the target response is performed. If we wish to increase the frequency with which a rat presses a lever, it is no use providing the reward half-an-hour after the response has occurred; the necessary association between lever-pressing and, say, food reward would simply not be made. Third, as well as being immediate, the reinforcement must be applied consistently. Under all but very extreme circumstances, the rat does not learn to press a lever as a result of a single reward for doing so but needs numerous rewarded trials until lever-pressing is acquired. It is best to reward every trial initially, for although learning can take place if rewards (or punishments) are more spread out, it is very much slower. However, once learned, a response may be maintained by occasional reinforcement.

Many psychologists have been attracted by Skinnerian research and have applied the rules to the modification of human behaviour. The degree of success which has been achieved has been surprising in view of the frequent criticisms of Skinner's approach as essentially simplistic and mechanistic. Perhaps the greatest changes that have been made in order to accommodate Skinner's system to work with humans have been in response to the obvious superiority of their thinking, memory and reasoning as well as their capacity to use and to understand language. These skills have had most effect on the second aspect of reinforcement

described above. As long as a person realizes that reinforcement will be contingent upon his behaviour within a
reasonable time, it may not be necessary for the reinforcement to be immediate. That individual will be able to think
about or anticipate the delayed outcome. When working with
children, however, some tangible reminder may be given of
the reinforcement to come, such as a gold star immediately
on completion of some school work as a token representing,
say, extra playtime during the day.

The types of problems to which reinforcement procedures
may be applied range from minor irritating habits to major
disorders which threaten the well-being or even life of the
sufferer. Many examples from the field of child-management
may be cited to illustrate the least severe end of this
scale.

Many young children go through 'phases' which are both
worrying and irritating to their parents but usually not
harmful in themselves. An example of this would be the
temper tantrums fairly frequently observed in toddlers. In
nearly all cases such episodes last a few weeks or at most
months and then disappear of their own accord. In a few
cases they persist much longer, or with greater severity,
and perhaps begin to disrupt family life. Providing the
cause is not due to some physical illness, one may attempt
to modify the behaviour by applying appropriate reinforcements. Very often it is found that the child receives a
great deal of attention when he has a tantrum, usually
because it is alarming and upsetting to his parents. On the
other hand, when he is occupied and behaving well, his
parents, sighing with relief, turn their attention to other
things, effectively ignoring good behaviour. Evidently the
child is being rewarded for having a tantrum but is punished
(as being ignored can be aversive) for being well behaved.
With these contingencies it is no wonder that such behaviour
becomes more frequent and good behaviour becomes rarer.
Tantrums may be modified simply by reversing reward and
punishment; his parents leave him to his own devices when he
has a tantrum but take great care to play with him and talk
to him when he is being good. Applied systematically, such
a straightforward alteration of reinforcements can have
amazingly rapid and beneficial effects.

Even relatively minor behaviour problems in children may
have more serious effects on their eventual welfare. One
form of difficulty that has been tackled fairly often in
this way is disruptive classroom behaviour. A child who is
frequently out of his seat, moving around and making a
noise, usually benefits less from his schooling than his
more appropriately behaved peers and is likely to fall
behind with his work. In addition he may become unpopular
with his companions as he upsets their work and interferes
with their games. In a busy classroom, such a child is often
reprimanded by the teacher when he is a nuisance but
receives very little attention for being 'good' since this
occurs infrequently and he rarely produces work of a high

enough standard to merit praise. Relatively mild chastise-
ments from the teacher may be more rewarding for the child
(being preferred to no attention at all) so the child is
rewarded for being disruptive and ignored for practically
everything else. As with the younger child, the task is to
reverse the contingencies. In this case it may not be possible for the teacher to ignore the bad behaviour entirely
but, usually, the amount of time and effort spent in the
reprimand can be reduced significantly so that the child
receives a minimum of attention for each disruptive act. At
the same time he is rewarded for appropriate behaviour and
an acceptable (although possibly lower than average) standard of work. If possible, the reward is given immediately
with attention and praise but may be supplemented by the use
of stars or marks for good conduct, and these tokens can be
exchanged for privileges at the end of the day. Usually the
co-operation of not only the teacher and pupil but also of
the entire class is required to make this procedure fully
effective.

The much-publicized condition of anorexia nervosa is an
example of a life-threatening state which may sometimes be
ameliorated by the use of reinforcement procedures. Patients
suffering from this disorder are most commonly girls in
their mid- to late-teens who have begun to diet excessively,
and now refuse to eat and sabotage attempts to feed them
by hiding the food or vomiting. Many lose so much weight
that they must be confined to bed. The main management
problem is to reinstate eating.

There is no single acceptable account of why a girl
begins to become anorexic but there is commonly evidence of
considerable social reinforcement for not eating once
serious dieting is under way, since serious weight loss
causes friends and relatives to become increasingly concerned and respond to refusals to eat by attention and
attempts to coax and persuade, and this attention contributes to the maintenance of not eating. Attempts have been
made to make positive reinforcement contingent upon eating
rather than not eating and, to do this, the patient has been
socially isolated and denied pleasures such as radio and
television in order to maximize the rewarding effect of
social contact. It has been arranged that a friendly therapist will eat each meal with the patient and converse with
her when, and only when, she eats a mouthful of food. Once
eating a meal has been established, the reward is made less
immediate by allowing the patient to earn time with the
therapist or friends after the meal has been eaten. She is
also allowed access to television, etc., in the same way.
This kind of procedure has been found to produce important
weight gain in a number of patients. When described in
outline it may appear that the patient is the passive
recipient of reinforcement, unaware of the contingencies
that have been planned, but this is far from the case, as
most patients become involved with the preparation of their
programmes, the negotiation of weight targets, amounts to
be eaten, planning rewards and agreeing to contingencies.

It is clear that reinforcement contingencies can be applied effectively to a wide range of behaviour problems in humans. As long as the contingencies are appropriately rewarding or punishing, and the consequences fairly immediate and consistent, the reinforcement is likely to be effective, but the chances of success will be increased if the person with the problem is involved in the construction and discussion of his own management programme.

conclusion

Behavioural approaches to change tend to lack appeal when compared to other methods. We would prefer, for example, to think that we are amenable to logic and reason and that if only the facts are made available to us we could change to be in accord with them. Or, in other contexts, we may find the dramatic aspects of psychoanalysis more compelling, with the eccentricities of human behaviour being explained as the result of mysterious and excitingly interesting forces. Certainly, behavioural approaches stand in sharp contrast and seem to inspire all the excitement of Latin conjugations!

On the other hand, while the techniques admittedly tend to apply about as well to animals as to man, their clarity and simplicity arises from sound experimental work and scientific thought, qualities which in any other context would be thought commendable. It is worth while to offer the example of bedwetting as a means of showing how such thinking offers distinct advantages over a more tortuous and complex account.

Psychoanalysts are inclined to regard bedwetting as merely the external sign of some inner turmoil. It has been regarded, for example, as a substitute for sexual gratification or a means by which a child can express aggression and resentment toward others. The behavioural formulation is starkly simple; individuals LEARN to be dry at night and some fail to acquire this skill. If the former view is correct, then simply removing the behaviour (bedwetting) would not cure the inner discontent; if the behavioural view is correct, however, then getting rid of the symptom would be a very useful thing.

Mowrer's (1938) simple device to unlearn bedwetting was in fact highly successful and is very widely used today. It deals directly with the symptom and in most cases bedwetting is eliminated. No evidence exists of any underlying pathological process of the kind postulated by the psychoanalyst.

Naturally, one example of a greater claim to effectiveness does not establish the general superiority of the behavioural approach, yet it does seem that such examples can be multiplied many times over. This is, in fact, what one would expect from a model constructed from painstaking laboratory experimental work and scientific formulations.

It is not, of course, that the approach or the techniques deriving from it, some of which have been briefly reviewed here, are either wildly successful or beyond criticism. There are, indeed, numerous difficulties and shortcomings and, as indicated earlier, one of the most serious of these is the partiality of the purely environmentalist viewpoint and the almost complete neglect of genetic/constitutional influences. Nevertheless, behavioural strategies now occupy a position of high importance for psychologists, and the influence of these strategies in many and diverse areas of application is still growing.

References

Cautela, J.B. (1966)
Treatment of compulsive behavior by covert sensitization. The Psychological Record, 16, 33-41.

Dawkins, R. (1978)
The Selfish Gene. Oxford: Oxford University Press.

Ellis, A. (1962)
Reason and Emotion in Psychotherapy. New York: Kyle Stewart.

Foa, E.B. (1976)
Multiple behaviour techniques in the treatment of transvestism. In H.J. Eysenck, Case Studies in Behaviour Therapy. London: Routledge & Kegan Paul.

Jones, M.C. (1924)
The elimination of children's fears. Journal of Experimental Psychology, 7, 383-90.

Mowrer, O.H. and Mowrer, W. (1938)
Enuresis: a method for its study and treatment. American Journal of Orthopsychiatry, 8, 436-59.

Munroe, R.L. (1955)
School of Psychoanalytic Thought. New York: Dryden Press.

Pavlov, I.P. (1927)
Conditioned Reflexes (Transl. Anrep). London: Oxford University Press.

Rachman, S. (1966)
Sexual fetishism: an experimental analogue. The Psychological Record, 16, 293-296.

Seligman, M.E.P. and Hager, J.L. (1972)
Biological Boundaries of Learning. New York: Appleton-Century-Crofts.

Skinner, B.F. (1953)
Science and Human Behavior. New York: Macmillan.

Vila, J. and Beech, H.R. (1978)
Vulnerability and defensive reactions in relation to the human menstrual cycle. British Journal of Social and Clinical Psychology, 17, 93-100.

Voegtlin, W.L. and Lemere, E. (1942)
The treatment of alcohol addiction. Quarterly Journal of Studies on Alcohol, 2, 717-803.

Watson, J.B. and Rayner, R. (1920)
Conditioned emotional reactions. Journal of Experimental Psychology, 3, 1-14.

Wolpe, J. (1969)
The Practice of Behavior Therapy. New York: Pergamon Press.

1. Describe the theoretical underpinnings of systematic desensitization as a treatment strategy to eliminate fear.
2. Drawing upon your personal experience, describe and discuss the incapacitating effect of anxiety on coping with a life problem you have had to face.
3. Describe the process of classical conditioning and how this process can account for the development of abnormal fears.
4. Discuss the differences between individuals in respect of their readiness to develop phobias.
5. To what extent can one argue that man is simply a product of his environmental experiences?
6. What are the implications of classical and operant conditioning for a crime prevention policy?
7. Describe the limitations of using aversive therapy as a means of changing behaviour.
8. What limitations do you perceive in attempting to change behaviour on the basis of experiences created in imagination?
9. Discuss the possible reasons behind the shift from the behavioural to a more 'cognitive' learning approach in dealing with problems of behaviour change.
10. Describe a behaviour modification technique that relies upon 'cognitive' learning.
11. What are the basic differences between 'cognitive' and behavioural strategies where behaviour change is concerned?
12. Describe a form of covert sensitization employed in the aversive control of thoughts.
13. In what sense can the behavioural approach be said to be hedonistic?
14. Responses and consequences are the two basic elements of operant training. Describe and discuss.
15. What are the basic requirements in providing reinforcement in order to secure effective behaviour change?
16. What criticisms of Skinner's approach can be offered?
17. To what extent do you think that we are affected in real life situations by the operation of reinforcement principles?
18. How could one apply an operant approach in a classroom to deal with disruptive class behaviour?
19. What are the main points of difference between the psychoanalytical and behavioural approaches?
20. List some of the common, everyday, psychological difficulties experienced and outline the behavioural strategies that might be useful in overcoming them.

Rachman, S. (1971) The Effects of Psychotherapy. Oxford: Pergamon Press.

    An account of the problems associated with psychotherapy and the way in which the behavioural approach deals with issues of treatment and training.

Kanfer, F.H. and Goldstein, A.P. (1975) Helping People Change: A textbook of methods. Oxford: Pergamon Press.
  An account of practical behavioural approaches to change.

Oakley, D. and Platkin, H. (1979) Brain, Behaviour and Evolution. London: Methuen.
  Undergraduate level synthesis of disciplines relevant to psychology. How evolutionary perspective can help our understanding of psychological questions.

Walker, S. (1976) Learning and Reinforcement. London: Methuen.
  Introductory text on key concepts to understanding behavioural approaches to change.

Boddy, A., Martin, F. and Jefferys, M. (eds) (in preparation) The Behavioural Sciences in General Practice. London: Tavistock.
  Primarily intended for GPs to enable the medical profession to acquire concepts relevant to their work so as to facilitate professional skill and expertise.

12

Counselling and Helping
Barrie Hopson

From a situation in the mid-1960s when 'counselling' was
seen by many in education as a transatlantic transplant
which hopefully would never 'take', we have today reached
the position of being on board a band-wagon; 'counsellors'
are everywhere: beauty counsellors, tax counsellors,
investment counsellors, even carpet counsellors. There are
'counsellors' in schools, industry, hospitals, the social
services. There is marriage counselling, divorce counselling, parent counselling, bereavement counselling, abortion
counselling, retirement counselling, redundancy counselling,
career counselling, psychosexual counselling, pastoral counselling, student counselling and even disciplinary counselling! Whatever the original purpose for coining the word
'counselling', the coinage has by now certainly been de-
based. One of the unfortunate consequences of the debasing
has been that the word has become mysterious; we cannot
always be sure just what 'counselling' involves. One of the
results of the mystification of language is that we rely on
others to tell us what it is: that is, we assume that we,
the uninitiated, cannot know and understand what it is
really about. That can be a first step to denying ourselves
skills and knowledge we already possess or that we may have
the potential to acquire.

It is vital that we 'de-mystify' counselling, and to do
that we must look at the concept within the broader context
of ways in which people help other people, and we must
analyse it in relation to objectives. 'Counselling' is often
subscribed to as being 'a good thing', but we must ask the
question, 'good for what?'

'Counselling' is only one form of helping. It is decidedly
not the answer to all human difficulties, though it can be
extremely productive and significant for some people, sometimes. Counselling is one way of working to help people
overcome problems, clarify or achieve personal goals. We can
distinguish between six types of helping strategies (Scally
and Hopson, 1979).

* Giving advice: offering somebody your opinion of what
  would be the best course of action based on your view
  of their situation.

* Giving information: giving a person the information he needs in a particular situation (e.g. about legal rights, the whereabouts of particular agencies, etc.). Lacking information can make one powerless; providing it can be enormously helpful.
* Direct action: doing something on behalf of somebody else or acting to provide for another's immediate needs; for example, providing a meal, lending money, stopping a fight, intervening in a crisis.
* Teaching: helping someone to acquire knowledge and skills; passing on facts and skills which improve somebody's situation.
* Systems change: working to influence and improve systems which are causing difficulty for people, that is, working on organizational development rather than with individuals.
* Counselling: helping someone to explore a problem, clarify conflicting issues and discover alternative ways of dealing with it, so that they can decide what to do about it; that is, helping people to help themselves.

There is no ranking intended in this list. What we do say is that these strategies make up a helper's 'tool-bag'. Each one is a 'piece of equipment' which may be useful in particular helping contexts. What a helper is doing is to choose from his resources whichever approach best fits the situation at the time.

There are some interesting similarities and differences between the strategies. Giving advice, information, direct action, teaching and possibly systems change recognize that the best answers, outcomes, or solutions rely on the expertise of the helper. The 'expert' offers what he feels is most useful to the one seeking help. Counselling, on the other hand, emphasizes that the person with the difficulty is the one with the resources needed to deal with it. The counsellor provides the relationship which enables the clients to search for their own answers. The 'expert' does not hand out solutions. This does not deny the special skills of the helper, but does imply that having 'expertise' does not make a person an 'expert'. We all have expertise. In counselling, the counsellor is using his expertise to help to get the clients in touch with their own expertise. Counselling is the only helping strategy which makes no assumption that the person's needs are known.

Teaching, systems change, and counselling are only likely to be effective if the 'helper' has relationship-making skills. Giving advice, information and direct action are likely to be MORE effective if he has them. Systems change is different in that it emphasizes work with groups, structures, rules and organizations.

The counsellor possibly uses most of the other strategies at some time or other, when they seem more appropriate than counselling. The other strategies would have an element of counselling in them if the 'helper' had the necessary skills. For example, a new student having difficulties making friends at school could involve a counsellor, in addition to using his counselling skills, teaching some relationship-building skills to the student, getting the staff to look at induction provision, making some suggestions to the student, or even taking him to a lunchtime disco session in the school club.

ho are the helpers?

Strictly speaking we are all potential helpers and people to be helped, but in this context it may be useful to distinguish between three groups.

Professional helpers
These are people whose full-time occupation is geared towards helping others in a variety of ways. They have usually, but not always, received specialist training. Social workers, doctors, teachers, school counsellors, nurses, careers officers and health visitors are a few examples. They define their own function in terms of one or more of the helping strategies.

Paraprofessional helpers
These people have a clearly defined helping role but it does not constitute the major part of their job specification or represent the dominant part of their lives, such as marriage guidance counsellors, priests, part-time youth workers, personnel officers and some managers. Probably they have received some short in-service training, often on-the-job.

Helpers in general
People who may not have any specially defined helping role but who, because of their occupational or social position or because of their own commitment, find themselves in situations where they can offer help to others, such as shop stewards, school caretakers, undertakers, social security clerks or solicitors. This group is unlikely to have received special training in helping skills. In addition to these groupings there are a variety of unstructured settings within which helping occurs: the family, friendships, and in the community (Brammer, 1973).

hat makes people good elpers?

In some ways it is easier to begin with the qualities that quite clearly do not make for good helping. Loughary and Ripley (1979) people their helpers' rogue's gallery with four types of would-be helpers:

* the 'You think YOU'VE got a problem! Let me tell you about mine!' type;
* the 'Let me tell you what to do' type;
* the 'I understand because I once had the same problem myself' person;
* the 'I'll take charge and deal with it' type.

271

The first three approaches have been clearly identified as
being counter-productive (Carkhuff and Berenson, 1976) while
the fourth one certainly deals with a person's problems but
prevents the person ever learning skills or concepts to
enable him to work through the problem on his own the next
time it occurs. The only possible appropriate place for this
person is in a crisis intervention. However, even this
intervention would need to be followed up with additional
counselling help if the needy person were to avoid such
crises.

Rogers (1958) came out with clearly testable hypotheses
of what constitutes effective helping. He said that helpers
must be open and that they should be able to demonstrate
UNCONDITIONED POSITIVE REGARD: acceptance of clients
as worth while regardless of who they are or what they say
or do; CONGRUENCE: the helper should use his feelings, his
verbal and non-verbal behaviour should be open to the client
and be consistent; GENUINENESS: he should be honest, sincere
and without façades; EMPATHIC: he should be able to let the
client know that he understands his frame of reference and
can see the world as he sees it, whilst remaining separate
from it. These qualities must be not only possessed but
conveyed: that is, the client must experience them.

Truax and Carkhuff (1967) put these hypotheses to the
test and found considerable empirical support for what they
identified as the 'core facilitative conditions' of effective helping relationships - empathy, respect and positive
regard, genuineness, and concreteness - the ability to be
specific and immediate to client statements. They differed
from Rogers in that whereas he claimed that the facilitative
conditions were necessary and sufficient, they only claimed
that they were necessary. Carkhuff has gone on to try to
demonstrate (Carkhuff and Berenson, 1976) that they are
clearly not sufficient, and that the helper needs to be
skilled in teaching a variety of life and coping skills to
his clients. The other important finding from Truax and
Carkhuff was that helpers who do not possess those qualities
are not merely ineffective, for they can contribute to
people becoming worse than they were prior to helping.

The evidence tends to suggest that the quality of the
interpersonal relationship between helper and client is more
important than any specific philosophy of helping adhered to
by the helper. This has been demonstrated to be the case in
counselling, psychotherapy and also teaching (Aspy and Roebuck, 1977). A recent review of the many research studies
on this topic would suggest, as one might expect, that
things are not quite that simple (Parloff, Waskow, and
Wolfe, 1978), but after a reappraisal of the early work of
Truax and Carkhuff and a large number of more recent
studies, the authors conclude that a relationship between
empathy, respect and genuineness with helper effectiveness
has been established. They also shed light on a number of
other factors which have been discussed periodically as
being essential for effective therapists (their focus was
therapy, not helping):

* personal psychotherapy has not been demonstrated to be a prerequisite for an effective therapist;
* sex and race are not related to effectiveness;
* the value of therapist experience is highly questionable; that is, someone is not necessarily a better therapist because he is more experienced;
* therapists with emotional problems of their own are likely to be less effective;
* there is some support for the suggestion that helpers are more effective when working with clients who hold values similar to their own.

What they do point out is the importance of the match between helper and client. No one is an effective helper with everyone, although we as yet know little as to how to match helpers with clients to gain the greatest benefits.

Helping and human relationships

Carl Rogers states very clearly that psychotherapy is not a 'special kind of relationship, different in kind from all others which occur in everyday life' (1957). A similar approach has been taken by those theorists looking at the broader concept of helping. Brammer (1973) states that 'helping relationships have much in common with friendships, family interactions, and pastoral contacts. They are all aimed at fulfilling basic human needs, and when reduced to their basic components, look much alike'. This is the approach of Egan in his training programmes for effective interpersonal relating (1975), of Carkhuff and Berenson (1976) who talk of counselling as 'a way of life', of Illich (1977) who is concerned with the de-skilling of the population by increasing armies of specialists, and of Scally and Hopson (1979) who emphasize that counselling 'is merely a set of beliefs, values and behaviours to be found in the community at large'. Considerable stress is placed later in this chapter on the trend towards demystifying helping and counselling.

Models of helping
Any person attempting to help another must have some model in his head, however ill-formed, of the process which he is about to undertake. He will have goals, however hazy, ranging from helping the person to feel better through to helping him to work through an issue for himself. It is essential for helpers to become more aware of the value-roots of their behaviours and the ideological underpinning of their proffered support.

The helper builds his theory through three overlapping stages. First he reflects on his own experience. He becomes aware of his values, needs, communication style, and their impact on others. He reads widely on the experience of other practitioners who have tried to make sense out of their observations by writing down their ideas into a systematic theory ... Finally the helper forges the first two items together into a unique theory of his own (Brammer, 1973).

Fortunately, in recent years a number of theorists and researchers have begun to define models of helping. This can only assist all helpers to define their own internal models which will then enable them in turn to evaluate their personal, philosophical and empirical bases.

CARKHUFF AND ASSOCIATES: Carkhuff took Rogers' ideas on psychotherapy and expanded on them to helping in general. He has a three-stage model through which the client is helped to (i) explore, (ii) understand and (iii) act. He defines the skills needed by the helper at each stage of the process (Carkhuff, 1974), and has also developed a system for selecting and training prospective helpers to do this. Since the skills he outlines are basically the same skills which anyone needs to live effectively, he suggests that the best way of helping people is to teach them directly and systematically in life, work, learning and relationship-building skills. He states clearly that 'the essential task of helping is to bridge the gap between the helpee's skills level and the helper's skills level' (Carkhuff and Berenson, 1976). For Carkhuff, helping equals teaching, but teaching people the skills to ensure that they can take more control over their own lives.

BRAMMER (1973) has produced an integrated, eclectic developmental model similar to Carkhuff's. He has expanded Carkhuff's three stages into the eight stages of entry, classification, structure, relationship, exploration, consolidation, planning and termination. He has also identified seven clusters of skills to promote 'understanding of self and others'. His list of 46 specific skills is somewhat daunting to a beginner but a rich source of stimulation for the more experienced helper.

IVEY AND ASSOCIATES (1971) have developed a highly systematic model for training helpers under the label 'microcounselling'. Each skill is broken up into its constituent parts and taught via closed-circuit television, modelling and practice.

HACKNEY AND NYE (1973) have described a helping model which they call a 'discrimination' model. It is goal-centred and action-centred and it stresses skills training.

KAGAN AND ASSOCIATES (1967) have also developed a microskills approach to counsellor training which is widely used in the USA. It is called Interpersonal Process Recall which involves an inquiry session in which helper and client explore the experience they have had together in the presence of a mediator.

EGAN (1975) has developed perhaps the next most influential model of helping in the USA after Carkhuff's and, indeed, has been highly influenced by Carkhuff's work. The model begins with a pre-helping phase involving attending skills, to be followed by Stage I: responding and self-exploration; Stage II: integrative understanding and

Figure 1

Model of helping
From Loughary and Ripley (1979)

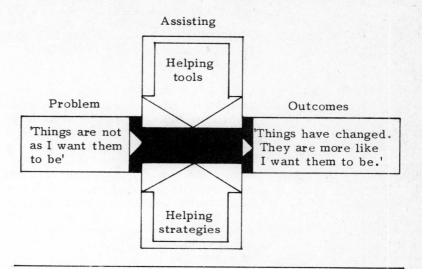

Assisting

Helping
tools

Problem

'Things are not
as I want them
to be'

Outcomes

'Things have changed.
They are more like
I want them to be.'

Helping
strategies

dynamic self-understanding; Stage III: facilitating action
and acting. The first goal labelled at each stage is the
helper's goal and the second goal is that of the client.

LOUGHARY AND RIPLEY (1979) approach helping from
a different viewpoint, which, unlike the previous theorists,
is not simply on the continuum beginning with Rogers and
Carkhuff. They have used a demystifying approach aimed at
the general population with no training other than what can
be gleaned from their book. Their model is shown in figure
1.

The helping tools include information, ideas, and skills
(such as listening and reflecting dealings). The strategies
are the plans for using the tools and the first step is
always translating the problem into desired outcomes. Their
four positive outcomes of helping are: changes in feeling
states, increased understanding, decisions, and implementing
decisions. Their approach does move away from the
counselling-dominated approach of the other models.

HOPSON AND SCALLY: we reproduce our own model in
some detail here, partly because it is the model we know
best and it has worked very effectively for us and for the
3,000 teachers and youth workers who have been through our
counselling skills training courses (Scally and Hopson,
1979), but also because it attempts to look at all the
aspects of helping defined at the beginning of this
chapter.

Figure 2 outlines three goal areas for helpers, central
to their own personal development. It also defines specific
helping outcomes. Helpers can only help people to the levels

Figure 2

Goals of helping

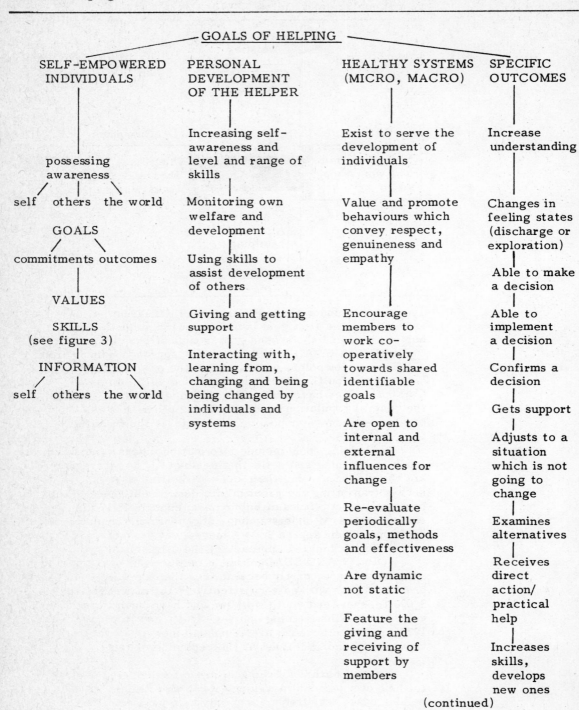

GOALS OF HELPING

SELF-EMPOWERED INDIVIDUALS	PERSONAL DEVELOPMENT OF THE HELPER	HEALTHY SYSTEMS (MICRO, MACRO)	SPECIFIC OUTCOMES
	Increasing self-awareness and level and range of skills	Exist to serve the development of individuals	Increase understanding
possessing awareness self others the world	Monitoring own welfare and development	Value and promote behaviours which convey respect, genuineness and empathy	Changes in feeling states (discharge or exploration)
GOALS commitments outcomes	Using skills to assist development of others		Able to make a decision
VALUES	Giving and getting support	Encourage members to work co-operatively towards shared identifiable goals	Able to implement a decision
SKILLS (see figure 3)	Interacting with, learning from, changing and being being changed by individuals and systems		Confirms a decision
INFORMATION self others the world		Are open to internal and external influences for change	Gets support
		Re-evaluate periodically goals, methods and effectiveness	Adjusts to a situation which is not going to change
		Are dynamic not static	Examines alternatives
		Feature the giving and receiving of support by members	Receives direct action/ practical help
			Increases skills, develops new ones

(continued)

276

Focus on
individual's
strengths
|
And builds on
them
|
Use problem
solving strate-
gies rather than
scapegoating,
blaming or focus-
sing on faults
|
Use methods which
are consistent
with goals
|
Encourage power-
sharing and enable
individuals to
pursue their own
direction as a
contribution to
shared goals
|
Monitor their own
performance in a
continuing cycle of
reflection/action
|
Allow people
access to those
whose decisions
have a bearing
on their lives
|
Have effective
and sensitive
lines of
communication
|
Explore differ-
ences openly and
use compromise,
negotiation and
contracting to
achieve a maxi-
mum of win/win
outcomes for all
|
Are always open
to alternatives

Receives
information
|
Reflects on
acts

of their own skills and awareness (Aspy and Roebuck, 1977). They need to clarify their own social, economic and cultural values and need to be able to recognize and separate their own needs and problems from those of their clients. Helpers see in others reflections of themselves. To know oneself is to ensure a clarity of distinction between images: to know where one stops and the other begins. We become less helpful as the images blur. To ensure that does not happen, we need constantly to monitor our own development. Self-awareness is not a stage to be reached and then it is over. It is a process which can never stop because we are always changing. By monitoring these changes we simultaneously retain some control of their direction.

From a greater awareness of who we are, our strengths, hindrances, values, needs and prejudices, we can be clearer about skills we wish to develop. The broader the range of skills we acquire, the larger the population group that we can help.

As helpers involved in the act of helping we learn through the process of praxis. We reflect and we act. As we interact with others, we in turn are affected by them and are in some way different from before the interaction. As we attempt to help individuals and influence systems we will learn, change, and develop from the process of interaction, just as those individuals and systems will be affected by us.

Having access to support should be a central concern for anyone regularly involved in helping. Helpers so often are not as skilled as they might be at saying 'no' and looking after themselves.

We would maintain that the ultimate goals of helping are to enable people to become self-empowered and to make systems healthier places in which to live, work and play.

Self-empowerment

There are five dimensions of self-empowerment (Hopson and Scally, 1980a).

*   Awareness: without an awareness of ourselves and others we are subject to the slings and arrows of our upbringing, daily events, social changes and crises. Without awareness we can only react, like the pinball in the machine that bounces from one thing to another without having ever provided the energy for its own passage.
*   Goals: given awareness we have the potential for taking charge of ourselves and our lives. We take charge by exploring our values, developing commitments, and by specifying goals with outcomes. We learn to live by the question: 'what do I want now?' We reflect and then act.
*   Values: we subscribe to the definition of values put forward by Raths, Harmin and Simon (1964): a value is a belief which has been chosen freely from alternatives after weighing the consequences of each alternative; it

is prized and cherished, shared publicly and acted upon repeatedly and consistently. The self-empowered person, by our definition, has values which include recognizing the worth of self and others, of being proactive, working for health systems, at home, in employment, in the community and at leisure; helping other people to become more self-empowered.

* Life skills: values are good as far as they go, but it is only by developing skills that we can translate them into action. We may believe that we are responsible for our own destiny, but we require the skills to achieve what we wish for ourselves. In a school setting, for example, we require the skills of goal setting and action-planning, time management, reading, writing and numeracy, study skills, problem-solving skills and how to work in groups. Figure 3 reproduces the list of life skills that we have identified at the Counselling and Career Development Unit (Hopson and Scally, 1980b) as being crucial to personal survival and growth.

* Information: information is the raw material for awareness of self and the surrounding world. It is the fuel for shaping our goals. Information equals power. Without it we are helpless, which is of course why so many people and systems attempt to keep information to themselves. We must realize that information is essential (a concept), that we need to know how to get appropriate information, and from where (a skill).

althy systems

Too often counsellors and other helpers have pretended to be value free. Most people now recognize that fiction. Not only is it impossible but it can be dangerous. If we honestly believe that we are capable of being value free, we halt the search for the ways in which our value systems are influencing our behaviour with our clients. If we are encouraging our clients to develop goals, how can we pretend that we do not have them too? Expressing these goals can be the beginning of a contract to work with a client for, like it or not, we each have a concept, however shadowy, for the fully functioning healthy person to which our actions and helping are directed.

As with clients, so too with systems. If we are working towards helping people to become 'better', in whatever way we choose to define that, let us be clear about what changes we are working towards in the systems we try to influence. Figure 2 lists our characteristics of healthy systems. Each of us has his own criteria so let us discover them and bring them into the open. Owning our values is one way of demonstrating our genuineness.

at is counselling?

Having identified six common ways of helping people, counselling will now be focussed on more intensively, which immediately gets us into the quagmire of definition.

279

Figure 3

Lifeskills: taking charge of yourself and your life

ME AND YOU

Skills I need to relate
  effectively to you

how to communicate effectively

how to make, keep and end a relationship

how to give and get help

how to manage conflict

how to give and receive feedback

ME AND OTHERS

Skills I need to relate
  effectively to others

how to be assertive

how to influence people and systems

how to work in groups

how to express feelings
  constructively

how to build strengths in others

ME

Skills I need to manage and grow

how to read and write

how to achieve basic numeracy

how to find information and resources

how to think and solve problems constructively

how to identify my creative potential
  and develop it

how to manage time effectively

how to make the most of the present

how to discover my interests

how to discover my values and beliefs

how to set and achieve goals

how to take stock of my life

how to discover what makes me do
  the things I do

how to be positive about myself

how to cope and gain from life transitions

how to make effective decisions

how to be proactive

how to manage negative emotions

how to cope with stress

how to achieve and maintain physical
  well-being

how to manage my sexuality

ME AND SPECIFIC SITUATIONS

Skills I need for my education

how to discover the educational options
  open to me

how to choose a course

how to study

SKILLS I NEED AT WORK

how to find a job

how to keep a job

how to change jobs

how to cope with unemployment

how to achieve a balance between my job
  and the rest of my life

how to retire and enjoy it

SKILLS I NEED AT HOME

how to choose a style of living

how to maintain a home

SKILLS I NEED AT LEISURE

how to choose between leisure optio

how to maximize my leisure opportun

how to use my leisure to increase m
  income

SKILLS I NEED IN THE COMMUNITY

how to be a skilled consumer

how to develop and use my political
  awareness

how to use public facilities

Anyone reviewing the literature to define counselling will quickly suffer from data-overload. Books, articles, even manifestoes, have been written on the question.

In training courses run from the Counselling and Career Development Unit we tend to opt for the parsimonious definition of 'helping people explore problems so that they can decide what to do about them'.

The demystification of counselling

There is nothing inherently mysterious about counselling. It is merely a set of beliefs, values and behaviours to be found in the community at large. The beliefs include one that says individuals benefit and grow from a particular form of relationship and contact. The values recognize the worth and the significance of each individual and regard personal autonomy and self-direction as desirable. The behaviours cover a combination of listening, conveying warmth, asking open questions, encouraging specificity, concreteness and focussing, balancing support and confrontation, and offering strategies which help to clarify objectives and identify action plans. This terminology is more complex than the process needs to be. The words describe what is essentially a 'non-mystical' way in which some people are able to help other people to help themselves (see figure 4).

Training courses can sometimes encourage the mystification. They talk of 'counselling skills' and may, by implication, suggest that such skills are somehow separate from other human activities, are to be conferred upon those who attend courses, and are probably innovatory. In fact, what 'counselling' has done is to crystallize what we know about how warm, trusting relationships develop between people. It recognizes that:

* relationships develop if one has and conveys respect for another, if one is genuine oneself, if one attempts to see things from the other's point of view (empathizes), and if one endeavours not to pass judgement. Those who operate in this way we describe as having 'relationship-building skills';
* if the relationship is established, an individual will be prepared to talk through and explore his thoughts and feelings. What one can do and say which helps that to happen we classify as exploring and clarifying skills (see figure 4);
* through this process an individual becomes clear about difficulties or uncertainties, and can explore options and alternatives, in terms of what he might do to change what he is not happy about;
* given support, an individual is likely to be prepared to, and is capable of, dealing with difficulties or problems he may face more effectively. He can be helped by somebody who can offer objective setting and action planning skills.

Figure 4

The Counselling Process

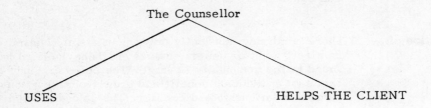

The Counsellor

USES   HELPS THE CLIENT

RELATIONSHIP BUILDING SKILLS	respect genuineness empathy	to feel valued, understood and prepared to trust the counsellor

EXPLORING AND CLARIFYING SKILLS	contracting open questions summarizing focussing reflecting immediacy clarifying concreteness confronting	to talk and explore to understand more about how he feels and why to consider options and examine alternatives to choose an alternative

	objective setting action planning problem-solving strategies	to develop clear objectives to form specific action plans to do, with support, what needs to be done

COUNSELLING IS HELPING PEOPLE TO HELP THEMSELVES

Counselling skills are what people use to help people to help themselves. They are not skills that are exclusive to one group or one activity. It is clear that the behaviours, which we bundle together and identify as skills, are liberally scattered about us in the community. Counselling ideology identifies which behaviours are consistent with its values and its goals, and teaches these as one category of helping skills.

What may happen, unfortunately, is that the promotion of counselling as a separate training responsibility can increase the mystification. An outcome can be that instead of simply now being people who, compared to the majority, are extra-sensitive listeners, are particularly good at making relationships, and are more effective at helping others to solve problems, they have become 'counsellors' and licensed to help. A licence becomes a danger if:

* those who have it see themselves as qualitatively different from the rest of the population;
* it symbolizes to the non-licensed that they are incapable, or inferior, or calls into question valuable work they may be doing, but are 'unqualified' to do.

It is important to recognize that labelling people can have unfortunate side effects. Let us remember that whatever the nomenclature - counsellor, client or whatever - at a particular time or place, they are just people. All, at some time or other, will be able to give help, at other times will need to seek or receive help. Some are naturally better fitted to help others; some by training can improve their helping skills. All, through increased awareness and skill development, can become more effective helpers than they are now.

Counselling is not only practised by counsellors. It is a widespread activity in the community and appears in several guises. Its constituent skills are described variously as 'talking it over', 'having a friendly chat', 'being a good friend' or simply 'sharing' with somebody. These processes almost certainly include some or all of the skills summarized in figure 4. Often, of course, there are notable exceptions: for instance, we do not listen well; we cannot resist giving our advice, or trying to solve problems for our friends; we find it difficult to drop our façades and roles. Counselling skills training can help reduce our unhelpful behaviours and begin to develop these skills in ourselves, making us more effective counsellors, as well as simply being a good friend. In almost any work involving contact with other people, we would estimate there is a potential counselling component. There is a need for the particular interpersonal skills categorized here as coun-selling skills to be understood and used by people at large, but particularly by all people who have the welfare of others as part of their occupational roles. Specialist 'counsellors' have an important part to play, but it is not

to replace the valuable work that is done by many who would
not claim the title. Having said that, people sometimes
think they are counselling, but in fact are doing things
very far removed: disciplining, persuading people to conform
to a system, etc.

Types of counselling

Developmental versus crisis counselling
Counselling can operate either as a RESPONSE to a situation
or as a STIMULUS to help a client develop and grow. In the
past, counselling has often been concerned with helping
someone with a problem during or after the onset of a crisis
point: a widow unable to cope with her grief, the school
leaver desperate because he has no idea what job to choose,
the pregnant woman with no wish to be pregnant. This is a
legitimate function of counselling, but if this is all that
counselling is, it can only ever be concerned with making
the best of the situation in which one finds oneself. How
much more ambitious to help people anticipate future
problems, to educate them to recognize the cues of oncoming
crisis, and to provide them with skills to take charge of it
at the outset instead of running behind in an attempt to
catch up! This is counselling as a stimulus to growth:
developmental as opposed to crisis counselling. All
successful counselling entails growth, but the distinction
between the two approaches is that the crisis approach
generates growth under pressure, and since this is often
limited only to the presenting problem, the client's
behavioural and conceptual repertoire may remain little
affected by the experience. There will always be a need for
crisis counselling in a wide variety of settings, but the
exciting prospect of developmental counselling for growth
and change has only recently begun to be tackled.

Individual counselling
As counselling was rooted in psychotherapy it is hardly
surprising that the primary focus has been on the one-to-one
relationship. There are a number of essential elements in
the process. The client is to be helped to reach his own
decision by himself. This is achieved by establishing a
relationship of trust whereby the client feels that the
counsellor cares about him, is able to empathize with his
problem, and is authentic and genuine in relating to him.
The counsellor will enter the relationship as a person in
his own right, disclosing relevant information about himself
as appropriate, reacting honestly to the client's statements
and questions, but at no time imposing his own opinions on
the client. His task is to facilitate the client's own
abilities and strengths in such a way that the client experiences the satisfaction of having defined and solved his
problem for himself. If the client lacks information on
special issues, is incapable of generating alternative
strategies, or cannot make decisions in a programmatic way,
then the counsellor has a function as an educator whose

skills are offered to the client. In this way the client is never manipulated. The counsellor is negotiating a contract to use some skills which he, the counsellor, possesses, and which can be passed on to the client if the client wishes to make use of them.

Individual counselling has the advantages over group counselling of providing a safer setting for some people to lower their defences, of developing a strong and trusting relationship with the counsellor, and of allowing the client maximum personal contact with the counsellor.

Group counselling

Group counselling involves one or more counsellors operating with a number of clients in a group session. The group size varies from four to sixteen, with eight to ten being the most usual number. The basic objectives of group and individual counselling are similar. Both seek to help the clients achieve self-direction, integration, self-responsibility, self-acceptance, and an understanding of their motivations and patterns of behaviour. In both cases the counsellor needs the skills and attitudes outlined earlier, and both require a confidential relationship. There are, however, some important differences (Hopson, 1977).

* The group counsellor needs an understanding of group dynamics: communication, decision making, role-playing, sources of power, and perceptual processes in groups.
* The group situation can provide immediate opportunities to try out ways of relating to individuals, and is an excellent way of providing the experience of intimacy with others. The physical proximity of the clients to one another can be emotionally satisfying and supportive. Clients give a first-hand opportunity to test others' perception of themselves.
* Clients not only receive help themselves; they also help other clients. In this way helping skills are generated by a larger group of people than is possible in individual counselling.
* Clients often discover that other people have similar problems, which can at the least be comforting.
* Clients learn to make effective use of other people, not just professionals, as helping agents. They can set up a mutual support group which is less demanding on the counsellor and likely to be a boost to their self-esteem when they discover they can manage to an increasing extent without him.

There are many different kinds of group counselling. Some careers services in higher education offer counsellor-led groups as groundwork preparation for career choices; these small groups give older adolescents an opportunity to discuss the interrelations between their conscious values and preferred life styles and their crystallizing sense of identity. Other groups are provided in schools where young people can discuss with each other and an adult counsellor those relationships with parents and friends which are so important in adolescence. Training groups are held for teaching decision-making skills and assertive skills. There are also groups in which experiences are pooled and mutual help given for the married, for parents, for those bringing up families alone and for those who share a special problem such as having a handicapped child. All these types of groups are usually led by someone who has had training and experience in facilitating them. The word 'facilitating' is used advisedly, for the leader's job is not to conduct a seminar or tutorial, but to establish an atmosphere in which members of the group can explore the feelings around a particular stage of development or condition or critical choice.

Another type of group is not so specifically focussed on an area of common concern but is set up as a sort of laboratory to learn about the underlying dynamics of how people in groups function, whatever the group's focus and purpose may be. These are often referred to as sensitivity training groups (e.g. Cooper and Mangham, 1971; Smith, 1975). Yet a third category of group has more therapeutic goals, being intended to be successive or complementary to, or sometimes in place of, individual psychotherapy. This type of group will not usually have a place in work settings, whereas the other two do have useful applications there. Obvious uses for this type of group occur in induction procedures, in preparation for retirement, in relation to job change arising from promotion, or in relation to redundancy. The second type of group is employed in training for supervisory or management posts, though one hears less about their use in trade unions.

Schools of counselling
Differences in theories of personality, learning and perception are reflected in counselling theory. It is useful to distinguish between five major schools.

1. PSYCHOANALYTIC APPROACHES were historically the first. Psychoanalysis is a personality theory, a philosophical system, and a method of psychotherapy. Concentrating on the past history of a patient, understanding the internal dynamics of the psyche, and the relationship between the client and the therapist are all key concerns for psychoanalysis. Key figures include Freud, Jung, Adler, Sullivan, Horney, Fromm and Erikson.

2. CLIENT-CENTRED APPROACHES are based upon the work of Rogers, originally as a non-directive therapy developed as a reaction against psychoanalysis. Founded on a subjective view of human experiencing, it places more faith in and gives more responsibility to the client in problem solving. The techniques of client-centred counselling have become the basis for most counselling skills training,

following the empirical evaluations by Truax and Carkhuff (1967).

3. BEHAVIOURAL APPROACHES arise from attempts to apply the principles of learning to the resolution of specific behavioural disorders. Results are subject to continual experimentation and refinement. Key figures include Wolpe, Eysenck, Lazarus and Krumboltz.

4. COGNITIVE APPROACHES include 'rational-emotive therapy' (Ellis), 'Transactional analysis' (Berne) and 'reality therapy' (Glasser), along with Meichenbaum's work on cognitive rehearsal and inoculation. All have in common the belief that people's problems are created by how they conceptualize their worlds: change the concepts and feelings will change too.

5. AFFECTIVE APPROACHES include 'Gestalt therapy' (Perls), 'primal therapy' (Janov), 're-evaluation counselling' (Jackins), and 'bioenergetics' (Lowen). These have in common the belief that pain and distress accumulate and have to be discharged in some way before the person can become whole or think clearly again.

There are many other approaches and orientations. The existential-humanistic school is exemplified by May, Maslow, Frankl and Jourard. Encounter approaches have been developed by Schutz, Bindrim and Ichazo, 'psychosynthesis' by Assagioli, 'morita therapy' by Morita, and 'eclectic psychotherapy' by Thorne. In the United Kingdom the biggest influence on counsellor training has been from the client-centred school. Behavioural approaches are becoming more common and, to a lesser extent, transactional analysis, Gestalt therapy and re-evaluation counselling.

Where does counselling take place?

Until recently counselling was assumed to take place in the confines of a counsellor's office. This is changing rapidly. It is now increasingly accepted that effective counselling, as defined in this chapter, can take place on the shop floor, in the school corridor, even on a bus. The process is not made any easier by difficult surroundings, but when people need help, the helpers are not always in a position to choose from where they would like to administer it. Initial contacts are often made in these kinds of environment, and more intensive counselling can always be scheduled for a later date in a more amenable setting.

What are the goals of counselling?

Counselling is a process through which a person attains a higher stage of personal competence. It is always about change. Katz (1969) has said that counselling is concerned not with helping people to make wise decisions but with helping them to make decisions wisely. It has as its goal self-empowerment: that is, the individual's ability to move through the following stages.

* 'I am not happy with things at the moment'
* 'What I would prefer is ...'
* 'What I need to do to achieve that is ...'
* 'I have changed what I can, and have come to terms, for the moment, with what I cannot achieve'.

Counselling has as an ultimate goal the eventual redundancy of the helper, and the activity should discourage dependency and subjection. It promotes situations in which the person's views and feelings are heard, respected and not judged. It builds personal strength, confidence and invites initiative and growth. It develops the individual and encourages control of self and situations. Counselling obviously works for the formation of more capable and effective individuals, through working with people singly or in groups.

In its goals it stands alongside other approaches concerned with personal and human development. All can see how desirable would be the stage when more competent, 'healthier' individuals would live more positively and more humanly. Counselling may share its goals in terms of what it wants for individuals; where it does differ from other approaches is in its method of achieving that. It concentrates on the individual – alone or in a group – and on one form of helping. Some other approaches would work for the same goals but would advocate different methods of achieving them. It is important to explore the inter-relatedness of counselling and other forms of helping as a way of asking, 'If we are clear about what we want for people, are we being as effective as we could be in achieving it?'

Counselling outcomes

This chapter has defined the ultimate outcome of counselling as 'helping people to help themselves'. A natural question to follow might be, 'to help themselves to do what?' There follows a list of counselling outcomes most frequently asked for by clients:

* increased understanding of oneself or a situation;
* achieving a change in the way one is feeling;
* being able to make a decision;
* confirming a decision;
* getting support for a decision;
* being able to change a situation;
* adjusting to a situation that is not going to change;
* the discharge of feelings;
* examining options and choosing one (Scally and Hopson, 1979).

Clients sometimes want other outcomes which are not those of counselling but stem from one or more of the other forms of helping: information, new skills, or practical help.

All of these outcomes have in common the concept of change. All counselling is about change. Given any issue or problem a person always has four possible strategies to deal with it:

* change the situation;
* change oneself to adapt to the situation;
* exit from it;
* develop ways of living with it.

counselling the best
ay of helping people?

In the quest for more autonomous, more self-competent, self-employed individuals the helper is faced with the question, 'If that is my goal, am I working in the most effective way towards achieving it?' As much as one believes in the potential of counselling, there are times when one must ask whether spending time with individuals is the best investment of one's helping time and effort.

Many counsellors say that time spent in this way is incredibly valuable; it emphasizes the importance of each individual, and hence they justify time given to one-to-one counselling. At the other end of the spectrum there are those who charge 'counsellors' with:

* being concerned solely with 'casualties', people in crisis and in difficulty, and not getting involved with organizational questions;
* allowing systems, organizations and structures to continue to operate 'unhealthily', by 'treating' these 'casualties' so effectively.

To reject these charges out-of-hand would be to fail to recognize the elements of truth they contain. One respects tremendously the importance that counselling places on the individual, and this is not an attempt to challenge that. What it may be relevant to establish is that counselling should not be seen as a substitute for 'healthy' systems, which operate in ways which respect individuality, where relationships are genuine and positive, where communication is open and problem-solving and participation are worked at (see figure 2). 'Healthy' systems can be as important to the welfare of the individual as can one-to-one counselling. It is unfortunate therefore that 'administrators' can see personal welfare as being the province of 'counselling types', and the latter are sometimes reluctant to 'contaminate' their work by getting involved in administrational or organizational matters. These attitudes can be very detrimental to all involved systems. The viewpoint presented here is that part of a helper's repertoire of skills in the 'tool-bag' alongside counselling skills should be willingness, and the ability, to work for systems change. Some counsellors obviously do this already in more spontaneous ways; for example, if one finds oneself counselling truants, it may become apparent that some absconding is invited by timetable anomalies (French for remedial groups on Friday afternoons?). The dilemma here is whether one spends time with a series of individual truants or persuades the designers of timetables to establish a more aware approach.

One realizes sometimes also that one may, in counselling, be using one's skills in such a way that individuals accept outcomes which possibly should not be accepted. For example, unemployment specialists in careers services sometimes see themselves as being used by 'the system' to help black youths come to terms with being disadvantaged. Such specialists ask whether this is their role or whether they should in fact be involved politically and actively in working for social and economic change.

Resistance to the idea of becoming more involved in 'systems' and 'power structures' may not simply be based upon a reluctance to take on extra, unattractive work. Some will genuinely feel that this approach is 'political' and therefore somehow tainted and dubious. It is interesting that in the USA during the last five years there has been a significant shift in opinion towards counsellors becoming more ready to accept the need to be involved in influencing systems:

> Their work brings them face to face with the victim of poverty; or racism, sexism, and stigmatization; of political, economic and social systems that allow individuals to feel powerless and helpless; of governing structures that cut off communication and deny the need for responsiveness; of social norms that stifle individuality; of communities that let their members live in isolation from one another. In the face of these realities human service workers have no choice but to blame those victims or to see ways to change the environment (Lewis and Lewis, 1977).

In this country, perhaps a deeper analysis is needed of the 'contexts' in which we work as helpers.

Can counselling be apolitical?

It is very interesting that in his recent book, Carl Rogers (Rogers, 1978) reviewing his own present position vis-à-vis counselling, indicates the revolutionary impact of much of his work as perceived by him in retrospect. Perhaps identifiable as the 'arch-individualist', Rogers signals now that he had not seen the full social impact of the values and the methodology he pioneered. He writes eloquently of his realization that much of his life and work has in fact been political, though previously he had not seen it in those terms. Counselling invites self-empowerment; it invites the individual to become aware and to take more control; it asks 'How would you like things to be?' and 'How will you make them like that?' That process is a very powerful one and has consequences that are likely to involve changing 'status quos'. Clearly processes that are about change, power, and control are 'political' (although not necessarily party political).

From this viewpoint counsellors are involved in politics already. As much as one may like there to be, there can really be no neutral ground. Opting out or not working for change is by definition maintaining the status quo. If the 'status quo' means an organization, systems or relationships which are insensitive, uncaring, manipulative, unjust, divisive, autocratic, or function in any way which damages the potential of the people who are part of them, then one cannot really turn one's back on the task of working for change. 'One is either part of the solution or part of the problem!' We have argued (Scally and Hopson, 1979) that counsellors have much to offer by balancing their one-to-one work with more direct and more skilled involvement in making systems more positive, growthful places in which to live and work.

o counsel or to teach? Counselling is a process through which a person attains a higher level of personal competence. Recently, attacks have been made on the counselling approach by such widely differing adversaries as Illich (1973) and Carkhuff (Carkhuff and Berenson, 1976). They, and others, question what effect the existence of counsellors and therapists has had on human development as a whole. They maintain that, however benevolent the counselling relationship is felt to be by those involved, there are forces at work overall which are suspect. They suggest:

* that helpers largely answer their own needs, and consciously or unconsciously perpetuate dependency or inadequacy in clients;
* helping can be 'disabling' rather than 'enabling' because it often encourages dependency.

For counsellors to begin to answer such charges requires a self-analysis of their own objectives, methods and motives. They could begin by asking:

* how much of their counselling is done at the 'crisis' or 'problem' stage in their clients' lives?
* how much investment are they putting into 'prevention' rather than 'cure'?

To help somebody in crisis is an obvious task. It is, however, only one counselling option. If 'prevention' is better than 'cure' then maybe that is where the emphasis ought to be. Perhaps never before has there been more reason for individuals to feel 'in crisis'. Toffler (1970) has identified some likely personal and social consequences of living at a time of incredibly rapid change. Many, like Stonier (1979) are forecasting unparalleled technological developments over the next 30 years which will change our lives, especially our work patterns, dramatically. There are so

many complex forces at work that it is not surprising that
many people are feeling more anxious, unsure, pessimistic,
unable to cope, depersonalized, and helpless. Helpers are at
risk as much as any, but are likely to be faced with ever-
increasing demands on their time and skills. Again, this
requires a reassessment of approaches and priorities, which
could suggest a greater concentration on the development of
personal competence in our systems. We need to develop more
'skilled' (which is not the same as 'informed') individuals
and thereby avert more personal difficulties and crisis. One
view is that this, the developmental, educational, teaching
approach, needs to involve more of those who now spend much
time in one-to-one counselling; not to replace that work but
to give balance to it.

Personal competence and self-empowerment, which are
the 'goals' of counselling, can be understood in many ways.
A recent movement has been to see competence as being
achievable through skill development. 'Life skills' are
becoming as large a band-wagon as counselling has become.

We are producing a series of Lifeskills Teaching
Programmes (Hopson and Scally, 1980b) which cover a range
of more generic personal skills: for example, 'How to be
assertive rather than aggressive', 'How to make, maintain
and end relationships', 'How to manage time effectively',
'How to be positive about oneself', 'How to make effective
transitions', etc. (figure 3). The programmes attempt to
break down the generalization of 'competence' into 'learn-
able' units, with the overall invitation that, by acquiring
these skills, one can 'take charge of oneself and one's
life'. We have the advantage, working in a training unit, of
being able to work directly with teachers and youth workers
on the skills this way. Aspy and Roebuck (1977) have identified that the most effective teachers are those who have,
and demonstrate, a high respect for others, who are genuine,
and display a high degree of empathy with their students.
Many professional counsellors therefore should have the
basic qualities required in teaching, and could make appre-
ciable contributions by being involved in programmes in the
community which encourage 'coping' and 'growth' skills. More
personally skilled individuals could reduce the dependence,
inadequacy and crises which are individually and collectively wasteful, and take up so much counselling time.

**Towards a 'complete
helper'**

The argument here is for the development of more complete
helpers, more 'all-rounders', with a range of skills and
'tool-bags' full of more varied helping equipment. It is
possible to work to increase the level of skill in each
particular helping technique and go for 'broader' rather
than 'higher' skill development. This diagram (figure 5)
could map out for individual helpers how they may want to
plan their own development.

On a graph such as this an effective teacher may be
placed typically along the line marked 'x'. A full-time

292

counsellor working in a school or workplace may typically be indicated by the line marked 'o'. An organization-change consultant may typically be somewhere along the dotted line.

Figure 5

Helpers' skills levels and possible approaches to increasing them

(what skills do I have and in which direction can I develop?)

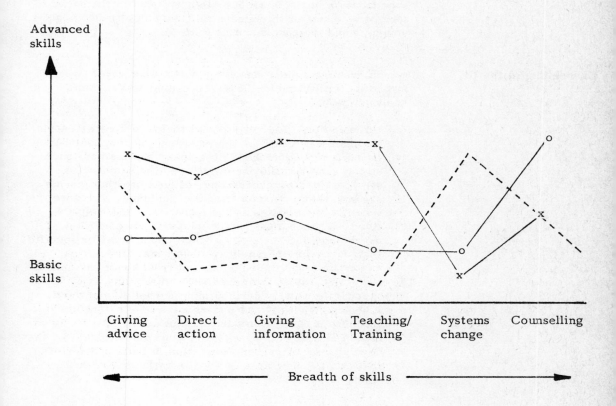

How much one wants to be involved in helping, at whatever level and in whatever form, obviously depends upon many factors. How much one sees helping as part of the roles one fills; how much helping is part of the job one does; how much one wants to be involved as a part-time activity; how much helping is consistent with one's values, politics and personality; all will have a bearing on where an individual may wish to be placed on the graph. One person may decide to specialize in a particular approach and develop sophisticated skills in that field. Another may go for a broader approach by developing skills from across the range. Yet another may at particular times develop new specialisms as a response to particular situations or as part of his own personal career development.

What is advocated here is that basic helping skills can be regarded as essential life skills. These skills can be made available to, and developed very fully in, professional helpers and in those for whom helping is part of their job specification in the workshop, in hospitals, in the social service agencies or in education. They can also be taught to young people in schools and at work.

Counselling in the UK

It is interesting that 'counselling' was a term rarely used in Britain until the mid-1960s. According to Vaughan's analysis (1976),

> three factors gradually tended to focus more attention on this area. One was the emergence throughout this century of a wider band of 'helping' professions, such as the Youth Employment Service, the social work services, and psychotherapy, as well as other 'caring' organizations, such as marriage guidance, and more recently such bodies as the Samaritans and Help the Aged. A second was the development of empirical psychology and sociology, which began to offer specific techniques for the analysis of personal difficulties; and a third was the rapid spread from about the mid-1960s onwards of the concept of counselling as a specific profession derived almost wholly from North America, where it had undergone a long evolution throughout the century from about 1910. Thus today we have a situation comparable in some ways to that of the development of primary education in Britain before the 1870 Act. A new area of specialization seems to be emerging.

It is just because a new area of specialization is developing that people already engaged in, or about to involve themselves in, counselling need to think carefully of where and how they wish to invest their time and resources. Counselling clearly is an important way of helping people, but it is not the only way.

References

Aspy, D. and Roebuck, F. (1977)
Kids Don't Learn from People They Don't Like. Amherst, Mass.: Human Resource Development Press.

Blocher, D. (1966)
Developmental Counseling (2nd edn). New York: Ronald
Press.

Bonnex, J.T. (1965)
Cells and Societies. Princeton University, NJ: Princeton
University Press.

Boy, A.V. and Pine, G.J. (1968)
The Counselor in the Schools. New York: Houghton
Mifflin.

Brammer, L.M. (1973)
The Helping Relationship. Englewood Cliffs, NJ: Prentice-
Hall.

Burnet, F.M. (1971)
Self-recognition in colonial marine forms and flowering
plants. Nature, 232, 230-235.

Carkhuff, R.R. (1969)
Helping and Human Relations. New York: Holt, Rinehart
& Winston.

Carkhuff, R.R. (1974)
The Art of Helping. Amherst, Mass.: Human Resource
Development Press.

Carkhuff, R.R. and Berenson, B.G. (1976)
Teaching As Treatment. Amherst, Mass.: Human Resource
Development Press.

Coombs, A., Avila, D. and Purkey, W. (1971)
Helping Relationships: Basic concepts for the helping
profession. Boston: Allyn & Bacon.

Cooper, C.L. and Mangham, I.L. (eds) (1971)
T-Groups: A survey of research. Chichester: Wiley.

Corey, G. (1977)
Theory and Practice of Counselling and Psychotherapy.
Monterey, Ca: Brooks/Cole.

Corsini, R. (ed.) (1977)
Current Psychotherapies (2nd edn). Itasca, Ill.: Peacock
Publications.

Egan, G. (1975)
The Skilled Helper. Monterey, Ca: Brooks/Cole.

Eibl-Eibesfeldt, I. (1971)
Love and Hate. London: Methuen.

Hackney, H.L. and Nye, S. (1973)
Counseling Strategies and Objectives. Englewood Cliffs,
NJ: Prentice-Hall.

Hoffman, A.M. (1976)
Paraprofessional effectiveness. Personnel and Guidance
Journal, 54, 494-497.

Hopson, B. (1977)
Techniques and methods of counselling. In A.G. Watts
(ed.), Counselling at Work. London: Bedford Square
Press.

Hopson, B. and Scally, M. (1980a)
Lifeskills Teaching: Education for self-empowerment.
Maidenhead: McGraw-Hill.

Hopson, B. and Scally, M. (1980b)
Lifeskills Teaching Programmes No. 1. Leeds: Lifeskills
Associates.

Illich, I., Zola, I.K., McKnight, J., Kaplan, J. and Sharken, H. (1977)
   The Disabling Professions. London: Marion Boyars.
Illich, I. (1973)
   Tools of Conviviality. London: Calder & Boyars.
Ivey, A.E. (1971)
   Microcounseling: Innovations in interviewing training. Springfield, Ill.: Thomas.
Jackins, H. (1965)
   The Human Side of Human Beings. Seattle: Rational Island Publications.
Kagan, N., Krathwohl, D.R. et al (1967)
   Studies in Human Interaction: Interpersonal process recall stimulated by videotape. East Lansing, Mich.: Educational Publication Services, College of Education, Michigan State University.
Katz, M.R. (1969)
   Can computers make guidance decisions for students? College Board Review, New York, No. 72.
Kennedy, E. (1977)
   On Becoming a Counsellor: A basic guide for non-professional counsellors. Dublin: Gill & Macmillan.
Lewis, J. and Lewis, M. (1977)
   Community Counseling: A human services approach. New York: Wiley.
Loughary, J.W. and Ripley, T.M. (1979)
   Helping Others Help Themselves. New York: McGraw-Hill.
Maslow, A. (1968)
   Toward a Psychology of Being (2nd edn). New York: Van Nostrand.
Mowrer, O.H. (1950)
   Learning Theory and Personality Dynamics. New York: Ronald Press.
Newell, P.C. (1977)
   How cells communicate. Endeavour, 1, 63-68.
Parloff, M.B., Waskow, I.E. and Wolfe, B. (1978)
   Research on therapist variables in relation to process and outcome. In S.L. Garfield and A.E. Bergin (eds), Handbook of Psychotherapy and Behavior Change: An empirical analysis (2nd edn). New York: Wiley.
Pietrofesa, J.L., Hoffman, A., Splete, H.H. and Pinto, D.V. (1978)
   Counseling; Theory, research and practice. Chicago: Rand McNally.
Proctor, B. (1979)
   The Counselling Shop. London: Deutsch.
Raths, L., Harmin, M. and Simon, S. (1964)
   Values and Teaching. Columbus, Ohio: Charles E. Merrill.
Rogers, C.R. (1957)
   The necessary and sufficient conditions of therapeutic personality change. Journal of Consulting Psychology, 21, 95-103.

Rogers, C.R. (1958)
> The characteristics of a helping relationship. Personnel and Guidance Journal, 37, 6-16.

Rogers, C.R. (1978)
> Carl Rogers on Personal Power. London: Constable.

Scally, M. and Hopson, B. (1979)
> A Model of Helping and Counselling: Indications for training. Leeds: Counselling and Careers Development Unit, Leeds University.

Sinick, D. (1979)
> Joys of Counseling. Mincie, Indiana: Accelerated Development Inc.

Smith, P.B. (1975)
> Controlled studies of the outcome of sensitivity training. Psychological Bulletin, 82, 597-622.

Stonier, T. (1979)
> On the Future of Employment. N.U.T. guide to careers work. London: National Union of Teachers.

Toffler, A. (1970)
> Future Shock. London: Bodley Head.

Truax, C.B. and Carkhuff, R.R. (1967)
> Toward Effective Counselling and Psychotherapy: Training and practice. Chicago: Aldine.

Tyler, L. (1961)
> The Work of the Counselor. New York: Appleton-Century-Crofts.

Vaughan, T. (ed.) (1976)
> Concepts of Counselling. London: Bedford Square Press.

Questions

1. Distinguish counselling from other forms of helping.
2. How can counselling and helping be 'demystified'?
3. How large a part do you think counselling does and should play in your work?
4. Distinguish between counselling and counselling skills.
5. Who are 'the helpers'?
6. What makes people effective helpers?
7. Compare and contrast two different models of helping.
8. What in your opinion are the legitimate goals of helping and why?
9. How useful a concept is 'self-empowerment' in the context of helping?
10. What are the advantages and disadvantages of individual and group counselling techniques?

Annotated reading

Corey, G. (1977) Theory and Practice of Counseling and Psychotherapy. Monterey, Ca: Brooks/Cole.
> This contains an excellent review of all the schools of counselling described in the chapter. There is an accompanying workbook designed for students and tutor which gives self-inventories to aid students in identifying their own attitudes and beliefs, overviews of each major theory of counselling, questions for discussion and evaluation, case studies, exercises

designed to sharpen specific counselling skills, out-of-class projects, group exercises, examples of client problems, an overview comparision of all models, ethical issues and problems to consider, and issues basic to the therapist's personal development.

Corsini, R. (ed.) (1977) Current Psychotherapies (2nd edn). Itasca, Ill.: Peacock Publications.
An excellent introduction to the main schools of psychotherapy by leading practitioners who have been bullied to stick to the same format. Covers psychoanalysis, Adlerian, client-centred, analytical, rational-emotive therapy, transactional analysis, Gestalt, behavioural, reality, encounter, experiential and eclectic. Contributors include Carl Rogers, Albert Ellis, William Glasser, Alan Goldstein, Will Schutz and Rudolf Dreikurs.

Vaughan, T.D. (ed.) (1975) Concepts of Counselling. British Association for Counselling, London: Bedford Square Press.
A guide to the plethora of definitions of counselling. Uneven, illuminating, with some useful descriptions of developments in the UK.

Index

Index

Index

Index